FOR GEORGE

BEST O' LUCK
TIGHT LINES
+
MANY HAPPY `WET' DAYS

Nov '00

Trout & Salmon
FLIES of SCOTLAND

Stan Headley

Photography by Terry Griffiths

Merlin Unwin Books

First published in Britain by Merlin Unwin Books, 1997
ISBN 1 873674 260

Text copyright © Stan Headley
Photos © Terry Griffiths

All rights reserved. No part of this publication may be reproduced, stored in a retrieval system or transmitted in any form or by any means, electronic, mechanical, photocopying, recording or otherwise, without the prior permission of Merlin Unwin Books.

Published by
Merlin Unwin Books
Palmers House
7 Corve Street, Ludlow
Shropshire SY8 1DB, U.K.

The author asserts his moral right to be identified as the author of this work.

British Library Cataloguing-in-Publication Data:
A catalogue record for this book is available from the British Library.

Designed and typeset in Caslon by Merlin Unwin Books.
Printed in Great Britain by Bath Press.

DEDICATION
For Catriona Alexandra and Nadine Margaret
my best and favourite patterns

Contents

Illustrations

Acknowledgements

A comprehensive listing of all the Scottish trout and salmon flies currently in use is a mammoth task. And, unfortunately, I'm no mammoth!

Flyfishing has a venerable tradition in this country, and many of our patterns are standards not only at home but throughout the world. But a current listing cannot just contain the standards, it must attempt to spot the up-and-coming patterns and also the ones which achieved standardhood in the recent past but are, as yet, not widely publicised.

It quickly became obvious to me that I was going to have to cast my net wide to gather in all the most informed sources of information the country had to offer. I was determined that this would be a work which would not fail due to lack of diligence or return.

The research side of my work has involved a great many people and I will attempt to repay my debt to each one by naming them below. I apologise unreservedly to anyone who finds his/her name unlisted. This is no reflection on your contribution, simply a reflection on my inability to do anything right !

Firstly, I must mention (in alphabetical order) those whose contributions have been above & beyond the call of duty: Davie 'Chaff' Chalmers, Alan Donaldson, Jimmy Fairgrieve, Ian Glassford, Franz Grimley, Davie McPhail, Jimmy Millar, Willie Miller, Alastair Murphy, Robert Rattray, Jim Smails and Davie Wood, all of whom provided flies of high quality, but also were pestered so unmercifully by me for additional patterns, information etc.

Secondly, there are those who not only provided flies, lists, and in-depth information on their local areas, but also put me in touch with invaluable sources of further information on their local areas: John Buchanan, Paul Buchanan, Ron Glass, Ian Hutcheon, Ken Kennedy, Stephen Leask, Davie Malcolm, Dave Mateer, Willie Mathieson, Bill McLenan, the late Jim Newlands (who sadly passed away whilst this work was in its infancy), Brian Peterson and Stuart Topp.

Those whose information on local pattern preference was also invaluable were: Michael Brady, John Buckland, Jock Dallas, Frank Durdle, John Kennedy, Ian Masson, Paul Panchaud, Ronnie Plunkett, Hugo Ross and Paul Young.

And finally, to those who won't need reminding of their contribution : Marlyn Astbury, Sandy McConnachie, Clive Chaddock, Keith Dunbar, Norman Irvine, Eddie McCarthy, and my dad, Ed Headley. On the production side, Tony Deacon and Tamsin Osler have been invaluable, while Terry Griffiths has produced some superb colour photos of the flies.

Having listed all those persons who played a vital part in this work, I feel somewhat of a fraud having my name on the front cover. To you all, my heartfelt thanks will have to suffice.

Introduction

When I was about 12 years old, I sat and looked on as Dunstan Hutchison was tying some flies for Loch Leven. Dunstan was a professional dresser from St Andrews and watching him produce those miracles from mere scraps of nothing was to alter the course of my life. A couple of years after this initial incident, I went out and caught a pound trout on a fly I had tied myself. It was a very simple fly with a rusty-brown body, tail and hackle, with a gold rib. I called it, in my boyish enthusiasm, the 'Rusty Nail'. Some fifteen years later, that same pattern took me a four and three quarter pound wild fish from Swannay, in Orkney.

Although I dabble a little at sea angling, sticking all sorts of smelly offerings on hooks, fishing for me has always been about flies. Most people tie flies to go fishing. I sometimes suspect that I've got it the other way round. For me, flies and fishing are inseparable and I get as much pleasure and satisfaction from tying a 'perfect' fly as in deceiving a particularly difficult fish. So, to be asked to supply a list of practical patterns in current use in Scotland, a country whose contribution to the World's history of fly fishing is unrivalled, is an honour impossible to quantify. It is comparable to leading a Scottish football team out onto the hallowed ground of Hampden.

There have been many pleasures in producing this work, but the greatest has been the alacrity and enthusiasm displayed by the many contributors of fly patterns, whom I have acknowledged elsewhere in the book. I asked them to supply me with examples of flies that they used on their particular waters; that were not just the bog-standards in common usage. I fully expected to have to re-tie some of them for photographic purposes, but the quality of flies which spilled from my morning mail was simply breath-taking. Without the help of these individuals, this would have been a poorer book and they should take as much pride in the finished article as I do.

Conversely, the least enjoyable part of the endeavour was discarding and omitting patterns from the final lists. My intention has been to list patterns that not only catch fish, but if at all possible, might stimulate the imagination of tomorrow's innovators. This is not an academic work. The detailed history and origin of every pattern will not be found, though I have attempted to give some advice on usage. I have, however, tried very hard to give correct attributions for new patterns. If any are wrongly accredited, then I can only apologise to those concerned.

In this hi-tech age of the Internet and digital TV, fly fishing is a route back to a simpler time, when man was closer to the natural rhythms of life. Time stands still beside a hill-loch or Highland river and the only passport required is a fly rod and a box of flies. If it is true that a day spent fishing is not subtracted from one's natural span, then perhaps I had better cut back a bit, or I'm going to live forever. I wish you many happy days and tight lines.

Stan Headley
August 1997

The Loch Flies

I have always thought that I could fairly accurately place the waters that a Scottish angler fished by looking through his boxes of loch wet flies. Big, bushy, colourful and wingless for the far North; drab, slim, sparse and winged from the South-West and Border regions. Central Belt patterns tend towards tinsel bodies, sparsely palmered; the Western Highlands like silver ribs and bodies; whilst the Isles patterns are notable for their dubbed bodies, heavily palmered, stoutly ribbed and with a hint of the Irish about them.

This area 'signature', as I call it, has become even more noticeable due to the phenomenal increase in anglers tying their own flies. In the past, when far fewer anglers 'rolled their own', fishers had to rely upon the shop-bought standard. Throughout the length and breadth of Scotland, anglers tended to use much the same selections from commercial sources. This is no longer so and each region of the country has its own preferred patterns. The list of Scottish loch flies currently in use is staggering. My own collections contain flies which are indispensable on certain, specific waters, but which hardly get a wetting anywhere else. There are others which are only used for very brief periods – perhaps just a few days – during the season. I am certainly not alone in this.

The biggest problem in compiling a comprehensive list of the loch flies in current use is not so much what to include, but which to leave out! Despite an attempt at objectivity, this catalogue will inevitably be tainted with the subjective and the indulgent. I apologise unreservedly to those who will undoubtedly find fault with my final selection. In my defence, though, I suggest that limited space is the true culprit.

This compilation of loch flies contains not only wet and dry flies, but also nymphs and lures that are currently in use. Moreover, they are not just the patterns for wild brown trout, but include those used for rainbow trout and also for salmon and sea-trout. There are those who consider the use of 'lures' anathema. To them, let me say that large, garishly colourful and multi-hooked 'flies' have always been used in Scottish loch fishing. The 'lures' of today are little different in concept to the Demons and Terrors of yesteryear ...though maybe some of the modern materials are a bit more startling! Personally, I don't much like 'lures' myself and would always prefer to use what I consider the more traditional Scottish flies. However, flyfishing has changed considerably this century. With increased population and leisure opportunity, added to the 'benefits' of modern transport, there is far greater angling pressure now. Water quality and habitat have deteriorated in some areas, while artificial stocking is widespread, notably with the alien rainbow trout. The use of modern 'lures' – many imported from the English reservoir scene – has spread into even the most traditional areas of Scotland. They have their place in the scheme of things and, with their undoubted popularity and wide usage, their inclusion in this volume is inevitable.

Loch fishing for salmon and sea-trout is an exciting, if minor, branch of stillwater fishing. The flies used are largely adapted from trout loch flies; indeed, many of them are the same. For this reason, I have included them here rather than in the section which deals with flies for salmon and sea-trout in rivers.

Aberdeen Angus *(A. Woolhouse)*

PLATE 1

Hook: Partridge L2A or SH1, 10-14
Silk: Brown
Tail: Bunch of ginger cock fibres
Body: In two parts: rear half Invicta yellow seal's fur or substitute, front red seal's fur or substitute
Body hackle: Palmered ginger cock hackle
Rib: Fine flat gold
Head hackle: Ginger hen hackle

This is a relatively new pattern, but with a fairly traditional look about it. Devised by Angus Woolhouse as an improvement on the Solwick, it has proved itself on browns and rainbows throughout the UK. It works best as a top dropper, but is worthy of experimentation elsewhere on the cast. I like it for early to mid season work. It may well be taken as a shrimp or sedge pupa. Try ribbing it with flat pearl for a very attractive variation.

Ace of Spades *(D. Collyer)*

PLATE 1

Hook: Partridge D4A or SH3, 8-14
Silk: Black
Body: Black chenille or, in small sizes, seal's fur or substitute.
Rib: Medium oval silver
Hackle: Natural guinea fowl hackle fibres
Wing: Two or four black hen hackles, one-and-a-half times the length of the hook shank, tied 'Matuka' style; i.e. bound along the top of the body with the ribbing
Overwing: A section of bronze mallard 'veiling' the hackle wing (it should be shorter than the hackle wing, but slightly longer than the body)

This very successful lure, developed by the late David Collyer, has stood the test of time. Although most usually considered as a lure for reservoir rainbows, I have seen it prove surprisingly effective in sizes 10 & 12 for wild brown trout in some very traditionally minded settings. It is fair to say that it is not commonly used in its smaller sizes, probably due to the degree of difficulty in tying it in miniature, but modestly sized specimens on the point of a team of wets will often prove successful.

Alexandra *(variant)*

PLATE 1

Hook: Partridge SH2, sizes 8-12
Silk: Black
Tail: Fluff from the base of a scarlet hen hackle, with a few strands of red Crystal Hair
Body: Flat silver, oval silver rib (optional)
Hackle: Black hen
Underwing: A slim bunch of red Crystal Hair strands
Overwing: Approx. 12 fibres of peacock sword

This traditional pattern is often over-looked by modern anglers. I have a feeling that the poor quality of commercial tyings, which are usually grossly over-dressed, may be to blame. Dressed as described, this is one of my favourites. Some claim it to be an unbeatable top-dropper pattern, but for me (and most others) it excels on the point, particularly in poor light and/or the late evening in very shallow water. (*see also* Silver Goat's Toe)

Allie Hardy *(Alastair Jamieson)*

PLATE 1

Hook: Partridge SH1/J1A, or Kamasan B175, 10 & 12

Tail: A tuft of fluorescent phosphor yellow floss (Glo-Brite, no.11)
Body: A mix of fiery brown and dark olive seal's fur
Hackle: One fiery brown and one olive cock hackle (matched in size). Two turns each at the head, then both palmered back down the body
Rib: Gold wire, wound in the opposite sense to secure the palmered hackles

Shetland patterns generally tend towards the brash side of garish! However, this offering from the far North, courtesy of Stephen Leask, is distinctly understated. It is a general purpose tool, but can be employed with advantage when trout are pre-occupied with daphnia.

Allrounder (J. Ketley)

PLATE 1

Hook: Partridge L2A/GRS2A, 10-14, or SH2 12-16
Silk: Black
Tail: A bunch of ginger cock hackle fibres
Body: Flat gold
Body hackle: Ginger cock hackle
Rib: Fine gold oval or wire
Wing: Well barred teal or widgeon

I have used this John Ketley pattern for many years now and its long-term consistency makes it worthy of inclusion. A general purpose pattern for loch work, it can often outfish its close cousin, the Wickham's Fancy.

Back-End Lure (W. Chalmers)

PLATE 1

Hook: Drennan Carbon Lure, 10
Silk: Black
Tail: Small bunch of pearl Crystal Hair
Body: Rusty orange chenille
Rib: Fine flat silver
Hackle: Throat of pearl Crystal Hair
Wing: Natural grey squirrel tail
Cheeks: Jungle cock

Wherever perch live in conjunction with trout, perch fry patterns are an important weapon in the angler's armoury. This offering comes from Loch Leven, where perch stocks fluctuate dramatically from year to year. At the time of writing, stocks of perch in Leven are good. This is an excellent pattern wherever trout may be found feeding on baby perch. As the name suggests, it is particularly useful when 'fry bashing' trout are encountered at the end of the season. (see also Leven Ghost)

Bibio

PLATE 1

Hook: Partridge L2A or SH1 or Kamasan B175, 8-14
Silk: Black
Body: In three parts – black, red and black – seal's fur or substitute

Body hackle: Black cock
Rib: Medium or fine oval silver, depending on size
Head hackle: Sparse, black hen – longer fibred than the body hackle

An Irish fly of great renown, the Bibio is usually attributed to Maj. Charles Roberts of the Burrishoole fishery, Co. Mayo. This pattern was originally designed for seatrout, in which capacity it excels on the Scottish West Coast lochs. In recent years, however, it has won acclaim as an indispensable pattern for both brown and rainbow trout.

Unusually, even when tied very badly, the Bibio is a pattern that will still catch fish. Shop-bought examples rarely, if ever, have the hen hackle at the head, but I firmly believe that it is a better fly for having one. It was most probably originated to imitate the natural heather fly, which abounds in certain upland areas. These insects are often blown off the heather on to the water and are much loved by hungry trout.

Variations which have the all-important mid band composed of claret or orange seal's fur have their adherents. Bushy flies of this type are often thought to be exclusively top-dropper candidates, but I find that the Bibio actually performs better as a point fly. (see Goat's Toe and Heather Fly)

Bibio (variant)

PLATE 1

Hook: Partridge L2A or SH1 or Kamasan B175, 8-14
Silk: Black
Body: In three parts – black, red, and black-seal's fur or substitute
Body hackle: Black cock
Rib: Medium or fine flat pearl lurex under the palmered hackle, with oval silver over the hackle
Head hackle: Longish, sparse, black hen

Pearl lurex has become an indispensable aid to the fly-tyer and it is used effectively to add new dimensions to traditional patterns. This is a very attractive fly with more flash and sparkle than the original, and it should be thought of as an addition to range rather than a replacement. Fish it on the point or top dropper.

Bibio, Claret *(Stewart Leslie)*

PLATE 3

Hook: Partridge L2A, J1A or SH1, 8-12
Silk: Black
Body: Mixed seal's fur or substitute, equal
measures of claret and scarlet
Hackle: Black cock: two turns at head, then
palmered
Rib: Medium oval silver

The mixing of claret and scarlet dubbing
produces a very effective colour shade: a view
strongly endorsed by Orcadian trout. Whenever
trout preferences shift to claret, try this fly. Its
simplicity and effectiveness make it a winner.

Bibio Emerger

PLATE 1

Hook: Partridge E1A or K14ST or Kamasan
B400, 12-16
Silk: Black or red
Body: In three parts as in a standard Bibio
Rib: Fine oval silver, or fine, clear monofilament
Hackle: Black hen

An immigrant from the English reservoir scene,
this is a very useful general purpose dry for
Scottish lochs and reservoirs. A great pattern for
novice tyers to dress, as the rougher & shaggier
the resultant fly, the better. I evolved my Black &
Claret from this pattern, and who is to say which
is the better of the two.

Black & Claret

PLATE 1

Hook: Partridge E1A or K14ST or Kamasan
B400, 12-16
Silk: Black
Body: In three parts – black, claret, black – seal's
fur, or substitute
Rib: Clear, fine nylon monofilament
Hackle: Sparse, straggly black hen, clipped
underneath.

This is my favourite dry fly for use on lochs or
reservoirs during hatches of dark midge. I usually
combine it on a two fly cast with a Black Blob, or
a small Black Hopper. Hatching midge often have
coloured areas within their bodies which,
although distinctly visible to trout via
transmitted light, are often missed by the human
eye. The colour claret has long been incorporated
in various dressings designed to imitate hatching
midges. I can vouch for the fact that the
efficiency of this pattern only serves to reinforce
the practice.

Black & Silver Lure *(Davie 'Chaff' Chalmers)*

PLATE 1

Hook: Kamasan B800, 10 & 12
Silk: Black
Tail: Bunch of relatively sparse black marabou
Body: Flat silver (no rib)
Wing: A relatively sparse bunch of black
marabou, extending to limit of tail
Eyes: Small silver bead chain (pair)

Flies of this type are becoming increasingly
important for loch fishing, particularly for
competition work, when conditions are tough
and fish are deep. This is a particularly effective
pattern, as the simplest of flies often are. For
early season work on Loch Leven I wouldn't be
without this one and 'Chaff' tells me that it
works consistently throughout the season. Don't
overdo the marabou – a very sparse tying works
best.
    Fish it on the top dropper on a sinking line
and expect solid confident takes 'on the hang'.

Black Blob

PLATE 1

Hook: Partridge L3A or K14ST, or Kamasan
B400, 12-14
Silk: Black
Body: Black seal's fur, or substitute, traditionally
ribbed with fine oval silver, but I prefer fine nylon
monofilament
Hackle: Short, straggly and sparse black hen

Simplicity seems to be an essential requirement
for a good dry fly and you won't find a dressing

5

much simpler than this. Whenever trout stomach contents are examined, there almost always seem to be one or two small, unidentifiable, black 'critturs' which have invariably been picked off the surface film. Trout seem to be fundamentally unable to refuse such objects. The Black Blob works brilliantly in this context and it is also worth a place during dark midge hatches.

Black Cat

PLATE 1

Hook: Kamasan Double B270, or in singles, Partridge SH1 8-12
Silk: Glo-Brite no.5 fluorescent floss, used as the tying thread
Tail: Tuft of black marabou – length dependent on size
Body: Fluorescent lime green chenille
Wing: Tuft of black marabou, extending as far back as the tail
Head: Built-up of tying floss, well varnished

This has become a standard lure for loch work in Scotland for both browns and rainbows. I like it in smallish sizes and have had success with it on some very 'traditionally minded' trout. It is normally fished on sinking lines, but will work all the way up to the surface. This black winged version seems more acceptable to wild trout than does its white-winged ancestor, the Cat's Whisker. Variations abound. (see also Black Cat (variant); White Cat; and Gold Cat)

Black Cat (variant)

PLATE 1

Hook: Drennan Traditional Wet, 8
Silk: Black
Tail: Tuft of black marabou, plus six strands of pearl Crystal Hair
Body: Fluorescent phosphor yellow chenille (Glo-Brite no.11)
Rib: Medium oval gold
Hackle: Brown partridge (optional)
Eyes: Pair of large silver bead chain eyes

The inclusion of the bead chain eyes radically affects the swimming action of this alternative to the standard Black Cat. The weight at the head gives the lure a sinuous, seductive action which can prove irresistible. However, it is a nightmare to cast (keep the leader relatively short) and virtually impossible to keep from diving to the depths. It is normally fished on weight-forward, sinking lines. It can be used effectively throughout the season, but particularly during periods when the fish are feeding at depth.

Black Kitten (Davie Malcolm)

PLATE 2

Hook: Kamasan B175, 10 and 12
Silk: Black
Tail: Tuft of black marabou
Body. Fluorescent lime green chenille
Wing: Tuft of black marabou, with shorter tuft of Glo-Brite no.5 floss over
Head: Three or four turns of gold metallic chenille or similar

This is a very clever pattern variation from Davie Malcolm's stable and one which has stood me in good stead amongst rainbows and daphnia-feeding brown trout. It is also a useful fall-back pattern for wild trout in difficult conditions, when sinking lines may offer the only hope of success.

Blae & Black

PLATE 2

Hook: Partridge L2A or Kamasan B170, 8-14
Silk: Black
Tail: Slim bunch of G.P. tippet fibres
Body: Black floss silk
Rib: Fine or medium oval silver, dependent on hook size
Hackle: Black hen
Wing: Paired slips of grey duck quill in large sizes; starling in the smallest sizes

Basically, this is a winged Black Pennell and although a venerable pattern, it is still in general use to this day. I can't say that it is a favourite of mine in this dressing, but I do have some success with a minor variant that uses a dyed yellow goose quill tail and has the hackle tied over the wing. This version is particularly useful in the late evening. The Blae & Black is a surviving remnant of a whole series of 'Blae' dressings, which are now no longer in general use. In some areas the Blae & Black is popular tied on a 'wee double' hook. (*see also* Colonel Downman

Bluebottle

PLATE 2

Hook: Partridge L2A, J1A, or G3A, 8-12
Silk: Black
Body: Royal blue chenille
Hackle: Longish black hen

In all my years investigating the contents of trout stomachs, I have yet to find a natural bluebottle. No matter, this pattern is a very good general purpose loch fly for trout and sea-trout. What they imagine it to be is beyond me, I'm afraid, but that won't stop me using it. All trout seem to be susceptible to blue coloured flies from time to time, particularly late in the season. Fish it on the top dropper and on a floating line. Other variations exist, but I think this is the best of them. (*see also* Zulu, Blue; Loch Ordie, Blue; and Donegal Blue)

Bogie

PLATE 2

Hook: Partridge SH2 or Kamasan B200, 12 & 14
Silk: fluorescent phosphor yellow floss (Glo-Brite no.11)
Tail: Tuft of fluorescent phosphor yellow floss
Body: Two layers of tying silk, with pearl Lurex over
Body hackle: Black cock
Rib: Very fine oval silver or wire
Head hackle: Longish black hen

This is a fly designed for the depths. It is somewhat like the proverbial 'little girl': when its good, its very, very good; but when its bad... In conditions of bright sunlight and when there is a hint of green algal coloration, this fly works very well in front of or instead of, mini-lures. I have also had some notable days using this pattern for wild browns, when fish have been feeding deep

and a sinking line was the only hope. (*see also* Pearly Green Palmer)

Booby Nymph (or White Cat)

PLATE 2

Hook: Partridge L2A/GRS2A or Kamasan B175, 10
Silk: White
Tail: White or yellow marabou
Body: Glo-Brite chenille, no.11
Wing: White marabou
Eyes: Tie in a suitable strip of Ethafoam, with a figure-of-eight lashing and trim to size and shape

Booby Nymphs have revolutionised many aspects of deep water trout fishing. By their inherent buoyancy, they can allow other flies of negative buoyancy to fish just above the loch bed when presented on a fast sinking line. In their own right, Boobies have an action all of their own when retrieved in short, sharp movements. Although this action seems lethally attractive to rainbow trout, wild brown trout, on the whole, are less impressed. The dressing behind the foam 'boobies' can be varied to suit conditions, and are limited solely by the tyer's's imagination.

Brown Palmer (A. McConnachie & I. Hutcheon)

PLATE 2

Hook: Partridge G3A or Kamasan B175, 10 & 12
Silk: Black or brown
Body: Claret chenille
Rib: Medium oval gold
Hackle: Dark red/brown cock-two turns at head, then palmered

Invented by Sandy McConnachie and Ian Hutcheon, this fly has been around so long in Orkney it is now almost considered a traditional pattern. The name is somewhat misleading since the fly is predominantly claret. Although an excellent general purpose pattern for peat water lochs, I have seen it do remarkable work on Loch Leven and English reservoirs. I can't give you many clues as to when exactly it will perform, but when it works it works well! I have had reliable sport with it when fish were taking hatching dark sedge.

Bruiser

PLATE 2

Hook: Partridge L2A or Kamasan B175, 8-12
Silk: Black
Tail: Flax blue wool
Body: Gentian blue wool
Rib: Fine oval silver
Hackle: Two cock hackles, one Gentian blue, the other natural black, palmered together

This is one of the great Kingsmill-Moore's patterns and I have to admit that I have never actually tied one myself. The reason that I include it here is that I once saw a bushy size 10 Bruiser perform a miracle on Spiggie loch, in Shetland, one flat calm evening during a hatch of very small midge. On that occasion, the Bruiser both moved and caught an absolute heap of fish. In its country of origin it is primarily a sea-trout pattern. It is very popular locally in the far North and West.

Bugs Bunny (Sandy Nicholson)

PLATE 2

Hook: Partridge SH2 or Kamasan B200, 12 & 14
Silk: Red
Tail: Tuft of rabbit fur, dyed fluorescent peach
Body: Flat silver, or pearl over fluorescent white floss
Rib: Fine oval silver or wire
Hackle: Fluorescent peach rabbit, tied as a beard
Wing: Long tuft of fluorescent peach rabbit fur, with a greater preponderance of guard hairs, plus a slim strip of holographic pearl tinsel either side

Peach has gained considerable popularity as a fly dressing colour in recent seasons, both for wild and stocked trout. It seems to be particularly effective in poor light conditions. I was present at the birth' of this pattern on Loch Leven, where it made a good impression on some trout feeding on perch fry. It has since proved very effective on wild trout waters for trout feeding on sticklebacks and when the water is turbid.

Although a far cry from more traditional patterns, I would strongly advise its inclusion in any general all-purpose fly collection. A useful variant has a tail of Glo-Brite no.11 floss and jungle cock cheeks.

I have little doubt that this will become a standard pattern.

Bumble, Claret

PLATE 3

Hook: Partridge L2A, J1A or SH1, 8-14
Silk: Black
Tail: Slim bunch of G.P. tippet fibres
Body: Dark claret seal's fur, or substitute
Body hackle: Two matched cock hackles, claret and black
Rib: Medium or fine oval gold, dependent on hook size
Head hackle: Blue jay fibres

The legacy of the late, great, Kingsmill Moore was a collection of wet flies which grow in popularity and fame as each season passes. The versatility of this particular pattern seems to be limitless, whether for salmon, sea-trout, browns or rainbows. I cannot imagine being without it, or one of its many varied forms.

Although the above dressing is excellent, I prefer mine ribbed with silver oval rather than gold, with a tag of flat silver under a tail of hot orange dyed G.P. tippets. Contrary to common usage, I do not believe that blue dyed guineafowl is an acceptable substitute for jay fibres – for this pattern at least.

I make no apology for listing the following important variations.

Bumble, Claret (fluorescent tag)

PLATE 3

Pattern as standard except
Tag: Two turns of flat silver under tail
Tail: Mixed fluorescent floss: Glo-Brite, nos. 7, 8, 11 and 12
Rib: Medium or fine oval silver

I was surprised to discover how effective a suitably altered Claret Bumble could be on daphnia-feeding brown and rainbow trout. It only serves to underline the versatility of this pattern. Varied as above and fished on all densities of lines, I consider this variation a nigh indispensable pattern when the fish are preoccupied with daphnia.

It is sometimes referred to as the 'Nice Arse Claret Bumble', which is a bit rude, maybe, but these things tend to stick.

Bumble, Claret (leggy version)

PLATE 3

Stuart Leslie has refined this pattern over the years. Pattern as standard except:

Hook: sizes 8 & 10
Tag: Two turns of flat silver under tail
Tail: G.P. tippets, dyed hot orange
Rib: Medium oval silver
Head hackle: Jay fibres over blue peacock neck hackle

This form of the Claret Bumble is a really good fly, to be fished as a top dropper in wild conditions of wind and wave, for sea-trout, salmon and wild browns. Takes can be savage under these conditions.

Bumble, Claret (Muddler)

PLATE 3

Hook: Partridge SH2, 12-16
Silk: Black
Tag: Two turns of flat silver
Tail: G.P. tippets, dyed hot orange, or mixed Glo-Brite fluorescent floss, nos 7, 8, 11 and 12
Body: Dark claret seal's fur, or substitute, or red Lurex, for a slimmer version
Body hackle: Pair of matched cock hackles, claret and black
Rib: Medium or fine oval silver
Head hackle: Blue jay fibres
Head: Fine dark roe deer hair, clipped to form a bullet-shaped head, retaining some of the fine tips as a collar or pseudo-hackle

Perhaps not the easiest fly to tie, particularly in its smallest sizes, but this fly is well worth the effort. It is an exceptional taker of surface-active fish in the late evenings and during the day when it is overcast. This is one of my favourites for Loch Leven and, indeed, on any other water where mini-Muddlers work well.

Bumble, Claret (slimline)

PLATE 3

Pattern as standard except:
Tag: Two turns of flat silver under tail
Tail: G.P. tippets, dyed hot orange
Body: Flat red Lurex
Rib: Fine oval silver

Trout frequently turn up their noses at bulky patterns, preferring flies with slim profiles. On such occasions, this is a good pattern when one wants a slimmer 'claret' fly. The red Lurex body darkens to claret under the influence of the palmered hackles. In conditions of light wind, or when dark midges are active, this variation can be supremely effective and I am confident that it will quickly gain widespread popularity.

Bumble, Golden Olive

PLATE 2

Hook: Partridge SH1 or L2A, 8-14
Silk: Brown
Tail: G.P. crest
Body: Golden olive seal's fur, or substitute
Body hackle: Two cock hackles, matched in size: golden olive and dark ginger
Rib: Fine or medium oval gold, depending on size
Head hackle: Blue jay

The secrets of tying this pattern successfully are as follow: a) Strip the fibres from the blue jay feather and tie them in at the head, extending forward over the eye, as the first tying step. When the rest of the fly is complete, stroke back the fibres and form the head; b) Maintain a slightly wider spacing than normal between the turns of body hackle; c) For very small sizes, omit the golden olive hackle, but pick-out fibres of the dubbing instead. Obey these rules and one can tie this pattern on almost any sized hook. The Bumbles are an enormously successful series of palmered wet flies, described by T.C. Kingsmill Moore in his brilliant book on Irish flyfishing, *A Man May Fish*. These flies continue to grow in popularity, particularly for wild fish. The Golden Olive Bumble seems to embody just about every element that stirs a trout's appetite and it would be one of my first selections on an unknown water. In its home country of Ireland it is generally accepted to have originated as a hatching mayfly imitator. I have found it excellent for browns, rainbows, sea-trout and salmon. This pattern seems to have no limits, though – strangely – Kingsmill Moore, the originator, did not rate it as a sea-trout fly. (*see* Golden Olive (parachute) Plate 18)

Bumble, Golden Olive (leggy version)

PLATE 2

Hook: Partridge SH1 or L2A, 8-14
Silk: Brown
Tag: Two turns of flat gold, under tail
Tail: G.P. crest
Body: Golden olive seal's fur, or substitute
Body hackle: Two cock hackles, matched in size: golden olive and dark ginger. The turns should be spaced rather further apart than for the standard Golden Olive Bumble dressing
Rib: Fine or medium oval gold, depending on size
Head hackle: Red G.P. pheasant body feather, behind blue jay

This is my favourite Golden Olive Bumble variant for the top dropper in a big wave. In such conditions, it considerably outshines the original. I haven't yet tried it on salmon or sea-trout. It also functions as a vague imitation of a hatching mayfly and is another example of the 'straggly' style of wet fly that is proving so deadly of late.

Bumble, Golden Olive (Muddler)

PLATE 2

Hook: Partridge SH2, 12-16
Tag: Two turns of flat gold
Silk: Brown
Tail: G.P. crest
Body: Golden olive seal's fur, or substitute

Body hackle: Two cock hackles, matched in size: golden olive and dark ginger
Rib: Fine or medium oval gold, depending on size
Head hackle: Blue jay
Collar/Head: Roe deer hair, spun and clipped to bullet shape

Dress the fly as one would a standard Golden Olive Bumble (with a gold tag, optional), but adjust the body length to leave enough space on the hook shank for a neat 'Muddler' head. Try to leave some fine tips of the deer hair to form a collar or 'pseudo-hackle'. When trout show a preference for feeding out in the open water of lochs or reservoirs and fairly close to the surface, mini-Muddlers are often lethal. The Golden Olive Bumble Muddler has proved particularly deadly. (*see also* Melvin Octopus; and Invicta)

Bumble, Hot-Orange

PLATE 2

Hook: Partridge SH1 or L2A, 8-14
Silk: Brown
Tag: Two turns of flat gold, under tail
Tail: G.P. crest
Body: Golden olive seal's fur, or substitute
Body hackle: Two cock hackles, matched in size: golden olive and hot orange
Rib: Fine or medium oval gold, depending on size
Head hackle: Blue jay

Adapted from the Golden Olive Bumble by local tackle dealer, W S Sinclair, this pattern has become a standard in the far North. Particularly good on peat-stained waters, it can be excellent tied on a longshank 10 or 12 and fished 'greased-up' during autumn 'Daddy' hatches. I was surprised to discover, during a trip to Ireland, that this dressing was referred to over there as the 'Orkney Bumble'.

Bumble, Ken's Golden Olive (K. Kennedy)

PLATE 2

Hook: Partridge SH3 long shank
Silk: Brown or black

PLATE 1

Aberdeen Angus, Ace of Spades, Adult Buzzer (Millar), Alexandra
Allrounder (Ketley), Allie Hardie, Amber Emerger, Amber Hopper
Black-End Lure, Bibio, Bibio (variant), Black & Claret, Bibio Emerger
Black & Silver Lure, Black Buzzer (Glassford), Black Blob, Black & Silver Muddler
Black Cat, Black Dunkeld, Black Cat (Chalmers' variant)

Tag: Two turns flat gold
Tail: G.P. crest, long
Body: Golden olive seal's fur
Body hackle: Golden olive and hot orange cock, palmered together
Rib: Fine oval gold
Head hackle: Blue peacock neck feather, wound as a hackle

At the back-end of the year, when Daddy Longlegs are featuring strongly on the menu, this pattern has done a lot of damage on the Orkney lochs. Personally, I like to give it a good dose of floatant and pull it through the wave tops. Others simply fish it as standard, but they do just as well with it. I recently discovered that this pattern has made the return journey back across the Irish Sea and been taken to the hearts of many Irish anglers who were fulsome in its praise.

Burleigh

PLATE 2

Hook: Partridge L2A or Kamasan B170, 10-14
Silk: Light yellow
Tail: Slim bunch of ginger cock hackle fibres
Body: Tying silk, well-waxed so as to darken the shade
Rib: Silver wire or very fine oval
Hackle: Light ginger hen, sparse
Wing: Starling, tied to lie close to the hook and with the natural curvature of the feather turning downwards.

This is a venerable pattern from Loch Leven, where it should still be highly efficient as its colouring strongly imitates that of the predominant midge species. It is not a million miles away from a pale Greenwell's Glory, which is one of the best wet flies for a flat calm on Leven. It is a pattern that could probably be used far more than it is today. (see Greenwell, Norm's)

Burton

PLATE 3

Hook: Partridge SH2 12 & 10
Silk: Black
Tail: G.P. crest

Body: In three parts: yellow, red, then black seal's fur, or substitute
Rib: Flat silver
Hackle: Dark furnace hen
Wing: Slips of cinnamon hen or turkey, overlying a central core of teal flank

This pattern originally came from Dumfriesshire's river Nith, as a sea-trout and salmon fly. Today, it is only as a loch fly that it continues to be regarded and particularly on Loch Lomond. Many of the patterns used on Lomond have a popularity peculiar to that loch. Such patterns include the Turkey series, the Mallard series, and the Haslam. Lomond patterns have a somewhat antiquated look to them, and rather complicated dressings.

Butcher

PLATE 2

Hook: Partridge L2A, 8-14, or small doubles, 12-16
Silk: Black
Tail: Traditionally: red ibis substitute. **Latterly:** fluffy fibres from the base of a scarlet hackle or scarlet cock hackle fibres
Body: Flat silver
Rib: Fine oval silver
Hackle: Black hen, dyed for preference.
Wing: Slips of mallard blue speculum feather

One of the most famous traditional patterns of all, the Butcher has been about for over a century and a half. It is said to have been invented by Messrs. Jewhurst and Moon, of Tunbridge Wells, Kent (of all unlikely places!). Mr Moon was a butcher by trade and the fly was apparently called the Moon's Fly until about 1938. Few consider it an absolutely indispensable pattern for browns or rainbows nowadays, but it maintains a very high esteem for sea-trout in rivers, estuaries and salmon in lochs. I used to be very fond of a size 14 Butcher, fished on its own, dead slow just below the surface, during midge hatches. In recent years, however, other options have come along and I use it much less. (see also Butcher, Bloody; Butcher, Kingfisher [variant]; and Butcher, Teal-Winged)

Butcher, Kingfisher

PLATE 9

Hook: Partridge SH2, 12-16, or Kamasan B175, 10-14
Silk: Black
Tail: Light blue (teal blue) hackle fibres
Body: Flat gold (brassy yellow, for preference)
Rib: Very fine oval gold, or wire
Hackle: Hot orange hen
Wing: Very lightly coloured slips from a mallard primary

Now, many people are going to shake their heads and think I'm wrong in claiming this dressing as the original. However, there are some very old references describing the Kingfisher Butcher as having a 'blae' wing and not the mallard blue speculum, as in the standard Butcher.

This dressing is a very effective general purpose trout fly, and I strongly favour it when olives are hatching in bright and windy conditions. It is also a very effective pattern for finnock sea-trout in estuaries and rivers.

Butcher, Kingfisher (wee double)

PLATE 9

Hook: Partridge SH2, 12-16, or Kamasan B175, 10-14, or 'wee doubles', 10-16
Silk: Black
Tail: Light blue (teal blue) hackle fibres
Body: Flat gold (brassy yellow, for preference)
Rib: Very fine oval gold, or wire
Hackle: Hot orange hen
Wing: Slips of mallard blue speculum feather

I really can not say that I am overly fond of this pattern, although it has done me some good for sea-trout. On its home waters of Loch Leven, where it used to be considered indispensable, it has never taken me a single fish. However, there are many anglers, particularly south of the Highland Boundary Line, who would include it in their essential selection, so perhaps the fault is mine.

Butcher, Leven (D. Chalmers & S. Headley)

PLATE 9

Hook: Partridge SH2, 14 & 12 or Kamasan B175, 12 & 10
Silk: Black
Tail: Fluorescent scarlet floss (Glo-Brite no.4)
Body: Flat silver
Rib: Very fine oval silver, or wire
Wing: Black marabou or dyed rabbit, with a single strip of holographic tinsel each side
Cheeks: Fluorescent scarlet floss (Glo-Brite no.4)

During the early summer of 1994 there was a rumour going the rounds that big baskets of fish were coming off Leven to a Bloody Butcher. 'Chaff' Chalmers and myself came up with this modernized version and had some success with it, particularly for brown trout. It does best as a day fly and, although effective at any time during the season, it seems best during the latter months.

Butcher, Teal-Winged

PLATE 15

Hook: Partridge SH2 or Kamasan B170, 12 & 14
Silk: Black
Tail: Bunch of scarlet or red hackle fibres
Body: Flat silver
Rib: Very fine oval silver
Hackle: Black hen
Wing: Strip of teal flank, rolled

I came across this pattern many years ago, when it was being touted as a sure-fire killer for English reservoirs. Willing to give any pattern a chance, I employed it on my home Orcadian waters where it became almost an over-night success. I must admit to being somewhat surprised as the Peter Ross, which it closely resembles, was much less successful in similar circumstances. To paraphrase the old saying: 'There's nowt so queer as trout'.

PLATE 2
Black Kitten, Blae & Black, Bloody Butcher, Bluebottle
Golden Olive Bumble, Hot-Orange Bumble, Ken's Bumble, Leggy Golden Olive Bumble
Golden Olive Bumble Muddler, Blushing Buzzer, Bogie
Booby Nymph, Brown Palmer, Bruiser, Bugs Bunny
Burleigh, Butcher, Hardy's Gold Butcher

PLATE 3
Burton, Near-Perfect Buzzer, CDC Caddis, CDC Emerger, CDC Hopper
CDC Sedge, Caenis Muddler, Camasunary Killer, Cardineal
Cat's Whisker (variant), Cinnamon & Gold, Clan Chief, Claret Buzzer (Millar)
Claret Bibio, Claret Bumble, Fluorescent Tag Claret Bumble
Claret Bumble (slimline), Claret Bumble (leggy), Claret Bumble Muddler

At first, I really liked this fly for shallow water and bright conditions and found it excellent in the slow periods of high summer. I don't use it for this role as much these days, but have come to regard it as a very useful dropper fly for fast-sinking lines. This is a fly worthy of serious consideration, particularly if you have problems catching on the Peter Ross.

Buzzer, Adult (J. Millar)

PLATE 1

Hook: Kamasan B160, 16
Silk: Black
Abdomen: Half a dozen dyed black deer hair fibres in a bundle, tied as a detached body
Wings: Pale badger cock hackle points, short
Thorax: Black mole fur, built into a small ball
Hackle: A good quality black cock hackle, wound through the thorax
Thorax cover: Crow or grey mallard wing quill

Jimmy Millar advises the use of this pattern when things get very tricky during very calm conditions, and the fish are feeding on tiny midge. Delicately constructed, this pattern really can prove a 'day-saver'.

Buzzer, Black (I. Glassford)

PLATE 1

Hook: Partridge K14ST, 10 – 14
Silk: Black
Tail: Fluorescent white floss (Glo-Brite no.16)
Abdomen: Two or three fibres of dyed black cock pheasant tail
Split shuck: Strands of flat pearl Mylar, tied in at tail, divided and brought up underneath the abdomen and tied in at the thorax
Abdomen Rib: Fine silver wire
Legs: Four strands of pearl Flashabou, tied to trail underneath
Wing bud: A short tuft fluorescent fire orange floss (Glo-Brite no.5)
Thorax cover: Dyed black cock pheasant tail fibres
Thorax: Black rabbit underfur
Hackle: Black hen
Breathers: As tail, split

Ian Glassford, himself, admits to wondering if such an elaborate dressing is really necessary. I don't know either, but I have used this successfully both north and south of the Border. I fish it on a sinking line in the middle of the cast between a mini-lure and something vaguely imitative, such as a Stick Fly or Gold Ribed Hare's Ear Nymph (see also Buzzer, Claret)

Buzzer, Blushing

PLATE 2

Hook: Partridge K14ST, 10-14
Silk: Black
Body: Two layers of tying silk, well varnished, leaving space for a small thorax of peacock herl
Wing Buds: Four strands of Glo-Brite No.8 each side, tied under the thorax and brought over as cheeks
Hackle: Shortish black hen, no more than two turns

This is one of the new generation of loch flies, in the modern imitative vein. Tied to represent a black midge pupa immediately prior to hatching, it should be fished static or very slow. When fish can be seen feeding on ascending midge pupae, this pattern is 'death on a hook'. It becomes very simple fishing: just chuck it at a rise and wait for the line to go tight. To be honest, it should be banned! (see also Buzzer, Near Perfect).

Buzzer, Guzzer (J. Millar)

Hook: Drennan Midge or Partridge K14ST, 12 & 14
Silk: Black
Body: Dark claret seal's fur, slim and tapered
Rib: Fine flat pearl Mylar (unstretched)
Thorax: As body, built up into a ball shape
Thorax cover: Cock pheasant tail fibres, dyed orange
Breathers: White baby wool, split and divided with a figure-of-eight whipping

Millar's nymphs and dry flies are amongst the most attractive that I have seen. The neatness and sparsity of his dressing style is the key to their success. He advises that the above pattern should be 'swung round on the wind, usually with a Pheasant Tail Nymph or a Gold Ribbed Hare's Ear on the point'. This fly is worth trying on a sinking line retrieved slowly amongst other imitative or semi-imitative patterns, or above a Booby Nymph. (*see* Heather Fly; and Pearly Bits)

Buzzer, Near Perfect

PLATE 3

Hook: Partridge K14ST, 10-14
Silk: Black
Body: Stripped peacock quill, well varnished
Cheeks: Fluorescent orange floss silk (Glo-Brite, no.8)
Thorax: Small build-up of peacock herl
Hackle: Short fibred grey dun hen, one turn only

Once the black midge of the early season have disappeared, they are generally followed by a lighter coloured, greyish midge. This pattern has been devised as a close-copy and it is extremely effective when fished static or very slowly amongst feeding fish. It is also worth a try fished on a short dropper below dry patterns.

CDC Caddis (D. McPhail)

PLATE 3

Hook: Partridge K14ST or similar, 10-14
Silk: Black or brown
Body: Dubbed, well mixed hare's ear
Wing: Two cul de canard feathers, tied looped, with a few fibres trailing as legs
Head: Well mixed hare's ear from base of wing to the hook eye

The winging method for this highly effective pattern is to tie in the cdc feathers by their points at the extreme posterior end of the body. Complete the body and then bring the feathers forward and tie them in, leaving just a little room for the construction of a head. Allow the bend of the feather to extend beyond the hook bend, and a few fibres to trail behind as legs.

This virtually unsinkable pattern can have a variety of body colours to suit the natural emerging insect. (*see also* CDC Sedge)

CDC Emerger (D. McPhail)

PLATE 3

Hook: Partridge K14ST or similar, 10-14
Silk: Black
Body: Cock pheasant tail fibres, wound
Rib: Fine copper wire
Hackle: Olive hen
Wing: One or two cdc feathers, tied 'loop style' over a couple of strands copper Crystal Hair (one either side)

The use of cul de canard (duck preen gland feathers) has made quite an impact upon stillwater dry fly design. The plumage has a peculiarly subtle appearance that gives a wonderfully good suggestion of insect wings. This method of looping the plumes allows a bubble of air to be trapped within the dressing, not only making the fly very buoyant whilst sitting deep in the surface film, but also creating a very natural looking imitation. Dressing materials should be adapted to represent the colours of emerging insects. (*see also* Emerger, Amber; and Bibio Emerger)

CDC Hopper (D. McPhail)

PLATE 3

Hook: Partridge K14ST or Kamasan B400, 10-14
Silk: Black
Body: Dark claret seal's fur
Rib: Very fine flat gold
Legs: Six knotted cock pheasant tail fibres, one-and-a-half times body length
Wing: One or two CDC feathers, looped

I normally prefer my Hoppers as simple as possible, and have had little success with augmented patterns. However, many of my acquaintances are strongly committed to CDC Hoppers because, they argue, no added floatant is required and the fly can sit semi-submerged in the surface film. There would seem to be a lot of sense in this, so perhaps I should review my own opinion. Adjust pattern coloration to suit conditions. (*see also* Hopper, Amber; Hopper, Black [dry])

PLATE 4
Claret Dabbler (variant), Coachman, Coachman Nymph, Coch-y-Bonddu
Coch Zulu, Cock Robin, Colonel Downman, Connemara Black
Cow Dung (Irvine), Craftye, Connemara Claret
Dark Mackerel, Damsel Fly Nymph (goldhead), Olive Dabbler
Diawl Bach, Doobry, Donegal Blue

PLATE 5
Doony Murdo, Dunkeld, Dunkeld Muddler, Extractor
Deepwater Dunkeld, Fiery-Brown Bibio, Fiery-Brown Emerger, Hare's Ear & Claret Emerger
Hare's Ear & Olive Emerger, Fleeuck, Fionn Spider
Fluo Green Midge, Fluo Soldier Palmer (1), Fluo Soldier Palmer (2)
Fluo Soldier Palmer Muddler, Fourwater Favourite, Frenzy

CDC Sedge

PLATE 3

Hook: Partridge E1A, GRS3A or K14ST, 10-14
Silk: Brown
Body: Well mixed hare's mask, with plenty of guard hairs
Rib: Fine oval gold or fine, clear monofilament
Wing: Four CDC feathers, tied flat over the body and extending just beyond the bend of the hook
Hackle: Medium red/brown hen, clipped flush underneath

I have taken some excellent bags of trout on this pretty little dry pattern since first I tied one about six years ago. Fished static or inched back it seems irresistible to wild browns and stocked rainbows. During sedge (caddis) hatches, this fly, along with the Sedgehog, would be my first line of attack. Do not grease the CDC wing until it becomes hopelessly bedraggled and, then, only very sparingly.

Caenis Muddler

PLATE 3

Hook: Partridge SH2, 14
Silk: Black
Body: Flat gold
Rib: Very fine oval gold
Wing: Tuft of fluorescent white marabou, extending no farther than the rear end of the body
Head: Fine roe deer hair, clipped to a bullet shape, retaining some fine tips as a collar

A major caenis hatch is the cause of hair-loss amongst most anglers. Catching trout that are feeding on caenis is always a problem and no single pattern will provide a complete solution. However, this little Muddler comes pretty close and has stood me in good stead for many years. Caenis feeders swim so high in the water that the angler's lures are frequently below their field of vision: quite often they are ignored because the fish simply don't see them. The buoyancy and water disrupting qualities of the Muddler head helps solve this problem. I also believe that gold-bodied flies, with touches of startling-white, are

effective against caenis feeders. (*see also* Tup's Indispensable [variant])

Camasunary Killer

PLATE 3

Hook: Partridge J1A or SH1, 8-12
Silk: Black
Tail: Royal blue wool
Body: In two parts: rear, as tail; front, fluorescent red wool
Rib: Medium oval silver
Hackle: Long black hen, tied full

This pattern, or its progenitor, was apparently devised by Stephen Johnson, of Jedburgh, whose family owned the Camasunary fishery on the Isle of Skye. As a sea-trout pattern it is held in high esteem and has largely been popularized by Peter Deane, doyen of professional fly dressers. It is very effective, particularly for estuary work, in which case I would strongly advise using corrosion-resistant hooks, such as the Partridge SH1. This pattern has been and continues to be much modified: I have seen it dressed with a palmered black cock hackle. Personally, I have always preferred to chop and dub wool bodies, rather than simply winding on a strand of wool yarn. I believe it produces a better looking fly.

Cardineal

PLATE 3

Hook: Partridge SH2, 10 & 12
Silk: Black
Tail: Bunch of scarlet hen hackle fibres
Body: Flat silver, or flat pearl Mylar over fluorescent white floss
Rib: Fine oval silver
Hackle: Scarlet hen
Wing: Slips of scarlet dyed duck, with well barred teal partially over

There is a Demon-style tandem called the Red Lure which, in my early youth, was extremely popular locally for sea-trout. This pattern is a miniature version of it, employing similar materials. It has a strong allegiance to the Silver Cardinal, which still has potential for sea-trout. I have used the above pattern to good effect in bright, windy conditions on brackish lochs and estuaries and I believe it is a fly worthy of far greater attention in such circumstances. (see also Teal, Blue & Silver).

Cat's Whisker (variant)

PLATE 3

Hook: Partridge D4A 6-10, for mini version SH1 10-12
Silk: Glo-Brite no.5 fluorescent floss as thread
Tail: Small tuft of white marabou
Body: Fluorescent lime green chenille
Wing: White marabou, reaching the end of the tail. A few strands of Flashabou or holographic tinsel won't hurt
Head: Build-up of tying thread, well varnished

The above dressing is essentially the Mini-White Cat, which I use a lot. I don't use the massive long shank versions, with bead chain eyes, as I believe that their employment is an admission of defeat. I will concede that this is entirely my own personal and subjective view. The White Cat (as it is largely known in Scotland) is a very effective pattern for both browns and rainbows in deep and/or discoloured water, or very bright conditions. When fish are pre-occupied with daphnia, lures of this type may be the only successful approach. Many colour variations abound, principally changing only wing and tail colourings. Orange and yellow are the most common colour changes. (see also Black Cat).

Cinnamon & Gold

PLATE 3

Hook: Partridge L2A or SH2, 8-14
Silk: Brown
Tail: In small sizes: a slim bunch of G.P. tippet fibres. In large sizes, omit entirely
Body: Flat gold
Hackle: Hen hackle, of a colour to match the wing
Wing: Slips of cinnamon coloured hen quill, or partridge tail

One of a very few ancient patterns which I consider to be indispensable in modern day flyfishing. A Cinnamon & Gold on the point will regularly take bigger than average fish from most waters and, in its larger sizes, is extremely effective for sea-trout and salmon from lochs. It is a must for those doldrums weeks in mid-season.

It interests me that the preferred shade of cinnamon differs from region to region. It would appear that, by and large, as one travels North the fly becomes increasingly dark. The versions used in the Northern Isles are virtually unrecognisable to our Southern cousins.

Clan Chief (John Kennedy)

PLATE 3

Hook: Partridge J1A or SH1, 8-12
Tag: Two turns of flat silver, under the tail
Tail: Fluorescent floss in two parts, scarlet over yellow. In large sizes, similarly coloured bunches of hackle fibres
Body: Black seal's fur or substitute
Body hackle: A black and a scarlet cock hackle, wound together
Rib: Medium oval silver
Head hackle: Long black hen

John Kennedy, from South Uist, has produced a number of modern classic loch-style patterns of which this is perhaps his most famous. Very much in the Kingsmill-Moore, 'Bumble' style, from Ireland, this fly demands a place in any fly box. It is my number one top dropper sea-trout and salmon loch pattern for wild, grey days. On its day, it is equally effective for wild brown trout. The fly shown is the salmon and sea-trout version.

Coachman

PLATE 4

Hook: Partridge L2A 10-14, or SH2 12-16
Silk: Black
Body: A single strand of bronze peacock herl, wound in butting turns
Rib: Very fine oval gold
Wing: Slim paired slips of white duck quill, tied low over the back and with the natural curve of the feather downwards

21

PLATE 6

G.P. Spider, Fritz Cat (goldhead), Ginger Quill (variant)
Goat's Toe, Gizmo, Goat's Toe (variant)
GRHE (variant), Hare's Ear Muddler, Gold Cat (Chalmers), Golden Banton Midge
Goldie, Grannom (variant), Green & Brown
Green & Gold Lure (Buchanan)

PLATE 7
Green French Partridge, Green Invicta, Green Palmer (Watt), Green Peter
Green Peter Muddler, Green Shredge, Greenwell's Glory, Greenwell Spider
Yellow-Tagged Greenwell, Norm's Greenwell, Grenadier, Grey Monkey
Grouse & Claret, Harrold's Grouse & Claret
Grizzle Lure (Murphy), Hare's Ear Shipman's, Hare's Ear Coch Zulu, Hammer Fly

Hackle: Rich, red/brown hen hackle or, optionally, black over the wing

This is another ancient pattern the popularity of which has suffered due to the poor quality of commercial examples. Tied as above, slim and simple, it is one of the best late evening/night flies available. The fuller, fatter dressing is said to imitate those big, fluffy moths which often descend in the late evening. I have never had any degree of success with 'fat' Coachmen and remain to be convinced that moths feature prominently on the trout's menu.

Fish this slim version slowly on the point, for maximum efficiency. I have found it good for both brown and rainbow trout, and also for river sea-trout in the evening.

Coachman Nymph

PLATE 4

Hook: Partridge K14ST, 12
Silk: Black
Tag: One turn of flat gold
Body: One very fine strand of peacock herl
Rib: Fine oval gold
Wing: Short tuft of white hen hackle fibres
Hackle: Short dark furnace hen, tied sparse

I came up with this pattern some years ago when a very small standard Coachman was doing exceptionally well with some midge feeding trout. I thought I might be able to improve upon the original for such conditions. Although this variation on the theme has been a great success, its progenitor is by no means redundant. I like to cast this pattern to visibly rising fish, in flat calms or the slightest of ripples and give it a few tweaks, or long slow pulls.

Coch-y-Bonddu

PLATE 4

Hook: Partridge L2A or GRS2A, 10-14
Silk: Black or brown
Tag: Two turns of flat gold
Body: Two strands of bronze peacock herl: one down the body in butting turns and one wound up in open turns

Rib: Very fine oval gold, or wire
Hackle: Dark furnace hen, tied long and sparse

Peacock herl bodied flies lack the respect they deserve mainly, I suspect, because English flytying pundits, who have the angling press by the ear, don't favour them much. The Coch-y-bonddu is a very effective, semi-imitative pattern for mid-summer use on any water. I find it will only work for me in top dropper position on a floating or intermediate line, but I rate it as a 'first eleven' player.

Tying note: Never twist herls into a rope, before winding the body. The resultant mess is ugly and opaque and there is no worthwhile improvement in durability achieved thereby. Use each herl as a dubbed thread and the result is a delicate, translucent and iridescent fuzz. The fine gold wire ribbing almost disappears into the herl and it is this which greatly enhances durability. (see also Palmered Coch; and Partridge Coch)
NB The above spelling is the one most generally used by British flyfishers. Strictly speaking, however, we should defer to Welsh speakers who insist that it should be Coch-a-bon-ddu (see Trout & Salmon Flies of Wales by Moc Morgan, Merlin Unwin Books 1996)

Coch Zulu

PLATE 4

Hook: Partridge J1A or SH1, 8-12
Silk: Black
Tail: Tuft of fluorescent red wool
Body: Black seal's fur, or substitute
Body hackle: One or two dark furnace hen hackles, dependent on hook size
Rib: Medium oval gold or narrow flat gold
Head hackle: A longish dark furnace hen hackle

Although this pattern is now strongly associated with Orkney, it was introduced here by the Welsh during the International Flyfishing Championships in the eighties and, I'm sure, they would claim Welsh origins for it. However, Hamish Stewart in The Book of the Seatrout (uncompleted at his death in 1914), claimed to have used a virtually identical pattern to good effect in the South Uist lochs for sea-trout. An older pattern called a Gold Zulu strongly resembles this tying, but has a peacock herl body and an oval gold rib. A very good wild trout pattern in its smaller sizes, its popularity is assured for it being at its best in the middle dropper position, a great rarity amongst flies of this ilk. John Kennedy tells me that this pattern is still popular for migratory fish in his South Uist lochs.

An alternative tail of fluorescent lime green floss or wool produces an excellent pattern for high summer on daphnia feeding trout.

Cock Robin (variant)

PLATE 4

Hook: Partridge L2A 8-14, or SH2 10-16
Silk: Black
Tail: A slim bunch of ginger cock hackle fibres
Body: In two halves: rear, Invicta yellow seal's fur or substitute; fore, scarlet seal's fur or substitute
Rib: Fine oval gold
Hackle: Ginger hen
Wing: Slips of hen pheasant secondary

Not so very far removed from its Irish ancestor, this pattern is a very successful sedge pupa imitation in waters of Scotland's Central Belt, such as Leven and other waters where sedge hatches are important. Flies with mixed bodies were very popular in my youth, but seem to have fallen from grace of late, as indeed have winged wet flies, to a greater or lesser extent. (see also Aberdeen Angus)

Colonel Downman

PLATE 4

Hook: Kamasan B405 or Partridge L2A, 10-14
Silk: Black
Tail: Longish red cock hackle fibres
Body: Black floss silk
Rib: Silver wire or very fine oval
Hackle: Black hen
Wing: 'Blae' duck or starling
Cheeks: Jungle cock

A very old and traditional Scottish pattern, Col. Downman's Fancy (as it is sometimes called) is a fair bet as a hatching black midge representation. It is very similar to the Blae & Black, a pattern which some authorities judge to be better with a red tail. David McPhail supplied the pattern shown and claims it is still popular in his native Ayrshire for both browns and sea-trout.

Connemara Black

PLATE 4

Hook: Partridge L2A 8-14, or SH2 10-16
Silk: Black
Tail: G.P. crest feather
Body: Black seal's fur, or substitute
Rib: Medium or fine oval silver, dependent on hook size
Hackle: Black hen, with a few fibres of blue jay in front
Wing: Bronze mallard

I often regard this fly as a 'Black Invicta' which, when you consider the dressing, is not far from the truth. A truly exceptional fly for all major game species and locations. For general use, I dress it in its traditional form. In small sizes, however, it makes a good semi-imitative midge pattern. For this cut down version, I use a black floss body, a slip of dyed yellow duck quill for a tail, omit the black hen hackle and tie the wing sparse and low over the back.

Many years ago, Ian Glassford of Motherwell sent me a pattern which he called a 'Connemara Claret' (Plate 4). This version was like the standard dressing, but had a claret seal's fur body with a fluorescent pink seal's fur throat and used a claret hen hackle. Dressed slim and long, I found it to be an excellent late evening pattern, fishing it amongst the stones when big browns were hunting stickle-backs in the shallows.

Cow Dung (Norman Irvine)

PLATE 4

Hook: Partridge J1A, 10 & 12
Silk: Brown
Body: Light olive green chenille
Body hackle: Ginger cock hackle
Rib: Very fine oval gold
Head hackle: Ginger hen

PLATE 8
Haslem, Heather Fly (Millar), Hedgehog, Black Hopper (dry)
Black Hopper (wet), Hot-Spot Peacock Palmer, Humbug, Hutch's Pennell
Hutch's Pennell Muddler, Invicta, Gold Invicta, Silver Invicta Muddler
Silver Invicta, Silver Invicta (variant), Silver Invicta Muddler (variant), Pearly Invicta
White-Hackled Invicta, Irishman's Claret

There are several Cow Dung fly patterns and, to a greater or lesser degree, all of them work. This, however, is the best I have come across and, moreover, it is possibly the easiest to tie.

The natural is a terrestrial fly and would never be found 'swimming' sub-surface. Nevertheless, trout can be conned into accepting this wet pattern whilst feeding on the real thing. However, this pattern possibly also suggests shrimp, sedge pupae or other food forms, which turns it from an interesting oddity into a general work-horse.

Chenille bodied trout flies are primarily a Northern Scottish phenomenon, but they do work very well, particularly as simple palmered patterns such as this. (see also Brown Palmer; and Bluebottle).

Craftye

PLATE 4

Hook: Drennan Wet Fly Supreme or Partridge SH1, 8 & 10
Silk: Black
Tail: Black marabou plus four strands of pearl Crystal Hair
Body: Phosphor yellow fluorescent chenille (Glo-Brite no.11)
Hackle: Two or three turns of black metallic chenille (Fritz)
Head: Gold bead

This is a somewhat augmented Black Cat, with the added attraction of the increasingly popular material 'Fritz'. This pattern is effective fished on sunk or intermediate lines for recalcitrant browns and rainbows, early and late in the season. (see also Shell Back Goldhead)

Dabbler, Claret (variant) (Sandy McConnachie)

PLATE 4

Hook: Partridge SH2, 10-14
Silk: Red
Tail: A slim bunch of cock pheasant tail fibres
Body: Dark claret seal's fur, or substitute
Body hackle: A matched pair of cock hackles: scarlet and claret

Rib: Medium or fine oval gold
Head hackle: Bronze mallard, tied to cloak the body and extending just beyond the bend of the hook.

I had had mixed results with the standard dressing of the Claret Dabbler (palmered with a ginger cock hackle) until Sandy gave me an example of his version. For our Scottish waters, at least, it seems a marked improvement on the original (with all due respect to Donald 'Dabbler' McLarn). This pattern is a must for conditions of low light, such as late evenings and on heavily overcast days. It works well in a middle dropper position, but in truth will perform well anywhere on the cast. (see also Dabbler, Oliver; and Dabbler, Silver)

Dabbler, Olive

PLATE 4

Hook: Partridge SH1, L2A or Kamasan B175, 8-12
Silk: Brown
Tail: Half a dozen cock pheasant tail fibres (from a melanistic bird for preference)
Body: Green olive seal's fur
Body hackle: Green olive cock hackle
Rib: Fine oval gold
Wing/Hackle: A 'cloaking' of bronze mallard

Few patterns can be realistically described as all-season flies, but this one has that distinction. From April until September it can be used to suggest shrimps, hatching sedges, hatching olives and even as a representation of small fry. I consider it an indispensable pattern for both wild and stocked trout.

Dabblers are often thought to be strictly top-dropper, bob flies. This is erroneous; they are very good fished in a variety of styles and modes and are worthy of much experimentation. (see also Dabbler, Claret; and Dabbler, Silver)

Dabbler, Silver (Stuart McTeare)

PLATE 14

Hook: Partridge SH2, 10-14
Silk: Red

Tail: Bunch of cock pheasant tail fibres
Body: Claret seal's fur, or substitute
Body Rib: Medium flat silver
Body hackle: Ginger cock, two turns at the head, then palmered
Hackle Rib: Fine oval silver, following the course of the flat ribbing (which is wound before the body hackle)
Hackle/Wing: Bronze mallard, cloaking the body and extending slightly beyond the bend

I hope Stuart will forgive me the few very minor variations I have imposed on his own Dabbler variant. I watched this fly extracting a succession of large browns from Ireland's Lough Sheelin in 1995 and reckoned it would do well back here. So far, it has yet to 'set the heather on fire', but it has taken me some good fish in difficult conditions. Stuart fishes it on point or bob, on a floating line, throughout the season. He does very well with this pattern when the Sheelin fish are feeding on fry. Surprisingly, I have had most success with it when I have fished it on a variety of sinking lines. (*see also* Dabbler, Olive)

Damsel Fly Nymph (goldhead) (A. Murphy)

PLATE 4

Hook: Kamasan B830, 12
Silk: Olive
Tail: Olive marabou
Body: SLF 'Finesse', dark damsel mix
Rib: Fine oval gold
Hackle: Olive dyed partridge hackle
Head: Gold bead

This pattern, sometimes referred to as an Olive Tadpole, is perhaps the most effective lure of its type. It will work even where no damsel fly has ever fluttered and, as a general purpose small stillwater pattern, it is hard to beat. It is worth remembering that the natural damsel nymph is a fast and agile underwater swimmer, so that it is well within the bounds of imitative realism to give it a 'bit of arm' on the retrieve. However, it will often work well just 'mooched' along the bottom using a slow 'figure-of-eight'. (*see also* Yellow-Eyed Damsel)

Dapping Daddy (J. Millar)

PLATE 38

Hook: Partridge K12ST or D3ST, 8 & 10
Silk: Black
Body: A slim bundle of natural deer hair, as a detached body
Legs: Six pairs of knotted cock pheasant tail fibres, three each side
Wings: Two cree cock hackle points, tied 'spent'
Hackle: Two long red game cock hackles, wound figure-of-eight around the wings

Dapping flies have come a long way since the 'flue-brushes' of bygone days. Even in early summer, when few crane flies are about, this pattern will bring up both salmon and sea-trout through the waves to investigate. Make sure that the legs are long and trailing, as this seems to maximise the allure of this pattern.

This sort of 'daddy' is popular on Loch Lomond and similar patterns are also on the Irish loughs for large brown trout. (*see also* Wee Man; Yellow-Tailed Daddy (DAP); Detached-Body Daddy; and Dry Daddy)

Dark Mackerel

PLATE 4

Hook: Partridge L2A 8-12 or SH2, 10-16
Silk: Black
Tail: A slim bunch of G.P. tippet fibres
Body: Flat red Lurex
Body hackle: Dark claret cock, tied sparse
Rib: Fine oval silver, very fine oval in small sizes
Wing: Bronze mallard
Head hackle: Longish dark claret hen

One of the best sea-trout patterns for both river and loch. In small sizes, it is also excellent for trout. Although worth a go anywhere the 'child of the tide' swims, the Dark Mackerel seems to be most popular where waters carry a peat stain, such as in the far North West.

The original fly was resurrected for Loch Leven by David Leslie and that most accomplished of anglers, Bill Currie, spotted its potential for sea-trout and salmon. His influence has been so great that the pattern is now almost exclusively linked with the migratory branch of the sport.

The above dressing is my own slight variation as Leslie's pattern often had no rib at all, or one of copper wire. The placing of the hackle over the wing is a practice I favour in winged patterns of large size.

This is a very old pattern (a dressing for it was found in an old notebook dating c. 1918) and a very good fly. I am certain it is worthy of far wider usage. (see also Irishman's Claret)

Detached-Body Daddy

PLATE 38

Hook: Partridge L2A, 10
Silk: Brown
Body: A slim bundle of natural deer hair, lightly bound with tying silk and varnished for durability
Legs: Six knotted cock pheasant tail fibres, three each side
Hackle: Long dark ginger cock
Head: Spun, clipped, medium fine roe deer hair

Daddy-Long-Legs hatches can cause trout to throw all caution to the wind. Sport can often be reduced when using dry patterns because of the time spent in drying-out sodden flies. In such situations, or when the naturals flies won't come out of the grass onto the water, I employ this pattern on the top dropper of a team of wet flies. As a dry fly, it is not quite as good as the Dry Daddy. Again, this fly can be very good for sea-trout and salmon in lochs. (see also Wet Daddy)

Diawl Bach

PLATE 4

Hook: Partridge SH2 or Kamasan B400, 12-16
Silk: Brown
Tail: Dark ginger hackle fibres
Body: One peacock herl wound in butting turns, over a wet varnished layer of tying silk
Hackle: Dark ginger hen, tied under the throat only.

I couldn't believe this fly was as good as people said it was until I gave it a fair trial. It is supposed to be one of the best midge pupa imitators. Frankly, it doesn't even vaguely resemble one! Nevertheless, very good when trout are on midge and I am now a firm believer. When trout are making those distinctive bulges when feeding on rising midge pupae just below the surface, fish a Diawl Bach (Welsh for 'Little Devil') on a floating or intermediate line. Retrieves should be in the range slow to 'not at all'.

A small variation incorporating a slim rib of flat pearl also makes it acceptable to trout feeding on shrimp. Fished slow on sinking lines it can also be remarkably effective when trout are feeding deep.

Donegal Blue

PLATE 4

Hook: Partridge J1A, G3A or SH1, 8-12
Silk: Black
Body: Kingfisher blue seal's fur, or substitute
Rib: Medium flat silver (robust)
Hackle: Long, sparse, black hen

Generally looked upon as a loch sea-trout and salmon pattern, I have found that the Donegal Blue works quite well for late season wild browns.

It is very popular in the Western Isles and, to a lesser extent, on the West Coast.

Donny Murdo (Ken Kennedy)

PLATE 5

Hook: Kamasan B170, 10-14
Silk: Brown
Tail: Tuft of creamy fur from a hare's mask
Body: Well-mixed hare's mask
Rib: Narrow flat gold
Hackle: Brown partridge
Head: Light coloured roe deer hair, spun and clipped, retaining some fine tips as a collar

Ken Kennedy took my Hare's Ear Muddler and adjusted it a bit. The result was this pattern which has proved to be an excellent mid-summer fly and excellent in the evening, particularly if caenis are on the move. This pattern works well for both wild and stocked trout and, in suitable sizes, may well prove effective for migratory fish.

The name comes from the Gaelic version of the children's TV programme, 'Danger Mouse', which is quite an apt name for this fuzzy little beauty.

Doobry

PLATE 4

Hook: Partridge J1A or SH1, 8-14
Tail: Fluorescent fire-red wool (Turrall's)
Body: Flat, 'brassy' gold
Body hackle: Black cock hackle
Rib: Very fine oval gold
Head hackle: Hot orange hen, with a longer black hen over: one turn of the black hackle through the hot orange

Fly design is a funny business. I created this pattern for a specific purpose on a specific loch. In all honesty, it was only a minor success in its original conception, but has now become a modern standard throughout the UK, particularly on Loch Leven and the English reservoirs.

Its commonest uses are as a general purpose loch-style pattern, for bright days on peat stained waters and as a salmon and sea-trout loch pattern.

Dry Daddy

PLATE 38

Hook: Partridge D4A, 10 or 12
Silk: Brown
Tail: Two knotted cock pheasant tail fibres, extending from the rear of the body
Body: Mixed hare's mask and hot-orange seal's fur, or substitute
Rib: Medium oval gold
Legs: Six knotted cock pheasant tail fibres – three on each side
Wing: Two honey dun hen hackle points, one each side tied in front of the legs and behind the hackle. The wings should be swept back to form a right angle between one another
Hackle: Long dark ginger cock hackle, trimmed flat underneath

This is my favourite dressing for a static, or twitched, dry imitation of a large crane fly (*Tipulidae*). It can be fished as a top dropper

pattern, but for this purpose I normally prefer the Detached Body Daddy.

With the hackle trimmed underneath and well greased, this fly will sit trapped in the surface film like a dead or dying natural insect. Irresistible! This pattern can be particularly effective for loch salmon and sea-trout in calmer conditions when wet flies are not proving very effective. For a dapping alternative, use the above dressing with a double hackle at the head, the natural curve of the fibres facing forward, left untrimmed underneath. (*see also* Dapping Daddy; Yellow-Tailed Daddy; and The Wee Man)

Dunkeld

PLATE 5

Hook: Partridge SH2, 8-14
Silk: Black
Tail: G.P. crest
Body: Flat, 'brassy' gold
Rib: Gold wire, or very fine oval
Hackle: Hot orange hen
Wing: Bronze mallard
Cheeks: Jungle cock eye feathers

For many years, I persevered with the Dunkeld, but couldn't catch a fish on it! That was, until I discovered an important rule in the use of jungle cock on trout flies: use the smallest possible, within reason.

The Dunkeld is essential in any collection of loch-style patterns. In its small sizes, this pattern may be the only solution for those difficult, mid-summer doldrums. It is the one to try before retiring beaten to the pub for an iced beer. Jungle cock is extremely expensive these days, but this pattern will work without it, particularly a variation palmered with a hot orange cock hackle. A silver bodied variant works very well for sea-trout and brown trout in brackish lochs.

Dunkeld, Black (D. Chalmers)

PLATE 1

Hook: Drennan Carbon Lure, 12 & 10
Silk: Black
Tail: Glo-Brite floss, no.11
Body: Flat silver

Rib: Silver wire
Hackle: A short bunch of hot orange marabou
Wing: Black marabou
Cheeks: Jungle cock

David 'Chaff' Chalmers has developed a wide range of patterns specifically for Loch Leven, but these flies have also proved themselves the length and breadth of the country. This is one of his most successful and popular patterns for sinking line work and he recommends its use throughout the season. (*see also* Dunkeld; Deep Water and Dunkeld; and Squirrel Tail)

Dunkeld (deepwater)

PLATE 5

Hook: Partridge R1A double, 8-14
Silk: Black
Tail: Fluorescent phosphor yellow floss or wool
Body: Flat gold or pearl Mylar over fluorescent orange floss
Rib: Fine oval gold
Hackle: Short tuft of hot orange marabou
Wing: Bronze mallard, or brown rabbit fur or marabou, plus a couple of strands of pearl crystal hair
Cheeks: Jungle cock eyes

This version of the Dunkeld is an excellent point fly for use on a sinking line when one has to go dredging for fish that are feeding deep, or sulking in the depths. The use of a heavy double hook helps fly presentation in this context.

Dunkeld Muddler

PLATE 5

Hook: Partridge SH2, 12-16
Silk: Black
Tail: G.P. crest or mixed fluorescent lime green and fluorescent peach floss
Body: Flat, 'brassy' gold
Body hackle: Hot orange hen hackle
Rib: Very fine oval gold
Wing: Slips of cock pheasant secondary
Head: Spun, fine roe deer hair, clipped to a bullet shape

I make no secret of my enthusiasm for the use of 'mini Muddlers' in loch style fishing. When fish are high in the water, they can be unbeatable. This one is a winner and I would use the G.P. crest tailed form during difficult, bright conditions and the fluorescent tagged form when fish are on daphnia or sub-surface midge and want to chase. I regard this pattern as almost indispensable for most waters. It is possibly one of the best floating and intermediate line wet flies for Loch Leven and surrounding waters.

Emerger, Amber

PLATE 1

Hook: Partridge K14ST, 10-14
Silk: Brown
Body: Amber seal's fur or sub.
Rib: Fine oval gold, or fine clear nylon monofilament
Hackle: Sparse ginger hen

This pattern is for use during hatches of pale coloured midges. Clipping the hackle flush underneath allows the fly to sit well down in the surface film. However, by leaving the hackle full and treating only the hackle with flotant, the fly can be fished semi-submerged. Such slight differences in presentation can be important on occasion.

Emerger, Fiery-Brown

PLATE 5

Hook: Partridge K14ST, 10-14
Silk: Brown
Body: Dark fiery brown seal's fur, or substitute
Rib: Fine, clear monofilament
Hackle: Dark red/brown hen, sparse and trimmed flush underneath

Fiery brown is a colour that seems particularly useful for dry patterns (in the 1996 season, over 75% of the fish I caught on dry flies were lured by patterns incorporating this colour). This pattern is one of my 'fail-me-nevers' and, in circumstances where there is no tangible evidence of fish preference, it would be one of my first choices.

Some years ago on Swannay we had hatches of tiny diptera, rather like very small house flies. I never had them identified to my satisfaction, but the Fiery-Brown Emerger was the fly to have on. Double figure catches of wild fish, averaging one-and-a-half pounds, in April, on dries? Now that's what I call good sport!

Emerger, Fiery-Brown Bibio

PLATE 5

Hook: Partridge K14ST, 12 & 14
Silk: Brown
Body: Rear: dark fiery brown seal's fur; front: light fiery brown/cinnamon seal's fur (or substitute)
Rib: Fine, clear monofilament
Hackle: Dark fiery brown hen hackle, two turns

I love to fish this pattern in conjunction with the Black & Claret in the early spring buzzer hatches and, later in the year, when fish are being a bit difficult. This fly is also a good bet when there is a wide range of potential food items trapped in the surface film and the angler has to choose something to cover all circumstances.

Emerger, Hare's Ear & Claret

PLATE 5

Hook: Partridge E1A or Drennan Emerger, 12-16
Silk: Black
Body: Two halves: rear – claret seal's fur, or substitute; fore – well-mixed hare's ear, including plenty of guard hairs
Rib: Clear, fine monofilament (over rear of body only)

Some year's ago, I was given a fly by English ace, Jeremy Clarke, which had a similar dressing to the above but in a Bibio format. I liked the look of it and it worked well, but the above dressing is more reliable on Scottish waters. I can only assume that it was designed to represent an adult fly crawling out of a shuck. Accordingly, the floatant should be applied *only* to the hare's ear front half, so that the untreated nether end can penetrate the surface film.

Although this pattern looks big, it is worth remembering that it imitates an emerger plus its shuck, so that the artificial can be at least twice the length of the adult insect.

Emerger, Hare's Ear & Olive

PLATE 5

The pattern is tied exactly as for the previous dressing, except that medium olive seal's fur replaces the claret seal's fur.

The olive version can be fished when olive midge or ephemerids are hatching, but it is also effective as a speculative pattern.

This 'half-and-half' format could easily be adapted and is – I am sure – worth experimenting with to suit particular waters and their resident insects. I would suggest the following: black, bibio, amber, scarlet and fiery brown.

Extractor (variant)

PLATE 5

Hook: Partridge L2A 8-12, or SH2 10-14
Silk: Black or brown
Tail: Slim bunch of G.P. red body feather fibres
Body: Flat gold
Body hackle: Lemon yellow cock
Rib: Very fine oval gold, or wire
Wing: Bronze mallard
Head hackle: Small G.P. red body feather, wound over wing

In 1991, I was bound for Lough Melvin in Ireland, and I tied up a version of this dressing, but without the palmered hackle. It didn't do much for me in Ireland, however, but occasionally it was put to use here in Orkney where it proved reasonably successful. I told Ken Kennedy about it and he got better results than I had done using the dressing shown here with the palmered hackle. This is a better dressing for general purpose work, particularly for working wave-lashed rocky shallows. It looks vaguely shrimp-like, which is what I suspect the trout take it for.

Fionn Spider (D. Mateer)

PLATE 5

Hook: Partridge J1A or Kamasan B175, 10 & 12
Silk: Black
Tail: Fluorescent lime green wool
Body: In two parts: rear, fluorescent lime wool; front, black seal's fur, or substitute
Rib: Fine oval silver
Hackle: Black hen

This is an unusual looking pattern from the West Highlands. Originally designed for traditional loch-style work, it is worth a try on a sinking line, above a mini-lure, for stubborn, deep-lying trout.

Fleeuck

PLATE 5

Hook: Partridge SH2 12 & 14, or Kamasan B175, 10 & 12
Silk: Black
Tail: Fluorescent lime green floss or wool, (my preference would be for mixed Glo-Brite floss, nos. 11 & 12)
Body: Flat gold
Body hackle: Hot orange cock (a deep rich colour)
Rib: Very fine oval gold, or wire
Head hackle: Hot orange hen, two turns

Bright, over-stated patterns on the top-dropper can frequently improve the odds when incorporating a 'lift and hold' technique with sinking lines for deep feeding or sulky trout. The Fleeuck was developed specifically for this purpose and has proved very successful. The name comes from the Orcadian dialect name for any old natural fly, with somewhat disparaging over-tones.

Fourwater Favourite

PLATE 5

Hook: Partridge D4A or Kamasan B400, 12-16
Silk: Black or brown
Tail: Tuft of long hair from a fiery brown dyed hare's mask

Body: Well mixed fur from a natural or fiery brown dyed hare's mask
Rib: Fine oval gold

This is a variation on the Gold-Ribbed Hare's Ear (GRHE) theme. It originated from the small stillwater scene in England, but has proved very useful in Scotland in similar environments. This fly can take fish at a variety of depths, but is almost always best when fished slowly.

Frenzy (D. McPhail)

PLATE 5

Hook: Partridge L2A or Kamasan B170, 10-14
Silk: Black
Tail: G.P. crest
Body: Flat gold
Rib: Very fine oval gold or wire
Hackle: Hot orange hen
Wing: Peacock sword fibres
Cheeks: Jungle cock eyes

This is a typical Scottish fancy pattern, which can lay some claim to imitative status when used to represent small perch fry. I have used this pattern successfully for wild trout on peat water lochs in bright conditions.

Tied tandem style, with a flash of red in the wing and a long G.P. topping over the top and it becomes a very old dressing known as a Mary Ann.

Fritz Cat [goldhead] (J. Millar)

PLATE 6

Hook: Kamasan B405, 10
Silk: Fluorescent white
Tail: White marabou, plus a few strands of pearl Crystal Hair (optional)
Body: Fluorescent phosphor yellow chenille (Glo-Brite, no.11)
Collar: A narrow band of fluorescent fire orange floss (Glo-Brite, no. 5)
Hackle: Two or three turns of yellow Fritz or Cactus chenille
Head: Gold bead

This pretty little mini-lure has great fish catching potential in the doldrums during mid-summer.

Many tyerss prefer to make the whole body length Fritz/Cactus chenille, but the supplier of this pattern, Jimmy Millar of Edinburgh, prefers the above dressing.

The pattern works well as a 'team member' fished on a sinking line, or singly on a long leader and a floating line. (*see also* Cat's Whisker; Craftye; and Light Bulb Goldhead)

G.P. Spider (D. Wood)

PLATE 6

Hook: Partridge L2A, 10 14
Silk: Black
Tail: A slim bunch of G.P. tippets
Body: Black floss silk
Rib: Sliver wire or very fine oval
Hackle: Light furnace (Greenwell) hen

The G.P., in this instance, stands for 'Greenwell Pennell'. Davie Wood, who kindly donated the pattern for the illustration, is sure that it is not an original or innovative dressing. However, since I can find no reference to it elsewhere, I have attributed it to him. He also states that it is a good traditional style pattern for midge time on all the Pentland Hill waters, including Glencorse and Gladhouse. Use on a floating or intermediate line. (*see also* Pennell Black; and Pennell, Hutch's)

Ginger Quill (variant)

PLATE 6

Hook: Partridge L2A or E1A, 12 & 14
Silk: Brown
Tail: A slim bunch of ginger cock hackle fibres
Body: Stripped peacock quill from eye feather
Rib: Very fine oval gold or wire
Body hackle: Small ginger cock hackle
Head hackle: Two turns of blue dun hen hackle

The original dressing included a blae wing and had no palmered hackle. In my view, however, this dressing, which has been about for some time, is superior. I really like it when pale midge are hatching in late spring and early summer. I was first shown this pattern by Brian Roberts, of Leicestershire, who scrapped the stripped quill and simply uses the tying silk to form the body. His version seemed perfectly effective despite the lack of the stripped quill body.

Gizmo

PLATE 6

Hook: Partridge SH2, 10-16, or Kamasan B175, 8-14
Silk: Blac6
Tail: A slim bunch of hot-orange dyed G.P. tippets
Body: Pearl Mylar on top of wet varnished tying silk
Rib: Very fine silver oval, or wire
Wing: Short bunch of grey partridge hackle fibres
Hackle: Black hen, sparse, tied over the wing

I used to refer to this pattern as a Teal & Green variant, but it is so far removed from the original as to make such a description ridiculous and confusing. But it is one of my top ten patterns, particularly during dark midge hatches and does very good work in its larger sizes as a speculative wet fly and as an imitator of very small fry. When pearl Mylar is wound over wet varnished black thread, a beautiful, reflective, silvery, metallic-green colour is produced. This mimics the appearance of a hatching midge during that stage of emergence when it pumps its body with gas in order to split the pupal skin. I took my first charr (Salvelinus alpinus) from Loch Borralie on this pattern, one late May evening. Although the fish were offered many things, they would only accept the Gizmo.

Goat's Toe

PLATE 6

Hook: Partridge J1A, 6-10
Silk: Black
Tail: Red wool
Body: Two strands of bronze peacock herl, with a good long flue: one wound up the body in butting turns; the other wound down in open turns
Rib: Red wool or floss
Hackle: Peacock blue neck feather

Another Irish import into Scotland, the Goat's Toe seems more popular here than in its country of origin. I suspect that this is another attempt to mimic the heather fly (*Bibio pomonae*), a close relative of the hawthorn fly (*B. marci*), both of which trout seem to find very tasty. The Goat's Toe is, perhaps, the most popular and successful sea-trout and salmon fly in use on the lochs of the Scottish West Coast and Isles. There is a variant which replaces the red rib with medium silver oval, but of which I have little knowledge. The original dressing had a red floss body, ribbed with a strand of peacock herl. This was terribly fragile, however, and the modern form is much more robust and tooth-resistant. Many would regard it as an essential and irreplaceable pattern for the sea-trout of the West. (*see also Bibio; and Ke-He*)

Goat's Toe (variant)

PLATE 6

Hook: Partridge SH2, 12
Silk: Black
Tag: Two turns flat gold, under the tail
Tail: A tuft of fluorescent fire red wool (Turrall's)
Body: Two bronze peacock herls (as in the previous dressing)
Rib: A thin strand of fluorescent fire red wool or floss
Hackle: A small metallic bottle-green peacock body feather, over two turns of long black hen hackle

In very bright weather, when trout are disinclined to come to come anywhere near the surface, this pattern may be the only recourse for the angler who insists on sticking with a floating line. It is also very effective in a good wave when patterns with 'fluff & fluster' are the answer. This version of the Goat's Toe is successful wherever used, even on English waters where the fish can be extremely disdainful of Northern wild trout patterns. The pattern differs from its ancestor not only in its use of fluorescent material, but also in replacing the blue peacock neck hackle with the bottle-green body feather. This seems to make it more acceptable to non-migratory trout. The two turns of black hen hackle are to support the peacock which tends to collapse on its own. The use of long, straggly head hackles of this type is a relatively recent evolution in trout flies and one that appears to be distinctly worthwhile. (*see also Silver Goat's Toe; Bumble, Claret (leggy); Bumble, Golden Olive (leggy); Octopus; Green French Partridge; and Wet Daddy*)

Goat's Toe, Silver

PLATE 14

Hook: Partridge SH2 12, or Kamasan B175 10
Silk: Black
Tail: Bunch of fluffy fibres from the base of a scarlet dyed hen hackle
Body: Flat silver
Body hackle: Short black cock
Rib: Very fine oval silver or wire
Wing: Bunch of peacock sword feather fibres, Alexandra style
Head hackle: bottle green peacock hackle

In a big wave, dull day, peaty water scenario, this pattern can be lethal to the point of embarrassment, fished on the top-dropper with a floating line. It can also be used on a fast sinking line, when you can try and kid yourself that it is not a 'lure'. The secret of this pattern's success lies in the mobility of the peacock neck hackle.

Although this version is very similar to an Alexandra, the pattern was named before it acquired a wing and looked more like the standard Goat's Toe. I believe that the effectiveness of this pattern is markedly enhanced by the inclusion of the sword tail wing.

This is a fly that I am sure would be worth experimenting with on salmon and sea-trout in lochs. (*see also Goat's Toe*)

Gold Butcher, Hardy's

PLATE 2

Hook: Partridge L2A, GRS2A, 8-14, or SH2 10-16
Silk: Black
Tail: A bunch of fluffy flue from the base of a scarlet hen hackle
Body: Flat gold
Rib: Fine oval gold
Hackle: Hot-orange hen
Wing: Paired slips of cinnamon quill

Although I don't use this pattern as much now as in the past, I still have a fondness for the Gold Butcher. It has taken many substantial brown trout and sea-trout for me and my friends. Like its close cousin, the Cinnamon & Gold, it does seem to have an uncanny ability to attract larger fish. In the past, this was regarded as an essential wet fly for waters such as Loch Leven and was also a great favourite for river and estuary sea-trout. It has rather slipped from favour and is seen only infrequently, mainly for salmon and sea-trout on Western lochs. For such work, I suggest tying the hackle in front of the wing.

Gold Cat (D. Chalmers)

PLATE 6

Hook: Drennan Traditional Wet, 8
Silk: Fluorescent yellow silk or fine floss (Glo-Brite no.11)
Tail: Yellow marabou, with gold Flashabou over the top
Body: Phosphor yellow chenille (Glo-Brite no.11)
Rib: Medium oval gold
Hackle: Brown partridge
Eyes: A pair of large silver bead chain beads

In the Central Belt of Scotland, medium and large lures of this general coloration are popular and necessary for the extraction of deep lying fish in bright daytime conditions. This is particularly so when the water is discoloured for any reason. The weight imparted by the 'eyes' gives added attraction due to the swimming action it imparts to the lure. Although frowned upon by the traditionalist, there can be no doubt that such lures are now an important part of the modern fly angler's armoury. (see also Black Cat (variant); Green & Gold Lure; Muddy McGregor; and Yellow-Eyed Damsel)

Gold Muddler (N. Irvine & S. Headley)

PLATE 11

Hook: Partridge SH2, 12-16, or Kamasan B175, 10-14
Silk: Black
Body: Flat gold
Rib: Very fine oval gold or wire

Wing: Slips of speckled cock pheasant secondary feather
Head: Fine roe deer hair, spun and clipped to a bullet shape, but retaining some of the fine points as a collar

In the late 1970s, I started using adapted Muddlers for loch-style wet flyfishing. From the start I was impressed with their ability to take wild trout in almost any circumstances and, ever since, they have remained a vital element in my fly selection. If compelled to name the most 'killing' mini-muddler pattern, this undoubtedly would be it. My long term boat partner, Norman Irvine, and I worked on refining the original Muddler Minnow for our purposes. After about twenty years of experimentation, this is the dressing we arrived at. Tied slim, sparse and small, ensuring that some of the deer hair tips are retained as a collar, this fly is 'death on a hook'. Over-dress it, or clip the head into a ball shape and the fly is far less effective, we find. It is at its best on the top dropper. Fished on the point, it seems to take fewer, but rather better fish. There are few days when this fly won't be in use: it works when fish are feeding on virtually anything and even when they are not feeding at all!

Gold Muddler (variant)

Hook: Partridge SH2, 12-16, or Kamasan B175, 10-14
Silk: Black
Tail: Fluorescent lime green floss (mixed Glo-Brite, nos. 11 and 12)
Body: Flat gold
Body hackle: Small ginger cock hackle
Rib: Very fine gold oval or wire
Wing: Slips of speckled cock pheasant secondary
Head: Fine roe deer hair, spun and clipped to a bullet shape, but retaining some of the fine points as a collar

This minor variation on the Gold Muddler serves when fish are feeding on daphnia. The addition of a fluorescent tag seems to trigger aggression under these circumstances. This version is also useful when algal discolouration restricts subsurface visibility and is especially good for rainbows. Perhaps this pattern is really a variation on a Wingless Wickham's, but to call it a 'Fluorescent Tagged Wingless Wickham's Muddler, with a Wing' is too horrible to permit.

Gold-Ribbed Hare's Ear
[GRHE] (variant)

PLATE 6

Hook: Partridge L2A, or Drennan Emerger, 12-16
Silk: Brown

Tail: Slim, short tuft of cream coloured hare's fur
Body: Mixed hare's mask fur, with plenty of guard hairs
Rib: Narrow, flat, metallic gold tinsel
Hackle: Sparse, short brown partridge

This is only a minor variation on the original, brought about by my inability to have confidence in a hackle-less pattern. Whilst this is an important rainbow and stocked brown trout pattern, I have never taken a real wild trout on it, which I find surprising, considering the number of hare's ear patterns which are essential for wild trout. Still, this is a very good fly to have in reserve and stocked rainbows increase their range yearly. This is a fly to be fished slowly almost all the time. however, one occasion springs to mind when some attractive over-wintered rainbows fell for this pattern ripped back at a hair-raising speed.

Golden Banton Midge
(Robin Brown)

PLATE 6

Hook: Kamasan B160 or Partridge K14ST, 12-16
Silk: Black or brown
Body: Pale hare's mask fur
Rib: Flat gold, closely ribbed
Wing: A short tuft of fluorescent white baby wool over two strands of pearl Crystal Hair
Hackle: Light furnace hen, tied over the wing

I liked this pattern as soon as I saw it and can well imagine fishing it behind a small Hare's Ear or Gold Muddler. I am advised that it is particularly effective during the summer months and, perhaps rather obviously, during buzzer hatches. It is not often one sees midge patterns with this style or colour of dressing, so would be worth having just to ring the changes. (*see also* Black, Buzzer; Coachman Nymph; Ginger Quill; and Hutch's Pennell)

Goldie

PLATE 6

Hook: Drennan Carbon Lure, 8-14
Silk: Black
Tail: A bunch of yellow hackle fibres
Body: Flat gold
Rib: Medium oval gold
Hackle: Yellow hen or cock
Wing: A slim bunch of dyed yellow squirrel under a similar tuft of dyed black squirrel tail

This is a lure designed by Bob Church which seems to be creating quite a following in the Central Belt region of Scotland. Yellow is often one of the few colours that will work when algal discolouration is restricting subsurface visibility. This is a nice slim lure and summer trout often show a preference for slim patterns. There is an orange variant which I believe is equally popular.

Grannom

PLATE 6

Hook: Partridge L2A or Kamasan B170, 10-14
Silk: Brown
Butt: Build-up of fluorescent lime green floss or thread, one quarter of total fly length and extending around hook bend
Body: Mixed hare's mask, with guard hairs included
Rib: Fine oval gold
Hackle: Medium red/brown hen
Wing: Speckled cock pheasant secondary

The natural insect (*Brachycentrus subnubilus*) which this pattern is supposed to imitate exists solely in running water! However, this pattern has been very successful for me in a wide range of lochs and stillwaters for many years. In big sizes, it makes for a good general purpose loch-style wet fly. In small sizes, it can be very effective for trout feeding on midge in very calm conditions, particularly if the bright green midge is about. Paired with a small Norm's Greenwell and you have a two fly cast that will take some beating in the above mentioned circumstances. I wouldn't be without this pattern in a midge hatch.

Green & Brown

PLATE 6

Hook: Partridge SH2, 12 & 14
Silk: Black
Body: Olive green ostrich herl
Rib: Fine oval gold
Hackle: Dark ginger hen
Back: Four strands of peacock herl, extending behind as a tail
Head: A few turns of peacock herl

A variation on Iven's Brown & Green Nymph, this pattern was adapted from the original to represent a freshwater shrimp. Shrimps (what the Americans call 'scuds') make up a very large proportion of trout food on most productive Scottish lochs. I have always felt that a good imitation for loch-style purposes is just waiting to be invented. Although this pattern has been very successful in the early months of the season, it is far from infallible and I have plans for some improvements to the pattern. (see also Jersey Herd)

Green & Gold Lure (Buchanan)

PLATE 6

Hook: Drennan Carbon Lure or Kamasan B830, 8-12
Silk: White
Tail: A substantial bunch of long gold Flashabou
Body: Glo-Brite chenille, no.11

This is an un-ashamed 'stocky-bashing' lure with plenty of movement and flash. Perhaps not for the purist, this can really save a blank on a put-and-take water where recently introduced trout might be the only fish to be tempted.

Green French Partridge

PLATE 7

Hook: Partridge J1A, 6-12
Silk: Black
Body: Bright green seal's fur, or substitute
Rib: Medium oval gold
Hackle: French partridge hackle, one-and-a-half times the body length

This is a very old hatching mayfly pattern from Ireland. John Kennedy, of South Uist, has a passion for Irish patterns and styles and has adapted the old pattern to create one of the best sea-trout and salmon flies used in the far North and West.

Bearing in mind the universal acceptance of the Green Peter for migratory fish in Scottish lochs and Irish loughs, perhaps it is not so surprising that this unlikely fly has such a good track record. It does have a lovely straggly quality about it and is a noted taker of big brown trout in the Isles.

Green Palmer (B. Watt)

PLATE 7

Hook: Partridge SH1, 12 & 14, or Kamasan B175, 10 & 12
Silk: Black
Tail: Bunch of green olive hackle fibres
Body: Green seal's fur, or substitute
Rib: Narrow flat pearl Mylar, not stretched
Body hackle: Green olive henny-cock hackle
Head hackle: Longish green olive hen hackle

Brian Watt of Shetland showed me this pattern a few years back. On that first acquaintance, it proved devastating on Loch Harray in discoloured, shallow water. This pattern has also carved a niche for itself on Stenness for big browns and for sea-trout.

Green Peter

PLATE 7

Hook: Partridge K2B, 8-12, or similar grub/sedge hook

Silk: Brown
Body: Mid-green seal's fur, or substitute
Body hackle: Ginger cock
Rib: Fine oval gold
Wing: Paired slips of hen or cock pheasant secondary
Hackle: Ginger hen, wound in front of the wing

When first introduced to this pattern, in the dim and distant past, I was assured that the fly works best when the body is carried around the bend of the hook. At the time, I was dubious, but after many years trying to disprove the theory, I am forced to admit that this seems to be the case. Tied on a sedge/grub hook, the curvature of the body is accentuated and this appears to enhance the fly's killing properties. It is important to try and get the wings to lie as close to the body as possible. I get round the problem by tying each slip in separately. This is a tricky manoeuvre, but one which prevents the wings from sticking up at right angles. Strictly speaking this is a variant, which has few similarities to its Irish ancestor. However, on this side of the Irish Sea it is almost always dressed thus. It is one of the few real 'indispensables' for wild trout, rainbows, salmon and sea-trout: a truly great bob-fly and well worth inclusion in any collection.

Green Peter Muddler

PLATE 7

The dressing is as for the Green Peter, but omit the head hackle and replace it with a head of spun, clipped and trimmed deer hair, leaving a few fine points as a collar.

It may seem indulgent to give this pattern a place to itself, but it is one of the most important and popular wet flies in the Scottish repertoire. In big sizes it is an efficient taker of wild trout and migratory species in the Highlands and Western Isles. In its smaller sizes, it is amongst the top-ten best patterns for stocked and wild trout in the more productive waters of the Central Belt and the Northern Isles. On Loch Leven, a minor variation incorporates a body of olive green chenille.

Green Priest

PLATE 13

Hook: Partridge L2A, 10-14
Silk: Black
Body: Green Lurex, over wet varnished layer of silk
Hackle: Sparse, longish black hen

One cold, grey, damp, 'driech' evening on Loch Hundland, I took a magnificent basket of trout on this pattern. It really was against all the odds and nothing else stimulated the slightest interest. Since then, it has become a last resort before final capitulation. In this role it has been extraordinarily reliable. The fly is probably a vague imitation of black midge pupae. Some people call it the Green Lurex Spider. (*see also* Teal & Green [variant])

Greenwell Spider

PLATE 7

Hook: Partridge L2A, 12 & 14
Silk: Pale yellow
Tail: Fibres of light furnace cock hackle
Body: Tying silk, well-waxed
Rib: Very fine oval gold, or wire
Hackle: Light furnace hen, sparse

Probably more popular nowadays in running water than on the loch, this pattern still has some adherents in the more traditional regions of the country. I would suggest that its usage would follow much the same criteria as for the standard, winged Greenwell.

Greenwell, Norm's
(Norman Irvine)

PLATE 7

Hook: Partridge E1A, 12 & 14
Silk: Pale yellow
Body: Tying silk, darkened slightly by rubbing between thumb and forefinger
Rib: Very fine oval gold, or wire
Hackle: Pale ginger hen, short & sparse
Wing: Palest slips of mallard primary, tied slim

It would be very hard to over-rate this pattern for the specific purpose of taking 'spooky' fish in near calm conditions, feeding on small, pale midge. The originator, prefers to use a pale golden floss for the body, but he is very 'pernickety' about shade and the above alternative has served me very well. He also frequently omits the rib. This fly is excellent wherever used, but particularly on productive waters where pale midge abound.

A few years back, Norm took a five pound Harray sea-trout on this fly in a totally flat calm – no mean achievement. (*see also* Greenwell's Glory; and Burleigh)

Greenwell's Glory

PLATE 7

Hook: Partridge L2A, 10-14
Silk: Light yellow
Tail: Fibres of light furnace cock hackle
Body: Tying silk, well-waxed
Rib: Very fine oval gold, or wire
Hackle: Light furnace hen, sparse
Wing: Starling, teal or mallard primary (originally, hen blackbird)

Greenwell's Glory is just about the most famous trout fly of all. It was first tied in 1854 by James Wright, of Sprouston on the Tweed, to a pattern suggested by a Durham cleric, one Canon William Greenwell. Although primarily a river pattern – and a very good one – it has made a very successful transition to the loch scene. Many claim it to be effective as a representation of hatching lake and pond olives, but this has not been my own experience. However, when pale olive midge are on the water, the Greenwell is an invaluable asset. For such purposes, make the wing as pale as possible and match the size to the natural.

When fish are visibly moving to surface insects in conditions of light wind, a delicately presented Greenwell can often out-fish the most cunning modern nymph or dry fly. It is one of the few 19th century patterns that will, undoubtedly, have an important place in the 21st!

The addition of a fluorescent phosphor yellow floss (Glo-Brite, no.11) tail produces the Yellow-

Tailed Greenwell: a superlative pattern for Loch Leven, and one which regularly takes very big trout from this water. (*see also* Greenwell, Norm's; and Kingfisher, Butcher)

Grenadier

PLATE 7

Hook: Partridge SH2, 10-16, or Kamasan B170, 10-14
Silk: Red
Body: Mixed: hot orange and amber seal's fur, or sub
Rib: Fine oval gold
Hackle: Ginger cock: two turns at the head and then palmered down the body

Variations on this pattern are legion and this is mine. I found that I could rarely score with a bright orange version, but softening the colour of the body transformed my opinion of the pattern. A very good general purpose weapon for rainbows and 'pelagic' browns on southern waters. It is also useful for wild browns on natural waters in the early months of the season.

Grey Monkey

PLATE 7

Hook: Partridge SH2, 10-16
Silk: Black
Tail: Fibres of teal
Body: In two halves: rear, yellow floss; front, grey seal's fur, or grey/blue rabbit underfur (originally, blue monkey)
Rib: Fine or medium oval gold (dependent on hook size)
Hackle: Blue dun hen
Wings: Starling or mallard primary
Cheeks: Jungle cock eyes (optional)

A pretty and venerable pattern, the Grey Monkey was once very popular in southern lochs. Nowadays, it is more important for sea-trout in river and estuary. It has the look of late evening and poor light about it and I am informed that it still has adherents on Loch Leven.

Grizzle Lure (A. Murphy)

PLATE 7

Hook: Kamasan B830, 12
Silk: Fluorescent yellow Danville's 'Flymaster'
Tail: White marabou
Body: Extra fine white 'Vernille' chenille
Body hackle: Grizzle, Metz cock saddle hackle
Rib: Silver wire
Head hackle: White hen
Eyes: Bead chain pair, painted fluorescent yellow

A mini-lure for all conditions, the Grizzle Lure works best as a point fly, fished very slowly with a figure-of-eight retrieve. For the method of painting the eyes please refer to the instructions for the Yellow-Eyed Damsel.

Grouse & Claret

PLATE 7

Hook: Partridge SH2, 10-16, or Kamasan B170, 10-14
Silk: Black
Tail: G.P. tippet fibres (dyed hot orange, optional)
Body: Dark claret seal's fur, or sub.
Rib: Fine or medium oval gold (dependent on hook size)
Wing: Grouse tail feather (or, as a substitute, slips from a melanistic hen pheasant secondary)
Hackle: Longish black hen, tied over the wing

I make no apology for stipulating that the hackle is tied in *front* of the wing in this version. In the bigger sizes, this makes for a definite improvement and in the smaller sizes, doesn't hurt one bit. Because of the difficulty in obtaining quality, well-marked, grouse tail feathers, I almost always use melanistic hen pheasant secondaries these days. The plumage is more robust than grouse tail and requires a well-trained eye to distinguish the substitute from the real thing. Some authorities give claret or red/brown for hackle colour, but I prefer black.

A very good sea-trout and salmon fly for Loch Lomond and other West Coast lochs. It also does tolerably well in small sizes when trout are feeding on dark midge. (*see also* Grouse & Claret (Harold's); Irishman's Claret; and Mallard & Claret)

Grouse & Claret Harold's

PLATE 7

Hook: Partridge JIA or SH1, 8 & 10
Silk: Black
Tail: Originally yellow wool (alternatively, Glo-Brite no.9)
Body: Dark claret seal's fur
Rib: Oval gold
Thorax: Two or three turns of a full-flued, bronze peacock herl
Hackle: Grouse neck feather, long and tied full

We have Eddie Young's fascinating book *Fisher in the West* to thank for the resurgence of interest in this rather obscure pattern. I have to admit that I have surprisingly little experience of it (I say 'surprisingly', because of my usual keenness for straggly, game-hackled patterns). I recently saw this fly remove a stunning sea-trout from a West Coast loch in bright sunshine, and virtual flat calm. Any pattern that can do that, even occasionally, is worthy of some investigation.

Although primarily a salmon and sea-trout pattern. I am quite sure that it should work well on wild browns, but perhaps in smaller sizes. (*see* also Grouse & Claret)

Hammer Fly (Davie Malcolm)

PLATE 7

Hook: Drennan Traditional Wet or Kamasan B175, 10 & 12
Silk: White
Tail: Fluorescent phosphor yellow floss (Glo-Brite no.11)
Body: Flat pearl Mylar over Glo-Brite no.11 fluorescent floss
Rib: Silver wire or very fine oval
Wing: White marabou over slim bunch of silver holographic tinsel
Head: Two or three turns of metallic gold chenille

Davie Malcolm's ability and success on Central Belt waters is well documented and the above

41

pattern is one of his favourites. He recommends it as a point fly on intermediate or sunk lines. (*see also* Black Kitten; Light Bulb [goldhead]; and Jungle Cock Viva [Claret variant])

Hare's Ear Coch Zulu (S. Leask)

PLATE 7

Hook: Partridge L2A or Kamasan B170, 12
Silk: Black or brown
Tail: Tuft of hot orange fluorescent floss (Glo-Brite no.6)
Body: Mixture of hare's ear and orange seal's fur, or substitute
Body hackle: Light furnace hen
Rib: Gold wire
Head hackle: Dark furnace hen

Some patterns have a basic 'fishiness' which is immediately apparent at first glance. This is one such. It has most of the features which I associate with a good all-round brown and rainbow trout pattern.

Hare's Ear Muddler

PLATE 6

Hook: Partridge GRS2A, 10-14
Silk: Brown
Body: Well mixed hare's mask fur
Body hackle: Ginger cock
Rib: Fine oval gold
Hackle: Brown partridge
Head: Light roe deer hair, spun and clipped to a bullet shape, leaving some of the fine points as a 'hackle'

Many people still believe that mini-Muddlers are just small lures. This pattern strongly contradicts that view. It is invariably at its best when fished slowly amongst fish feeding on hatching insects. The combination of Muddler head, with the hare's ear fur and hackle seems to suggest the confusion of metamorphosis. Interestingly, colour match seems to matter very little with this pattern, as it works very well in a dark or black midge hatch. It is also excellent during sedge, caenis and olive hatches, or simply as a prospecting 'try it and see' pattern. If corixae

(water boatmen) are on the menu, this would be one of my first choices, along with Silver Invicta. (*see also* Donny Murdo; Gold Muddler; and Gold-Ribbed Hare's Ear, Muddled)

Hare's Ear Shipman's

PLATE 7

Hook: Partridge E1A or Drennan Emerger, 10-14
Silk: Primrose or fluorescent yellow thread
Body: Light, well mixed hare's mask fur
Rib: Fine nylon monofilament
Tufts: Fluorescent white floss, or 'cul de canard' plumes

In mid-summer, when caenis and pale midge are frequently predominant, this pattern can be an essential part of a loch fisher's armoury. I prefer the version with fluorescent white floss tufts for caenis feeders, but the dressing using CDC plumes allows the fly to be fished without floatant and it therefore lies well down into the surface film. I find that it is worth having both types at hand.

Surprisingly, all Shipman's patterns can be effective 'pulling' flies, greased or un-greased. This is particularly true with this pattern, especially during the dreaded caenis hatch. (*see also* Caenis Muddler; and Tup's Indispensable)

Haslam

PLATE 8

Hook: Partridge SH2, 12 & 10
Silk: Black or brown
Tag: Flat silver
Tail: G.P. crest
Butt: White wool or fluorescent floss
Body: Flat silver
Body hackle: Badger cock, palmered
Rib: Medium oval silver
Head hackle: Blue jay
Wing: Hen pheasant tail (occasionally hen pheasant secondary slips)
Horns: Traditionally, blue macaw, but slim slips of blue dyed goose, laid over the wing will serve

As is typical with many of the flies associated with Loch Lomond, this pattern has rather an

PLATE 9
Jersey Herd (variant), Jungle Cock & Silver, Kate McLaren, Kate McLaren (variant)
Ke-He, Black Ke-He, Orange Ke-He, Kingfisher Butcher (variant)
Kingfisher Butcher, Kingfisher Butcher (wee double), Knouff Lake Special, Lawfield Nobbler
Leven Butcher, Leven Ghost, Leven Spider, Leveret
Leven Stinger

intricate dressing. When all is said and done it looks to me rather like a 'snazzy' Silver Invicta.

In Wales, the Haslam has a reputation as a sea-trout and salmon fly and particularly on the River Dovey. (*see also* Burton)

Heather Fly (J. Millar)

PLATE 8

Hook: Kamasan B170 or Partridge K14ST, 12
Silk: Black
Body: Black seal's fur, extending slightly round hook bend, slim in the abdomen and built up at the thorax
Rib: Fine copper yarn, over abdomen only
Legs: Dark orange dyed cock pheasant tail fibres, knotted: two on either side
Wing: Teardrop shaped Lureflash pearl film, protruding from under the thorax, and extending beyond the hook bend
Hackle: Four turns of black cock hackle wound through the thorax and clipped flat underneath

Jimmy Millar, of Edinburgh, proffers this as his number one dry pattern for loch work and I have little reason to doubt him. It is a very attractive fly, which has all the features one normally looks for in a first class dry pattern. The use of the flat pearl film as a winging material is both innovative and exciting.

This is intended to be a close copy of the natural Heather Fly (*Bibio pomonae*), which is blown onto the water in August and September. I have no reason to think it would fail as a general purpose pattern outside that season. (*see also* Hopper, Black [dry]; and Pearly Bits)

Hedgehog (A. Nicolson)

PLATE 8

Hook: Partridge L2A, 8-12
Silk: Colour irrelevant, normally black
Body: Seal's fur or Partridge SLF of various colours, wound between the wing bunches
Wing: Bunches of deer hair tied along the top of the hook shank
Head: Muddler style, created from the waste butts of the last bunch of winging material

When tying in the bunches of deer hair, make sure to lay a turn of dubbed thread over the roots to prevent excessive splaying of the fibres. Space the bunches close together to maximise both the buoyancy and the surface disrupting effect of the finished fly.

The fly depicted here is the Orange Hedgehog, which has a strong following on Loch Leven, where I saw it work wonders in 1995. I also like claret, hare's ear and green seal's fur versions.

Very few flies have arrived on the scene with quite the impact of Sandy Nicolson's Hedgehog. It was perhaps the most popular fly in Orkney during the 1995 season. I caught fish with it on Lough Sheelin, in Ireland, and know it took salmon from the Delphi Fishery, when nothing else was having much effect. Greased-up, but fished like a wet fly, it pulls fish up to the top like nothing else I have ever seen. I expect to hear a lot more of this fly in the future (*see also* Sedgehog)

Hopper, Amber

PLATE 1

Hook: Partridge E1A or L3A, 10-14
Silk: Brown
Body: Amber seal's fur, or sub.
Rib: Medium or fine oval gold
Legs: Six knotted cock pheasant tail fibres, three on each side
Hackle: Ginger hen

When dressed 'fine and sparse', this pattern makes a very effective general purpose dry fly. Dressed heavily and in large sizes, it is a first rate top-dropper pattern during hatches of Daddy Long Legs hatches. In such circumstances one would fish it greased-up, but fished 'wet'. (*see also* Hopper, Black; Hopper, Claret; and Hopper, CDC)

Hopper, Black (dry)

PLATE 8

Hook: Partridge E1A or K14ST, 12 & 14, or Kamasan B400, 10 & 12
Silk: Black

Body: Black seal's fur, or substitute
Rib: Fine oval silver, or fine monofilament
Legs: Six knotted, dyed black pheasant tail fibres – three each side
Hackle: Black hen, straggly and not too full.

This is an indispensable dry fly for lochs and reservoirs. Use it when black flies are evidently on the menu; when fish are not being particularly selective; or when conditions suggest dries even though no surface feeding is apparent. Brown trout, in particular, rarely pass up the chance of an easy meal lying inert in the surface film, even when they are not generally feeding at this level. This pattern is well worth a try on sea – trout lochs when calm weather conditions do not favour the standard wet fly approach. Arguments rage amongst anglers as to whether the legs of hopper patterns should extend above or below the body, or horizontally out to the sides. In all honesty, it depends to a great extent on how the angler wishes his fly to be presented and also on how the flotant is applied. I will, however, let you into a little secret. Most reservoir matchmen tie the legs above the body.

Other successful variations on the Hopper theme (for both brown and rainbow trout) include: Hopper, Amber Hopper, Claret; Hopper, Hare's Ear; and Hopper, Fiery Brown (with either natural or dyed legs)

Hopper, Black (wet)

PLATE 8

Hook: Partridge E1A or Drennan Emerger, 10 & 12
Silk: Black
Body: Abdomen: black seal's fur, or substitute, ribbed with drawn fine pearl Lurex
Thorax: Glo–Brite no.2, unribbed.
Legs: Six knotted, dyed black pheasant tail fibres – three each side and extending in the horizontal plane.
Hackle: Black hen

It was with some surprise that I learned that Hoppers were very effective patterns when fished wet and not even necessarily near the surface. I suspect that they are taken for midge (chironomid). Whatever the reason for their acceptability, these relatively recently developed 'Underwater Hoppers' are worth some more attention and experimentation. Fished behind surface disrupting patterns, such as Hedgehogs and Muddlers, on a floating line amongst rising trout on Loch Leven, they have proved lethal, especially during midge hatches. They are also well worth a try when using sinking lines. A claret variation with a Glo-Brite no.5 'hot-spot' and a fiery-brown version with a fluorescent peach 'hot-spot' are also proven killers.

Hot-Spot Peacock Palmer

PLATE 8

Hook: Partridge J1A or SH1, 10 & 12
Silk: Black
Body: Bibio-style: peacock herl, then fluorescent fire red wool, then peacock herl again
Rib: Medium gauge copper wire
Hackle: Ginger cock, two turns at head, then palmered

In the early and late part of the season, when fish can be locked on to freshwater shrimp in the shallows, this pattern and its near cousin, the Peacock Palmer, can be lethal.

There is a parasite which affects Gammarus species and shows up as a bright reddish-orange patch about midway down the body. There is some belief amongst scientists that the parasite causes the behaviour of infected shrimp to attract predators (i.e. trout) in order to complete the life cycle. This pattern is an attempt to mimic the parasitized shrimp. Whether fish accept it as such is arguable, but the fly is very successful, nonetheless. (see also Peacock Palmer)

Humbug

PLATE 8

Hook: Partridge SH1, 10 & 12
Silk: Black Tail: Tuft of black marabou, over white marabou, over three strands of pearl Crystal Hair
Body: Flat silver
Wing: Three strands pearl Crystal Hair, over black marabou, over white marabou

PLATE 10

Lightbulb (goldhead), Loch Ordie (wet), Anorexic Loch Ordie, Blue Loch Ordie
Dark Loch Ordie, Machair Claret, Mallard & Claret, Malloch's Favourite
March Brown, Palmered March Brown, Silver March Brown, McLeod's Olive
Melvin Octopus, Loch Ordie (dapping fly), Mini-Stick

PLATE 11
Montana Nymph (goldhead), Jarret's Glory, Morning Glory
Gold Muddler, Muddler Minnow, Muddled Hare's Ear, Mulraney Pig
Murrough (variant), New Nymph (Wood), Octopus, Orangeman
Orange Rory, Olive & Silver Lure (Chalmers), Orange Zulu
Mr Softie, Ossie's Owl (variant), Muddy McGregor

Head: Two turns of fluorescent chenille (normally lime green, but white, peach, orange and red, on occasion)

This pattern was devised for wild trout feeding on daphnia or out in deep water and it has worked well locally. It hasn't had a great deal of exposure as I prefer not to use patterns of this type for wild trout, if at all possible. A bit snooty, I know, but we all have our little foibles. It has done well, fished on the middle dropper, between a Black Kitten and a White Cat and was designed as a 'half-way house' between these two excellent mini-lures.

Invicta

PLATE 8

Hook: Partridge L2A or GRS2A, 8-14
Silk: Brown
Tail: G.P. crest
Body: Invicta yellow (light amber) seal's fur, or substitute
Body hackle: Ginger cock
Rib: Fine or medium oval gold, depending on hook size
Beard Hackle: Blue jay fibres
Wing: Hen pheasant secondary

The Invicta was devised by James Ogden, of Cheltenham. One of the most popular stillwater flies of the 1970s and '80s, it seems now to have slipped from favour slightly. This is probably due in some part to the growing popularity of the Golden Olive Bumble, which is very similar and, in my opinion, a better fly.

The Invicta's limited uses today for loch trout would include, as a hatching sedge pattern in the late evening of mid-summer and as a shrimp imitator early and late in the year. There are, in my view, better contenders for these roles. The pattern has also retained a degree of popularity, in big sizes, for migratory fish on the West Coast and in the Isles.

Most of the second-generation 'spawnings' of this pattern are now much more popular than the original. (see also Invicta, Green; Invicta, Silver; Invicta, Gold; Invicta, White-Hackled; and Orangeman)

Invicta, Gold

PLATE 8

Hook: Partridge L2A or GRS2A, 8-14
Silk: Black
Tail: G.P. crest
Body: Flat gold
Body hackle: Small ginger cock
Rib: Fine oval gold
Hackle: Blue jay fibres, tied as a beard
Wing: Slips of hen pheasant secondary, or speckled cock pheasant secondary feather

Just because a fly can catch fish from time to time does not necessitate its inclusion in a list of 'essential' patterns. I have had some very good evenings with the Gold Invicta, particularly on Loch Leven, but have never been convinced that any of the many other palmered, gold bodied flies would not have done as well. However, in deference to its magical, silver, first cousin and because so many of my accomplices are keen on it, I have included it here. (see also Invicta, Silver; Invicta, Green; and Invicta)

Invicta, Green

PLATE 7

Hook: Partridge SH2, 10-16, or L2A, 8-14
Silk: Brown
Tail: G.P. crest
Body: Green olive seal's fur, or substitute
Body hackle: Pale olive green or golden olive cock
Rib: Fine oval gold
Head hackle: Blue jay fibres, tied as a beard
Wing: Matched slips of well marked hen or cock pheasant secondary feathers

The Green Invicta is a good general purpose fly, which is at its best early to mid season.

Invicta, Pearly

PLATE 8

Hook: Partridge L2A or Kamasan B170, 8-14
Silk: Black
Tail: G.P. crest

Body: Flat pearl Mylar over two layers of tying silk
Body hackle: Ginger cock, palmered
Rib: Very fine oval silver, or wire
Beard Hackle: Blue jay
Wing: Hen pheasant secondary slips

Although it might be considered a variant of the much-lauded Silver Invicta, this pattern deserves its own place in the pantheon of successful wet flies. It is an excellent pattern the whole year round for all types of salmonids.

A variation incorporating a palmered green olive body hackle is a good imitation of a freshwater shrimp and is also well worth inclusion in any collection. (*see also Pearly Wickham's*)

Invicta, Silver

PLATE 8

Hook: Partridge L2A, GRS2A or Kamasan B170, 8-14
Silk: Black
Tail: G.P. crest
Body: Flat silver
Body hackle: Ginger cock
Rib: Very fine oval silver or wire
Throat: Blue jay fibres
Wing: Well marked hen or cock pheasant secondary (hen pheasant tail, in the original dressing)

This derivation of Ogden's famous Invicta is also known in some parts as the Silver Knicker. It is perhaps one of the most versatile loch/stillwater flies for all Scottish game species. Rainbow trout, sea-trout and salmon seem unable to resist it whenever it is offered, but browns seem to like it best from mid-summer onwards. It can take fish when used on lines of any density, but I suspect it does best on floating and intermediate lines. For wild trout, try fishing it in rocky shallows on bright days and late evenings, where it seems to be perfectly acceptable as a stickleback fry imitator. It is also quite useful in small sizes as a point fly when trout are feeding on pale midge, or sometimes as a corixa imitator.

A useful and popular variation replaces the golden pheasant crest tail with a tuft of fluorescent phosphor yellow floss. (*see also Invicta, Silver(variant); Invicta; Invicta, Green; Invicta, White-Hackled; Invicta, Gold and Orangeman*)

Invicta, Silver (variant)

PLATE 8

Hook: Partridge SH2 or Kamasan B175, 10-14
Silk: Brown
Tail: G.P. crest or fluorescent phosphor yellow floss
Body: Flat pearl Lurex wound over wet varnished fluorescent white floss
Body hackle: Badger cock
Rib: Very fine silver wire
Throat: Blue jay
Wing: Pale buff coloured cock pheasant secondary
Cheeks: Jungle cock eyes

Variations on the ubiquitous Silver Invicta are legion, but I devised this one for fry feeding rainbow trout. The pattern is lighter in colour than the original and the pearl over white body was intended to try and portray the translucency of tiny fish fry.

On the right occasions, this pattern pulls rainbows like magic, particularly when they are in a chasing mood. Fished on high density sinking lines it makes a valuable contribution as a dropper fly above mini-lures.

Invicta, Silver Muddler

PLATE 8

Hook: Partridge SH2 or Kamasan B175, 10-14
Silk: Black
Tail: G.P. crest
Body: Flat silver
Body hackle: Ginger cock
Rib: Very fine silver oval or wire
Throat: Blue jay (optional)
Wing: Well marked hen or cock pheasant secondary
Head: Pale deer hair, spun and clipped to produce a bullet shaped head, retaining some of the fine points as a collar

PLATE 12
Owl, Palmered Coch, Parmachene Belle, Parmachene Belle (hairwing)
Partridge Coch, Peacock Palmer, Peach Doll (variant)
Pearly Peach Doll, Peach Palmer, Peach Muddler
Pearly Bits, Black Pennell, Black Pennell (variant), Pearly Green Palmer
Pheasant Tail Nymph (Sawyer), Peterson's Pennell, Peter Ross

PLATE 13
Poacher, Popeye, Priest (variant), Green Priest (below)
Professor, Rainbow Attractor, Qualifier,
Seal's Fur Palmer, Shipman's Buzzer CDC (variant), Ruthven Palmer
Sedgehog, Shuttlecock
Shredge, Shellback Goldhead, Silver Cardinal

Mini-Muddlers are very effective for sea-trout and salmon and for both brown and rainbow trout. Where such flies work, this is an essential pattern. When the fish are evidently active at the surface, fish this pattern on the top or middle dropper.

Invicta, Silver (Muddler variant)

PLATE 8

This version is tied identically to the Silver Invicta Variant (i.e., with pearl over white body, etc.), but leaves out the jungle cock cheeks and includes a head and collar of spun and clipped white deer hair.

When the un-Muddled Silver Invicta (variant) is attracting fish as a point fly, but failing to take them, this pattern, fished on the top, will often finish the job by converting the follows into takes. This version is very good as a sinking line pattern in very bright conditions when bait fish have sought deeper water. Unfortunately, I have found that perch are equally attracted to it under such circumstances.

Invicta, White-Hackled
(W.S. Sinclair)

PLATE 8

Hook: Partridge L2A or Kamasan B170, 8-14
Silk: Brown
Tail: G.P. crest
Body: Invicta yellow seal's fur, or substitute
Body hackle: Ginger cock
Rib: Fine oval gold
Wing: Paired slips of hen pheasant secondary
Hackle: Longish white hen, wound in front of the wing (an under hackle of blue jay is optional)

This pattern was devised by Orcadian angler W.S. (Billy) Sinclair some years ago and has now become a popular and indispensable pattern for the loch angler. It is well regarded in all regions of Scotland and has successfully emigrated to Ireland and England.

Fished as a dropper fly on a floating line, in breezy conditions, the White-hackled Invicta will pull wild fish even on those difficult summer days of bright sun and wind. In small sizes, it is a first

choice during evening sedge hatches on Loch Leven. In larger sizes, it is very popular on the sea-trout and salmon lochs of the West Coast and Western Isles. (*see* Invicta; and White-Hackled Orangeman)

Irishman's Claret

PLATE 8

Hook: Partridge L2A, 8-14, or Kamasan B170 10-14
Silk: Black
Tail: G.P. tippets (dyed hot orange for preference)
Body: Dark claret seal's fur, or substitute
Body hackle: Dark claret cock hackle
Rib: Fine or medium oval gold, dependent on hook size
Wing: Bronze mallard
Head hackle: Longish dark claret hen, tied in front of the wing

Many years ago, I was introduced to this pattern by Brian Roberts, an English ex-international, who had picked it up on his travels. I have since developed a very strong regard for the Irishman's Claret and consider it to be the very best winged wet fly of this coloration. For late evenings and overcast days I regard it as nearly indispensable and I know of no water where it will not perform. It is also a first-class fly for the middle dropper, a position in which few flies do their best.

This pattern is clearly a derivation of the Mallard & Claret but, in my opinion, it is superior: no doubt blessed with hybrid vigour. A minor variation with a teal wing is a pretty and effective alternative.

For salmon and sea-trout in the Far West, this pattern deserves a rigorous testing.

Jersey Herd (variant)

PLATE 9

Hook: Partridge SH2, 12-16
Silk: Black
Tail & Back: Four strands of peacock herl tied in at head, brought over the body and tied in at the hook-bend. Trim the ends of the herls to leave about a quarter inch for the tail

Body: Flat gold
Rib: Fine oval gold
Hackle: Hot orange hen, kept well under the hook shank
Head: Three or four turns of peacock herl

The origin of this pattern as a 'lure' from the English reservoirs has probably much to do with its lack of popularity North of the Border. However, tied in small sizes and fished as a nymph or wet fly, it is worthy of more attention. I particularly like this fly for very early season work, when it appears to accepted as a shrimp, or even a cased-caddis. In bright March-April weather, I fish it slowly on the point, in shallow water over a hard bottom, with a high expectation of success.

Tom Ivens's original dressing, with the copper body, I find less effective, but a minor variation with a red Lurex body and a claret hackle can be very good in poor light. (*see also* Green & Brown)

Jungle Cock & Silver

PLATE 9

Hook: Partridge L2A, 8-14, or SH2, 10-16
Silk: Black
Tail: Slim bunch of G.P. tippet fibres
Body: Flat silver
Rib: Very fine oval silver, or wire (optional)
Wing: Paired jungle cock eye feathers
Hackle: Sparse black hen, tied in front of the wing

This pattern is a bit of a pain to tie, because jungle cock eye feathers are remarkably resistant to lying in the desired plane. Nevertheless, this pattern is well worth the effort. As a traditional wet fly imitation of hatching midge, it is hard to beat, particularly in small sizes. Flies with silver bodies appear to mimic the gas-bloated bodies of dark midge, in the process of hatching. Partnered with a Gizmo or a Coachman and thrown to visibly feeding fish on a floating line, this pattern makes a nonsense of close-copy imitations.

In its larger sizes it is effective as a general purpose wet fly for trout, sea-trout and salmon.

There is a black bodied version which seems to have few supporters in Scotland.

Kate McLaren

PLATE 9

Hook: Partridge J1A, L2A or SH1, 8-14
Silk: Black
Tail: G.P. crest
Body: Black seal's fur, or substitute
Body hackle: Black cock, in quite widely spaced turns
Rib: Fine or medium oval silver, dependent upon hook size, again widely spaced.
Head hackle: Ginger, or red hen, tied long & full

One of the great wet flies for sea-trout, salmon, brown and rainbow trout, it was originally tied by William Robertson, of Glasgow. Kate McLaren was the mother of the late Charles McLaren, longtime proprietor of the Altnaharra Hotel, on Loch Hope and renowned sea-trout fisher. Designed originally for the sea-trout of the far North West, this pattern has crossed many boundaries and is indispensable.

It seems to improve the fly if the turns of hackle and ribbing are relatively widely spaced. I was first made aware of this one day when John Kennedy's fly was catching fish, whilst my own (more closely palmered) renderings were being consistently ignored. I have stuck to this style of dressing ever since, with no regrets. A couple of turns of flat silver under the tail does no harm at all, particularly in the smaller sizes.

Kate McLaren (variant)

PLATE 9

Hook: Partridge J1A or SH1, 10-14
Silk: Black
Tag: Two turns of flat silver, under the tail
Tail: Fluorescent lime green floss (mixed Glo-Brite, nos. 11 & 12)
Body: Black seal's fur, or substitute
Body hackle: Black cock
Rib: Fine oval silver
Head hackle: Ginger hen (hot orange as an alternative)

The 'Kate' has become a firm favourite on Loch Leven and associated waters and is often used on sunk-lines. The passion in this area for

53

PLATE 14
Silver Dabbler (McTeare), Silver Goat's Toe, Silver Muddler
Soldier Palmer, Soldier Palmer Muddler, Sooty Olive, Sooty Olive (variant)
Stick Fly, Squirrel Tail Dunkeld, Suspender Nymph, Teal & Black
Teal Blue & Silver, Teal & Green (1), Teal & Green (2), Teal & Green (3)

PLATE 15

Teal-Winged Butcher, Ted's Olive, Treacle Parkin, Tup's Indispensable (variant)
Viva, Technocat, Gold Viva
Cactus Head Viva, Viva Spider, Jungle Cock Viva, Jungle Cock Viva (claret)
Matson's Pennell, Watson's Fancy, Wet Daddy, White-Hackled Orangeman
White Weazel, Wickham's Fancy (variant), Wingless Wickham's, Wingless Wickham's (variant)

fluorescent tails inevitably led to the above variation. I know of a few very successful anglers who rarely, if ever, omit this pattern from their casts when searching 'down below' for fish. The version with the hot orange hackle is highly rated by some.

Ke-He

PLATE 9

Hook: Partridge L2A, J1A or G3A, 8-14
Silk: Black
Tail: Red wool, under slim bunch of G.P. tippets
Body: Two peacock herls: one tied up the hook shank in butting turns; the other tied down the hook in open turns (NOT twisted together)
Rib: Very fine oval gold, or wire (must not be obtrusive)
Hackle: Dark ginger hen, full and long.

The Ke-He was the collaborative invention in the 1930s of two anglers, Messrs. Kemp and Heddle, from whom it derives its name. The popularity of many flies takes off like a sky-rocket, only to decline rapidly, in a similar manner. This, unfortunately, was the case with the Ke-He. Even on its home waters, in Orkney, the Ke-He is now rarely fished with great success, though once it was rated very highly, particularly as a mid-summer pattern. However, its half-brothers, the Black Ke-He and, to a lesser extent, the Orange Ke-He, are still popular.

The original dressing had a dyed red hackle and no wool tail and was (I strongly suspect) tied to imitate the Heather Fly (*Bibio Pomonae*).

Ke-He, Black

PLATE 9

Hook: Partridge J1A, L2A or SH1, 8-14
Silk: Black (red is an attractive alternative for bigger sizes)
Tag: One or two turns flat silver
Tail: Tuft of fluorescent or ordinary red wool, under a small bunch of G.P. tippet fibres
Body: Two strands of full-fibred bronze peacock herl. One herl is wound in butting turns down the shank. The second herl is wound over the first and back up the shank. Do not twist the herls together

Rib: Fine oval silver or wire
Hackle: Black hen, straggly and long.

The original Ke-He was devised, apparently, to imitate some bees that were being blown on to Orkney's Loch Harray and driving the trout wild. This version of the Ke-He excels for trout on peat water lochs at any time and on any water in the late evening. It is a very effective pattern for loch salmon and sea-trout. I like to fish it on the point for trout and on the middle dropper for salmon and sea-trout. For the late evening and salmon/sea-trout work, I prefer the fluorescent tail and usually combine this variation with hot-orange dyed tippets. I find it a better general purpose pattern than the original Ke-He. (*see also* Ke-He, Orange).

Ke-He, Orange

PLATE 9

Hook: Partridge J1A/G3A/SH1, or Kamasan B175, 8-12
Silk: Red
Tag: Two turns of flat silver
Tail: Dyed orange G.P. tippets over fluorescent fire red wool (Turrall's)
Body: Two long flued peacock herls, one wound up the shank in butting turns and the other wound down the hook in open turns
Rib: Very fine oval gold, or wire
Hackle: Longish hot orange hen

This is a relatively modern variation on the original Ke-He. It is a very good pattern for saving an otherwise hopeless day. In very bright weather this makes a good tail fly, particularly on peaty water.

It is also very popular in the far North for sea-trout in brackish and salt water. In the past it has also served me very well, in small sizes, for reservoir rainbows. (*see also* Wormfly, Orange)

Knouf Lake Special

PLATE 9

Hook: Partridge SH2 or Kamasan B200, 10 & 12
Silk: Primrose
Tail: Thick bunch of G.P. tippet fibres

Body: Bronze peacock herl
Rib: Fluorescent yellow floss
Hackle: Longish dyed yellow partridge hackle

This improbable looking pattern was brought back from Canada by John Buchanan, of Gargunnock. He rates it as a sedge pupa pattern and it must be said that it has certain characteristics in common with the Yellow Owl, which I have always considered to be a sedge pupa imitator.

Lawfield Nobbler (B. Peterson)

PLATE 9

Hook: Kamasan B175, 8 & 10
Silk: Colour irrelevant
Tail: Scarlet/red marabou
Body: Phosphor yellow fluorescent chenille (Glo-Brite, no.11)
Body hackle: Hot orange cock, palmered
Rib: Fine or medium oval silver
Head: Split lead shot, painted black with white eye spots

Lead-headed lures of this type are not as popular as they once were for general trout fishing. Pigs to cast, 'nobblers' have been largely supplanted by Goldheads, which are rather more manageable. However, lead-heads do possess a quite uniquely accentuated action underwater and are still favoured by some, particularly for small stillwaters. It is for this purpose that Brian Peterson of Greenock offers this pattern.

Leven Ghost (D. Chalmers)

PLATE 9

Hook: Partridge SH3 longshank, 8
Silk: Black
Body: Pearsall's orange floss silk
Rib: Fine flat silver
Hackle: White marabou, tied as a beard and extending to the bend of the hook
Wing: Four strands bronze peacock herl, with two G.P. crest feathers over; two olive cock hackles on each side (convex sides outwards)
Cheeks: Jungle cock eyes

This may be a variation on an American streamer pattern, the Gray Ghost, originally tied by Mrs Carrie Stevens in about 1924. Streamers of this style used to be very popular throughout Scotland, but this popularity has declined dramatically over the last thirty years or so with the ascendancy of hair wings, marabou, etc. Davie Chalmers assures me that, when fish are on perch fry, this pattern is 'second to none'. (*see also Back-End Lure*)

Leven Spider

PLATE 9

Hook: Partridge GRS2A or Kamasan B170, 10-14
Silk: Glo-Brite no.5 (fire orange)
Tail: Lime green fluorescent floss (mixed Glo-Brite, nos. 11 & 12)
Body: Flat gold
Rib: Very fine oval gold, or wire
Hackle: Sparse black hen, shortish
Head: Built-up tying silk, well-varnished

A few years back, I fished a day and evening on Loch Leven with an Edinburgh angler who fished a team of three of these Leven Spiders. At first he fished them on a sinking line, later on an intermediate and then, finally, a floater. He never changed his flies, only his line density, and built up a huge basket of fish throughout the session. Any fly that can perform such a feat on this challenging water is worthy of much respect and the pattern is now a standard on Central Belt lochs and reservoirs.

Variations include pearl and silver bodies; red and peach tails and lime green heads.

Leven Stinger (D. Chalmers)

PLATE 9

Hook: Kamasan B270 Double, 12 & 10
Silk: Black
Tail: Fluorescent scarlet floss (Glo-Brite, no.4)
Body: Flat silver
Rib: Fine oval silver
Wing: Slim bunch of pearl Flashabou over four peacock herls
Cheeks: Bunches of Glo-Brite, no.4

PLATE 16
Woodcock & Green, Wormfly, Wormfly (longshank variant)
Black Wormfly (longshank variant), Black Wormfly, Orange Wormfly
Yelow-Eyed Damsel, Xmas Tree, Yellow Owl, Yellow Owl Muddler
Zulu, Blue Zulu, Brown Zulu (Leslie), Gold Zulu
Pearly Zulu, Red Zulu, Simline Zulu

Though perfected for use on Loch Leven, I have little doubt that this pattern should prove useful on other waters where flies of this type are popular. A spin-off from the Leven Butcher, the Stinger fishes best from the start of the season to mid-summer. Fish it on a fast sinking line when the water is clear.

Substitute the peacock herl with white marabou or dyed rabbit fur for an alternative daytime pattern for difficult conditions.

Leveret

PLATE 9

Hook: Partridge SH1 or Kamasan B175, 10 & 12
Tail: Fluorescent floss or yarn, of varying colours
Body: Well mixed hare's mask fur, with plenty of guard hairs, well scrubbed out
Rib: Fine flat gold (optional)

The Leveret is an extension of the Gold Ribbed Hare's Ear theme and is a useful pattern throughout the season, especially the first half. Fish it on a floating or intermediate line.

The dressing is simplicity itself, but really benefits from using the 'dubbing loop' technique to make best use of the hare's fur for the body. This should be well 'scrubbed' to achieve an extra shaggy effect, with the long guard fibres giving a suggestion of legginess in place of a hackle.

Light Bulb [goldhead] (D. Malcolm)

PLATE 10

Hook: Drennan Wet Fly Supreme, 10 & 12
Silk: White
Tail: Fluorescent yellow marabou
Body: Rear half: flat pearl over fluorescent green floss; front half: fluorescent orange seal's fur, or substitute
Wing: White marabou, with two strands of pearl Crystal Hair over, tied to protrude from under the fluorescent orange seal's fur
Head: Gold bead

Another of Davie Malcolm's top half-dozen mini-lures for Central Belt waters. This very pretty little pattern which should find acceptability amongst most stocked water trout. The fly in the illustration uses a gilt plastic, rather than a metal bead.

Loch Ordie (dapping)

PLATE 10

Hook: Partridge J1A, 6-10
Silk: Colour irrelevant, usually black
Hackle: Hen or henny-cock hackles, tied with the concave sides facing forwards: (from rear) black; dark ginger; ginger; white. The last hackle slightly longer.

NB: Traditionally a 'flying' treble was included, but this is now considered optional.

This is one of a very few old dapping patterns still to be regularly used for big browns, salmon and sea-trout in the far North West and the Islands. In the old days, some remarkably big flies were dressed for dapping, but modern trends have seen great reductions in size.

The original pattern had only ginger and white hackles, but the above minor variation is a marked improvement. Soft hackles, such as hen or henny-cock, hold floatant better and longer than high quality, glassy cock hackles. Moreover, hen hackles pick up more wind, making them useful in even light breezes.

A useful variant has a series of black hackles finished off with a ginger head hackle.

Loch Ordie (wet)

PLATE 10

Hook: Partridge L2A or SH1, 8-14
Silk: Colour irrelevant, usually black
Hackle: Hen hackles tied in to slope *backwards* down the hook shank. The colour sequence is as for the dapping version: black, dark ginger, white

This is an Orcadian variation on the Loch Ordie for use as a wet fly. Used as a wave-tripping top dropper, it is particularly successful in the wild and windy weather which is such a feature of the Northern Isles. Treated with floatant, it has an endearing habit of popping to the surface at the end of the retrieve, prompting savage strikes from trout. It has become well loved on the lochs of the West as a sea-trout and salmon fly. (*see also Loch Ordie, Blue; and Hedgehog*)

Loch Ordie, Anorexic (*Ian Hutcheon*)

PLATE 10

Hook: Partridge GRS2A, 10-14
Silk: Black
Hackle: One longish ginger hen wound in two-thirds of the way up the hook shank, with one slightly shorter white hen in front

Dressed light and airy, this variation on the original can be considered a pattern in its own right, as it performs a totally different role. This version should be used with delicacy when light wind or flat calm conditions coincide with hatching midge or sedge. The slim and sparse nature of the fly responds best to a gentle retrieve. Under the right conditions, this can be a very productive pattern.

Variations with black and dark ginger hackles are also useful.

Loch Ordie, Blue (*Norman Irvine*)

PLATE 10

Hook: Partridge L2A, 8-12
Silk: Black
Hackle: Four or five black hen hackles, with one 'teal' blue hen hackle at the head

Many experienced fly fishermen shy away from flies with lots of blue in them, considering the colour to be 'unnatural'. They ought to try a day out in a boat with Norman bringing up great slabs of brown trout to his blue version of the Loch Ordie. Very much a peat water fly, it can be outstanding on its day. Incidentally, if you immerse something blue in peaty water, it actually looks green. I would guess that this pattern would be well worth a try for sea-trout in a loch. (*see also Loch Ordie, Anorexic; Loch Ordie, Dark; and Loch Ordie*).

Loch Ordie, Dark

PLATE 10

Hook: Partridge L2A or GRS2A, 10-14
Silk: Black or brown
Hackle: One or two furnace hen, with one black hen in front, or simply two furnace hen hackles

This important variation on the Loch Ordie has largely supplanted the original, here in Orkney. Fished high and slow in the water, it mimics hatching midge and small, dark sedge.

The dressing should be light and concentrated close to the hook eye, almost in the style of a low-water salmon fly. A small butt of either fluorescent red or lime green floss is often incorporated, which does no harm at all.

Machair Claret (*John Kennedy*)

PLATE 10

Hook: Partridge J1A or Drennan Wet Fly Supreme, 8-12
Silk: Black
Tail: A jungle cock eye feather, shiny side down
Body: Dark claret seal's fur, or substitute
Body hackle: Paired cock hackles, claret and black
Rib: Medium or fine oval gold, size dependent
Head hackle: Longish black hen
The inclusion of an expensive jungle cock eye, as an essential part of this dressing, means that the Machair Claret is unlikely to become universally popular. That is a pity, because the fly is very good for brown trout, sea-trout and salmon in the Western Isles. The pattern is another one of John Kennedy's excellent inventions, in which the Irish influence is strong.

Mallard & Claret

PLATE 10

Hook: Partridge L2A, GRS2A or Kamasan B170, 8-14
Silk: Black
Tail: G.P. tippets
Body: Dark claret seal's fur, or substitute
Rib: Fine oval gold

Hackle: Dark ginger/medium red brown hen
Wing: Bronze mallard

One of the country's most popular flies, the Mallard & Claret is excellent for all game species and in most situations. There seem to be few limitations in its ability to mimic natural food items. It is effective for trout feeding on midge, sedge and shrimp and it works throughout the season. Moreover, its effectiveness doesn't seem to be restricted by light or weather conditions.

I have a suspicion that a black hackle, rather than a dark red game, actually improves this pattern, but this may be heresy! (see also Grouse & Claret; Dark Mackerel; and Irishman's Claret)

Malloch's Favourite

PLATE 10

Hook: Partridge L2A or GRS2A, 10-14
Silk: Black
Tail: Ginger cock hackle fibres
Body: Stripped peacock quill, tipped with a turn of flat silver
Hackle: Blue dun hen
Wing: Slips of woodcock primary from the trailing edge, shiny side out

This is a fly pattern from the esteemed old tackle dealers, Malloch's of Perth, which family firm has produced generations of expert loch fishers. It dates from the 19th century. This fly is still worth a go today, if tied light and sparse. Quill bodies imitate the finely segmented bodies of midge pupae admirably and the other elements of this pattern are also strongly suggestive of midge. This pattern has strong past associations with Loch Leven and neighbouring waters. (see also Buzzer, Near Perfect)

March Brown

PLATE 10

Hook: Partridge L2A/GRS2A or Kamasan B170, 8-14
Silk: Brown, yellow or, sometimes, orange
Tail: Brown partridge hackle fibres, sparse
Body: Well mixed hare's mask over yellow dubbing
Rib: Very fine oval gold, or wire

Hackle: Brown partridge
Wing: Hen pheasant secondary

There have been many patterns offered in imitation of the ephemerid species commonly called the March Brown. This insect *only* lives in running water, but this hasn't precluded the usefulness of the artificials on stillwaters. I find this particular pattern suits my purposes very well. The underbody of yellow dubbing gives the fly a somewhat olive cast, as the fibres emerge through the hare's fur.

In smaller sizes, it is very good for use on fish rising to unidentified food forms. In its larger sizes, I like it as a top dropper pattern in a big wave, when the more bushy flies typically offered in such conditions have failed. On lochs and reservoirs it is an excellent imitator of a wide range of invertebrates: sedges, olives, shrimps and hoglice. In one or other of its forms, I consider it indispensable. (see also Palmered March Brown)

March Brown, Palmered

PLATE 10

Hook: Partridge L2A, GRS2A or Kamasan B170, 8-12
Silk: Brown
Under-dub: Sparse dubbing of yellow seal's fur, or substitute
Over-dub: Well mixed hare's mask
Body hackle: Ginger cock hackle
Rib: Fine oval gold
Head hackle: Longish brown partridge hackle

I designed this pattern along the lines of an old recipe for the March Brown, which incorporates an under-dubbing of yellow mohair. The effect of the yellow under-dubbing showing through the hare fur produces a natural olive cast to the fly that is virtually impossible to achieve by other means.

As a general purpose loch fly, this pattern is in a league of its own. Fish it when trout are rising to a wide variety of surface fly: when they are on hatching olives or sedges, or even on shrimp and hoglice. As a static wet fly, fished under stationary dry patterns, it is an efficient taker of suspicious and sophisticated rainbows.

On peat water lochs, I sometimes omit the yellow under-dub and use just the sandy coloured fur from the base of the hare's ear. This seems to produce a better pattern for this type of water. In both forms, I consider these palmered versions of the March Brown to be indispensable. (see also March Brown)

March Brown, Silver

PLATE 10

Hook: Partridge L2A or Kamasan B170, 10-14
Silk: Black or brown
Tail: Brown partridge hackle fibres
Body: Flat silver, ribbed with very fine oval silver or wire
Hackle: Brown partridge hackle
Wing: Dark, well marked hen pheasant secondary

Prior to the arrival of the Silver Invicta, this was my favoured pattern for wild browns in shallow water as a stickleback fry imitator. I rarely use it now. My researches show that it still maintains a degree of popularity, particularly on rivers.

McLeod's Olive

PLATE 10

Hook: Partridge L2A or GRS2A, 10-14
Silk: Brown
Tag: One or two turns of flat gold, under tail
Tail: Green olive cock hackle fibres
Body: Green olive seal's fur
Rib: Very fine oval gold, or wire
Hackle: Green olive hen
Wing: Grey mallard or starling

Although it would be natural to assume that this pattern is an attempt to imitate members of the ephemerid tribe of 'olives', I have found it largely useless in this capacity. It is, however, a successful shrimp and sedge pupae representation and on any of the waters where green patterns are considered essential, it is worth a 'swim'.

It is a very old fly, long associated with Loch Leven and other Central Belt waters.

Midge, Fluorescent Green

PLATE 5

Hook: Partridge K14ST, 12 & 14
Silk: Fluorescent lime green floss (Glo-Brite, no.12)
Body: Two layers of the tying thread
Cheeks: Four strands of fluorescent white floss, either side
Thorax: Green peacock herl (the best material is found at the extreme tip of a peacock sword feather)
Hackle: One turn of honey dun hen

The simplest midge pupae patterns are usually the best and this the embodiment of simplicity. In the bleak mid-summer, when insect hatches dwindle to the odd outbreak of tiny midge, this pattern can 'save your bacon', if fished slow and high in the water. For brown trout it only seems to work when the natural bright green midge are actually about, but for rainbows it will score at almost any time.

Mini-Stick

PLATE 10

Hook: Partridge K14ST or Kamasan B200, 12 & 14
Silk: Brown
Butt: Tapered lime green fluorescent floss
Body: Single peacock herl, wound in touching turns
Rib: Fine oval gold
Hackle: Two turns of dark furnace hen

This versatile pattern works well on lochs and reservoirs, for both wild brown trout and rainbows. Fish it on a floating line for surface active fish, or on a sinker when there is evidence of fish feeding on ascending nymphs or pupae. It is particularly good for fish feeding on sedge pupae, or as a point fly to add some variety to a team of midge pupae imitations. When employed on a sinking line, using the 'lift & hang' technique, an extended 'hang' with this fly will often be rewarded by solid takes. (see also Stick Fly)

Mr Softie (A. Murphy)

PLATE 11

Hook: Partridge L2A, 8
Silk: Fluorescent yellow Danville 'Flymaster'
Tail: Yellow marabou
Body: Fine, yellow cactus chenille
Back: Yellow Ethafoam

The Booby Nymph has had a tremendous impact upon stillwater fly fishing over the past few years, particularly for rainbow trout. Love them or loathe them, buoyant flies of this type are here to stay. It was only a matter of time until variations on the original concept came along. Alastair Murphy informs me that this fly is a proven fish killer. It can be tied in a variety of colours, and it has a different action in the water to those of the standard 'Booby-eyed' construction. (*see also* Popeye)

Montana Nymph (goldhead)

PLATE 11

Hook: Kamasan B405 or Partridge L2A, 10 & 12
Silk: Black
Tail: Bunch of black cock hackle fibres
Body: Black chenille
Thorax: Fluorescent phosphor yellow chenille (Glo-Brite, no.11)
Hackle: Black cock, palmered through thorax only
Thorax cover: Black suede chenille
Head: Gold bead

The original dressing was designed to imitate large dark stonefly nymphs of Northern America. However, the pattern crossed 'the pond' and acquired a fluorescent (cf. a plain yellow) thorax. For a decade, at least, it has been one of the most popular and successful reservoir patterns used in Britain.

The Montana takes both wild and stocked fish all over Scotland and I know of Orcadian anglers who wouldn't be seen dead without one on the cast when fishing certain waters. The standard version is the one most commonly encountered, but this 'beaded' version will no doubt gain in popularity, as have all the other 'Goldhead' patterns.

For small-stillwaters, fish singly on a long leader via a floating or intermediate line. For loch work, fish as a point fly on sinking or intermediate lines.

Morning Glory (Francis Jarrett)

PLATE 11

Hook: Partridge SH1 or Kamasan B175, 10-14
Silk: Black
Tail: Tuft of fluorescent blue floss (Glo-Brite, no.14)
Body: Flat gold
Body hackle: Hot orange cock, two turns at head then palmered
Rib: Very fine oval gold, or wire
Wing: Natural grey squirrel tail

This is an adaptation of that popular Leven fly, the Kingfisher Butcher. I am not a great fan of hair-winged trout flies but, for this one, I'm prepared to make an exception. I prefer it for sea-trout, rather than their stay-at-home brown trout cousins.

A minor variation, known as Jarrett's Glory, after its inventor Francis Jarrett of Cowdenbeath, has a wing of white and black marabou (the white twice the length of and *under* the black). It is a very effective mini-lure for rainbows and daphnia feeding brown trout.

Muddled Hare's Ear

PLATE 11

Hook: Partridge SH2, 12-16
Silk: Brown
Tail: Fibres of lemon wood duck, or dyed 'silver' mallard substitute
Body: Well mixed hare's mask
Rib: Very fine oval gold
Hackle: Brown partridge (omit in small sizes)
Wing: Lemon wood duck (or substitute), rolled or folded
Cheeks: Jungle cock eyes
Head: Very fine roe deer hair, spun and clipped, retaining some fine points as a collar
The success of this pattern makes the daunting task of tying it worth while. In its small sizes, this

pattern is lethal on a floating line amongst midge-feeding trout, regardless of whether the insects are dark or light. In the larger sizes, I like it for late evenings when sedge are on the go and for general purpose work.

As an alternative to wood duck, I would suggest finely marked brown partridge for the small sizes, and the 'wrong' side of a bronze mallard feather in the larger sizes. I'm afraid that the jungle cock eyes are essential, as they represent the wing buds, but artificial 'eyes' may work. (see Hare's Ear Muddler; and Donny Murdo)

Muddler, Black & Silver

PLATE 1

Hook: Partridge SH2 or D4A, 10-14
Silk: Black
Tail: A bunch of black hen hackle fibres or dyed rabbit
Body: Flat silver
Rib: Fine oval silver
Wing: Bunch of black hen hackle fibres, or dyed rabbit, tied over a small bunch of pearl crystal hair
Head: Black deer hair, clipped to a bullet shape, retaining some of the fine tips at the rear as a 'ruff' or pseudo-hackle

On its day this fly can be a 'life-saver'. I well remember one occasion fishing on Loch Boardhouse with the renowned Brian Leadbetter. Conditions seemed hopeless – brilliant sunshine and strong wind – and I opined as much. However, Brian took this as a challenge and we set out to try and beat the conditions. In the end, I managed to catch three good trout, all on the Black & Silver Muddler, whilst Brian, despite his undoubted skills, failed even to move a fish.

This really is a great point fly in tough, bright conditions, or at any other time.

Muddler Minnow

PLATE 11

Hook: Partridge D4A, 8-12
Silk: Brown
Tail: Folded slip of oak turkey or hen pheasant quill

Body: Flat gold
Rib: Fine oval gold
Underwing: Bunch of grey squirrel hair
Wing: Slips of 'oak' turkey or hen pheasant
Head: Deer hair, spun and clipped, retaining some of the hair points as a collar, or false hackle

This is Don Gapen's original pattern, designed to imitate the cockatush, or muddler – a small bullhead-like goby found in North American streams. The fly was introduced to Britain in the 1950s by Tom Saville, the Nottinghamshire tackle dealer, amongst others.

The original Muddler has spawned a whole race of flies, which have in common – if *nothing* else – the spun and clipped deer hair head. In its larger sizes, the original is largely redundant for general British requirements, which is hardly surprising. However, in the North-West and the Western Isles, it is still very popular and effective for salmon and sea-trout in lochs. In these waters, a copper body is often preferred.

Muddler Muddler

Hook: Partridge SH2 or J1A, 10-14
Silk: Black or brown
Body: Flat silver
Rib: Very fine or fine oval silver
Wing: Buff coloured cock pheasant secondary
Head: Fine, pale deer hair, spun and clipped to a bullet shape, retaining some fine points as a collar

Very simple patterns are often the best. Mini-Muddler patterns, such as this, are simplicity itself and are very effective for traditional loch-style fishing. They have proved to be excellent, vaguely imitative patterns, for when trout are feeding on shrimp, midge and sedges.

Although the above would suggest a simplified Silver Invicta Muddler, it became an essential part of my repertoire long before I had come across any of the Silver Invicta spin-offs. In a late evening hatch on Loch Leven, this is one of the patterns I would confidently reach for. (see also Gold Muddler; Bumble,Claret Muddler; Caenis Muddler; Hare's Ear Muddler; Green Peter Muddler; Muddled Hare's Ear; Dunkeld Muddler; Soldier Muddler; and Yellow Owl Muddler).

Muddy McGregor (J. Buchanan)

PLATE 11

Hook: Drennan Carbon Lure or Partridge SH3, 10 & 12
Silk: Red
Tail: Red or scarlet hen hackle point
Body: Fluorescent phosphor yellow chenille (Glo-Brite, no.11)
Hackle: Red or scarlet hen hackle, tied in at throat only
Wing: Fluorescent yellow marabou

This is a lure for dirty or discoloured water and devastatingly effective on 'stockies'. The antithesis of subtlety and restraint, it is, nevertheless, very effective in its own way.

Mulraney Pig (D. McPhail)

PLATE 11

Hook: Partridge G3A or Kamasan B170, 10-16
Silk: Black
Tail: G.P. crest (omitted in the original version)
Body: Black floss or seal's fur, with slim bunch of peacock sword fibres tied down over the body, as a back
Rib: Fine oval silver (not over the peacock sword fibres)
Wing: Slim bunch of Amherst pheasant tippet fibres
Hackle: Black hen, tied in front of the wing

Davie McPhail assures me that this slightly augmented Irish import is a worthwhile pattern for use against the sea-trout and browns of Ayrshire. I had heard mention of this pretty pattern before, but this is my first viewing of it. It looks as though it could be used in a loch-style mode against midge feeders.

Murrough (Stephen Leask)

PLATE 11

Hook: Partridge E1A or Kamasan B400, 10 & 12
Silk: Black
Body: Spun deer hair, clipped to a cigar shape
Wing: Squirrel tail hair, dyed hot orange (either splayed over the body or divided)
Hackle: Rich dark ginger hen, tied in front of the wing

Murrough is the Irish name for either of the great red sedges *Phrygania grandis* and *P. striata*). Greased-up and fished on the top-dropper, this pattern is capable of seducing the most cynical of brown trout. This version's Shetland origins would indicate that it is a fly for a good, windy day, and that is indeed the case. It fishes best from mid to late season. (*see also* Hedgehog)

New Nymph (D. Wood)

PLATE 11

Hook: Kamasan B405, 10-14
Silk: Black
Tail: Olive grizzle marabou, over Glo-Brite no.11 fluorescent floss
Body: Well mixed hare's mask fur
Rib: Yellow Twinkle
Thorax: Fluorescent phosphor yellow floss (Glo-Brite, no.11)
Hackle: Yellow dyed grey speckled partridge

Davie Wood, of Kirkliston, brought this pattern together using aspects of Damsel Fly nymphs and a Jeremy Hermann pattern which he had seen in use. He likes it mid season on floating and intermediate lines and reckons it to be vaguely imitative rather than representing anything in particular. It certainly has that 'fishy' look.

Octopus

PLATE 11

Hook: Partridge K2B or Kamasan B420, 8-12
Silk: Black
Body: Green olive seal's fur (Green Peter green)
Body hackle: Ginger cock
Rib: Fine oval gold
Head hackle: Small golden pheasant red body feather, wound

This pattern was devised to answer the problem I had in trying to make the Green French

Partridge work effectively here in Orkney. It is a half-way house between the aforementioned and a Green Peter.

It will take fish in a variety of conditions and on varying line densities but it fishes best as a bob-fly in windy conditions, when it should be dragged across the wave tops. It has taken browns and rainbows all over the UK for me and others. In big sizes, it has been excellent for loch sea-trout and salmon. (*see* also Melvin Octopus)

Octopus, Melvin

PLATE 10

Hook: Partridge K2B or Kamasan B420, 8-12
Silk: Brown
Tag: Two turns of flat gold
Tail: Tuft of fluorescent phosphor yellow floss (Glo-Brite, no.11)
Body: Golden olive seal's fur, or substitute
Body hackle: Paired cock hackles, green olive and golden olive
Rib: Fine oval gold
Head hackle: Yellow rump feather from a Golden Pheasant

I designed this pattern as a hatching mayfly imitator for Lough Melvin, in Ireland, in 1991. On a return visit in 1995, I was pleased to see it being used by the locals and it still adequately fulfils its purpose. In the intervening years I have heard of it being used, with good result, for Scottish trout in similar circumstances.

Make the turns of the body hackle quite widely spaced: three turns on a size 10 hook is about right. The head hackle should flare at right angles to the hook, rather than being swept back. (*see* also Bumble, Golden Olive; and Octopus)

Olive & Silver Lure (D. Chalmers)

PLATE 11

Hook: Drennan Carbon Lure or Partridge SH3, 10
Silk: Black
Tail: Bunch of fluorescent scarlet floss (Glo-Brite, no.4)
Body: Flat silver
Rib: Silver wire or very fine oval

Wing: Olive marabou over four bronze peacock herls
Cheeks: Fluorescent scarlet floss (Glo-Brite no.4)

A mid to deep water daytime lure for brown trout in the earliest and latest months of the year.

Orangeman

PLATE 11

Hook: Partridge SH2 or Kamasan B170, 10-14
Silk: Red
Tag: A couple of turns of flat gold (only in larger sizes)
Tail: G.P. crest
Body: Invicta yellow seal's fur
Body hackle: Hot orange cock
Rib: Fine oval gold
Head hackle: Beard of blue jay fibres (in larger sizes, tie as a full collar wound in front of the wing)
Wing: Slips of cock or hen pheasant secondary

I had been fishing this one for years and calling it the Orange Hackled Invicta until I discovered it was a very popular and time-served Loch Lomond pattern. On Lomond it is effective for salmon and sea-trout, but it does not have such a reputation elsewhere. I know it best as a fly for brown trout in the early months of the year and for browns and sea-trout in brackish water throughout the year. I see no reason why it should not be effective for the rainbows of the South and the Central Belt. (*see* also Invicta; Invicta, Green Invicta, White-Hackled and Orangeman, White-Hackled)

Orange Rory (Peter Gunn)

PLATE 11

Hook: Partridge L2A or Kamasan B175, 8-12
Silk: Black
Tail: Bunches of hackle fibres, black over hot orange
Hackle: Series of alternating black and hot orange hen hackles, *always* starting with black at the tail and finishing with hot orange at the head.

This is a startling, non-imitative patterns that works well on fish feeding on daphnia in bright weather. Although bearing strong resemblance to the Loch Ordie in its construction, it fulfils entirely different functions.

I was first introduced to this pattern on Lough Melvin, where it seduced numbers of the indigenous 'sonaghan' trout during difficult weather conditions. It is also effective at the back end of the season, when wild trout can be particularly 'pernickety' in their preferences for fly pattern.

Ossie's Owl

PLATE 11

Hook: Partridge K14ST or Kamasan B100, 10-14
Silk: Black
Tail: Fluorescent phosphor yellow floss (Glo-Brite, no.11)
Body: One peacock herl, wound in butting turns
Rib: Four strands of Glo-Brite no.11 Floss twisted together and wound as a single 'rope' in open turns
Hackle: Brown or grey partridge hackle, tied long and sparse

Leven anglers are convinced that the Yellow Owl and its descendants (of which this is one) imitate the large midge which hatch from the loch in the mid-summer months. I have strong doubts that this is the case. To my mind, the Owl series of flies is far more suggestive of sedge pupae than of chironomids. The only obvious midge feature is the curved body (a shape shared by emerging sedge pupae). However, since midge hatches are often concurrent with sedge emergence, who can really be certain?

Regardless of what exactly the trout take it for, Ossie's Owl is a very successful variation on its progenitor. It works well on floating or intermediate line in late evening rises on Leven.

A Muddler-headed version, known as Ossie's Muddled Owl, is worthy of inclusion in any fly box destined for Loch Leven in the summer. (see also Yellow Owl; Yellow Owl Muddler; and Owl)

Owl (D. Chalmers)

PLATE 12

Hook: Partridge K2B or Drennan Sedge, 10 & 12
Butt: Fluorescent lime green floss (Glo-Brite, no.12), varnished
Tail: A slim bunch of brown partridge hackle fibres
Body: Two bronze peacock herls, wound
Rib: Fine oval gold
Hackle: Long brown partridge hackle

Mention the name 'owl' in Scottish fishing circles and the well informed will know the subject concerns the phenomenal hatches of large chironomids which take place on Loch Leven. The insects are known there as 'owls' (and also, 'curly bums').

This pattern has a striking resemblance to the Grannom, which I know to be a very successful pattern for such hatches, but it is sufficiently different to warrant its own, distinct inclusion in this list. This is an evening fly for the period from mid-June to August. (see also Ossie's Owl; Yellow Owl; and Yellow Owl Muddler)

Palmered Coch

PLATE 12

Hook: Partridge L2A or Kamasan B170, 10-14
Silk: Black or brown
Tag: Two turns of flat gold
Body: Long flued peacock herl, wound in butting turns
Body hackle: Rich red/brown cock
Rib: Very fine oval gold or wire
Head hackle: Longish dark furnace hen

I have frequently found trout in a mood to accept very dark flies, but totally refusing offerings that were entirely black. Under such circumstances, this is the pattern I reach for. It is very much a floating line pattern and only seems to work for me on the top dropper. It is very good on peaty waters throughout the season and in clear water lochs from mid-season to late. The fly is also worth a try when dark sedges are about and I have known it do well in 'falls' of cow-dung flies. (see also Coch-y-Bonddhu; and Partridge Coch)

Parmachene Belle (variant)

PLATE 12

Hook: Partridge SH2, 10-14
Silk: Red
Tail: Bunches of hackle fibres, red over white
Body: Yellow seal's fur (yellow floss in the original)
Rib: Fine or medium oval gold, size dependent (silver in the original dressing)
Hackle: Red and white hen, mixed
Wing: In three parts: Two tufts of white squirrel tail, with one tuft of dyed red squirrel tail sandwiched between. In very small sizes, use dyed rabbit fur. (The original dressing had married strips of white/red/white duck or goose quill)

The Parmachene Belle is a very old fancy pattern from the USA. Garish wet fly patterns, such as this, are not very popular today, but this fly still has its uses. I have seen some spectacular sea-trout and brackish water browns fall for its charms and salmon are also reputed to be susceptible. There is also a story about it creating havoc amongst Leven trout on one particularly difficult day.

Perhaps not the easiest fly to tie, particularly in its original form, the Parmachene Belle is still worthy of a place in a general purpose fly box. It is no bad thing to keep one's hand in with some of the traditional tying techniques, such as marrying wing slips. The hairwing variant of the Parmachene Belle (see Plate 12) is much easier to construct, of course.

Partridge Coch

PLATE 12

Hook: Partridge L2A/GRS2A or Kamasan B160, 10-14
Silk: Black or brown
Tag: One or two turns flat gold
Body: One long flued peacock herl, wound in touching turns
Rib: Very fine oval gold, or wire
Hackle: Brown speckled partridge hackle

I believe that this pattern was brought to Orkney by a Welshman, sometime in the early 1980s.

Since then, it has established itself as a general pattern that imitates nothing in particular, but which has a generally 'foody' sort of look about it. It is a great mid-summer pattern that often succeeds in difficult conditions. Fished on a middle dropper, with a Coch-y-Bonddu or a Palmered Coch on the bob, it can often solve some pretty knotty high summer problems. A slight variation incorporating a grey speckled partridge hackle is equally effective on its day.

Peach Doll (variant)

PLATE 12

Hook: Partridge SH2 or Kamasan B200, 10 & 12
Silk: Red
Body: Chopped and dubbed mixture of fluorescent orange and amber flosses (Glo-Brite, nos. 7 & 8)
Rib: Fine oval gold
Back & Tail: Mixed strands of Glo-Brite flosses, nos. 7 & 8

I always thought that some of the versions of the Peach Doll that I have seen looked rather wan and faded. This version, using the two colours of Glo-Brite floss produced a more vivid peach colour. My philosophy is this: if the pattern is supposed to be a 'shocker', then don't hold back.

In dirty water, very poor light, or simply when fish are stale and show no interest in more traditional dressings, I resort to the above pattern and give it a 'turbo-charged' retrieve. It will take wild trout, but it is noticeably better on stocked fish. It is at its best fished on intermediate and sinking lines. (see also Peach Doll, Pearly; and Peach Palmer)

Peach Doll, Pearly

PLATE 12

Hook: Partridge SH2 or Kamasan B200, 10-14
Silk: Red
Body: Two layers of flat pearl Mylar over a layer of tying silk
Back & Tail: Mixed strands of fluorescent orange and amber floss (Glo-Brite, nos. 7 & 8)

This is a useful alternative to the Peach Doll. Not quite as effective as the original for fishing in deep or heavily discoloured water, but it is frequently superior as a 'pulling' fly in the upper layers when fish require this sort of approach. It is at its best in mid-summer, for rainbow trout.

Peach Muddler

PLATE 12

Hook: Partridge SH2 or Kamasan B175, 10-14
Silk: Red
Tail: Mixed fluorescent orange and amber flosses (Glo-Brite, nos. 7 & 8)
Body: Chopped, mixed and dubbed fluorescent flosses – as for tail
Hackle: Palmered ginger cock
Rib: Fine oval gold
Head: Spun and clipped fine deer hair retaining some fine points as a collar, or false hackle

When trout are keen to chase and are stimulated by surface disrupting patterns, this is one to try, particularly in dull light conditions. It works best on intermediate and floating lines. Again, this is mainly a rainbow trout pattern, but occasionally it can be very effective for both browns and sea-trout.

Peach Palmer

PLATE 12

Hook: Partridge SH1/J1A or Kamasan B175, 10 & 12
Silk: Red
Tail: Tuft of mixed Glo-Brite flosses nos. 7 & 8
Body: Chopped, mixed and dubbed, fluorescent orange and amber flosses (Glo-Brite, nos. 7 & 8)
Thorax: Chopped and dubbed fluorescent fire orange floss (Glo-Brite, no.5)
Hackle: Ginger cock, two turns at the head, then palmered
Rib: Fine oval gold

This very efficient pattern is for those who would like a more traditional looking alternative to a Peach Doll. An early and late season pattern, it also comes into its own in discoloured water conditions, whether due to algae or mineral turbidity. It is usually used on sinking lines, but occasionally on floaters. It works best for rainbows, but sometimes also on browns.

Peacock Palmer (Norman Irvine)

PLATE 12

Hook: Partridge L2A 10 & 12 or SH2 12 & 14
Silk: Brown
Body: One long peacock herl, tied in at head and wound down the shank in butting turns, then back up the hook in open turns
Hackle: Medium red/brown cock, two turns at head, then palmered
Rib: Fine flat gold

Think of drifting close to shore, over hard ground, on a Northern loch and this is the pattern my imagination sticks resolutely on the point. I believe that fish take it for a shrimp or, perhaps, a cased caddis. Regardless of whatever it imitates (or doesn't), this is a very successful pattern for wild trout.

Although I prefer it on the point, the Peacock Palmer works well in the middle position.

A pattern very similar to this was popular in the early part of the 20th century and was known as the Red Palmer. Because of possible confusion with the Soldier Palmer, Norman named this pattern with regard to its main material component. (see also Hot-Spot Peacock Palmer)

Pearly Bits (J. Millar)

PLATE 12

Hook: Kamasan B170 or Partridge K14ST, 14
Silk: Black
Body: Black seal's fur, tied slim in the abdomen and bulkier at the thorax
Wing: Two strips of flat pearl Mylar, suitably cut and tied in to give a realistic delta-winged shape
Hackle: Two turns of soft black cock

Sometimes one sees a fly pattern and immediately thinks 'I've got to give that a go!' This is just such a pattern. Whether the pearl wings make a heap of difference is debatable, but how could you fail to have confidence, with this pattern sitting out there in a pin-ripple, whilst trout are munching their way through a hatch of black midge? (*see also* Black Hopper; Bibio Emerger; Black Blob; and Heather Fly)

Pearly Green Palmer

PLATE 12

Hook: Partridge SH2 or Kamasan B200, 10-12
Silk: Fluorescent lime green thread
Tail: Tuft of mixed fluorescent phosphor yellow and lime green (Glo-Brite, nos. 11 & 12)
Body: Two layers of tying thread, with flat pearl Mylar over
Hackle: Light green olive, two turns at head, then palmered
Rib: Very fine oval silver, or wire

When waters are discoloured by green algae, patterns of this hue are often very effective. Fluorescent green also seems to have strong attraction for fish feeding on daphnia or, obviously, insect species of similar coloration.

Some years ago, an extraordinary occurrence on Loch Leven confirmed that this pattern was something rather special. Whilst checking to see whether my leader was tangled and drawing it, fly by fly, from the water, a trout of over two pounds shot out of the water and took the fly as it hung at least 18 inches above the surface! I have to say, though, that I generally prefer to fish the fly *below* the surface, on intermediate or sinking lines, in conjunction with mini-lures.

Pennell, Black

PLATE 12

Hook: Partridge J1A or Kamasan B175, 8-14
Silk: Black
Tail: Slim bunch of G.P. tippet fibres
Body: Traditionally black floss, but ever-increasingly seal's fur or substitute
Rib: Medium or fine silver oval, depending on hook size
Hackle: Longish, sparse black hen

Possibly the leading contender for the title of 'The Fly Found in Most Fly Boxes', it was invented by the redoubtable Victorian angler, H. Cholmondeley-Pennell. Although perhaps losing some of its popularity as a trout fly, its reputation amongst salmon and sea-trout loch fishers is still as strong as ever. For such work, dress the fly with a dubbed body, include a silver tag and tie the hackle bigger and bushier. If you don't mind straying even further from the original dressing, a palmered cock hackle wound down the body works wonders. For trout, the sparser this pattern is tied, the better it seems to work. (*see also* Pennell, Black (variant); Blae & Black; and Pennell, Peterson's)

Pennell, Black (variant)

PLATE 12

Hook: Partridge L3A (light wire), 12
Silk: Black
Tail: Four hot-orange dyed G.P. tippet fibres
Body: Two layers of the tying silk, tied in touching turns
Rib: Very fine oval gold
Hackle: Very sparse black cock

This version should be tied as slim as possible: positively anorexic! If one can resist the temptation to overdress it, this version is deadly. My boat partner, Norman Irvine, picked up this pattern from somewhere about ten years ago and it has been taking boatloads of fish ever since. Fish it slowly on a floating line as part of a team, or even at depth on a sinker. You may be pleasantly surprised to discover how such a skinny and insignificant little fly can sometimes be irresistible. This is a good example of fly pattern evolution.

Pennell, Hutch's (Ian Hutcheon)

PLATE 8

Hook: Partridge GRS2 or 3A, 10-14
Silk: Black
Tag: Two turns flat silver under the tail
Tail: Slim bunch of G.P. tippets (dyed hot-orange, optional)
Body: One peacock herl, wound in butting turns from the tail to the hackle position (I prefer to use the green herls from the back of a sword feather)
Rib: Very fine oval silver, or wire

Hackle: Longish black hen, with a shorter white hen in front – both sparse

Dress this pattern in a 'minimalist' style with as little material as possible and you have a killing 'loch-style' fly for dark midge hatches. Ian's dressing cleverly suggests several of the important elements of a hatching midge pupa. The short white hackle at the head may be breathers, or something of the adult insect breaking out from the pupal shuck.

Since this pattern has appeared on the scene it has created much interest and, for the months of April, May and June, many now regard it as indispensable. (see also Pennell, Black; Pennell, Black [variant]; and Ginger Quill)

Pennell, Hutch's (Muddler)

PLATE 8

Hook: Partridge SH2, 14 & 16
Silk: Black
Tag: Two turns flat silver, under tail
Tail: Slim bunch of hot orange dyed G.P. tippets
Body: Fine peacock herl from sword-tail
Rib: Very fine oval silver, or wire
Hackle: Longish black hen
Head: Fine, white deer hair, retaining a few fine points

This adaptation of the original was designed to enhance features already present and make the pattern look more 'buggy'. On its day it can even outshine its parent. It is a very good top-dropper, fished with a standard Hutch's Pennell below, for those who don't mind all their eggs in one basket!

Pennell, Matson's (Dick Matson)

PLATE 15

Hook: Partridge SH2, 12 & 14
Silk: Black
Tail: Tuft of fluorescent neon magenta floss (Glo-Brite no.1)
Body: Very sparsely dubbed black seal's fur, or substitute
Rib: Silver wire or very fine oval
Hackle: Longish, sparse black hen

Dick Matson lives on the shores of Loch Swannay, which he treats as a 'laboratory' for perfecting his fly patterns. This one has, without doubt, had a great impact on Swannay trout and its fishermen. It is a reliable taker of quality fish throughout the season. It is particularly good when fish are on black midge, but this is not a pre-requisite for its use. It is well worth a try on any water where black flies are normally successful. (see also Zulu, Slimline; Pennell, Black; and its other variants).

Pennell, Peterson's

PLATE 12

Hook: Partridge L2A/SH1 or Kamasan B175, 8-12
Silk: Black
Tag: Two turns of flat silver, under the tail
Tail: A slip of dyed yellow goose or duck
Body: Black seal's fur, or substitute
Body hackle: Short black cock hackle
Rib: Fine or medium oval silver, depending on size
Head hackle: Bottle-green peacock neck feather

I designed this pattern during my 'straggly hackle' period, as a half-way house between the Connemara Black and the Goat's Toe. It was named after the Scottish team manager, Brian Peterson, who made it work even better than I could.

In a big wave, it is a very good top-dropper pattern for wild brown trout in the Highlands and Islands, but it has achieved even more acclaim for sea-trout and salmon. In fact, during the 1996 season, it was my 'number one' seat-trout pattern, outfishing even the indispensable Claret Bumble.

A variation incorporating a fluorescent phosphor yellow tail (Glo-Brite, no.11) is useful for sinking line work. (see also Pennell, Black)

Peter Ross

PLATE 12

Hook: Partridge L2A or Kamasan B170, 8-14
Silk: Black
Tail: G.P. tippets (dyed hot-orange is my

preference)
Body: In two parts: rear, flat silver; fore., red seal's fur or substitute
Rib: Fine oval silver over the rear (silver) half of the body only
Hackle: Black hen
Wing: Barred teal flank feather

This famous fly was devised by one Peter Ross, of Killin, in Perthshire, as a variation on the Teal & Red. Loved by some, loathed by many, the Peter Ross still maintains a popularity in Scotland and elsewhere. Its original uses as a fry imitator, or even as a midge pupa representation, have been superseded by more realistic patterns. Nevertheless, on the more traditional lochs of the North and West, it still works well, especially when the better trout start 'mooching' about in shallow water late in the evening.

I rarely use it for brown trout nowadays, but I still rate it very highly for sea-trout and salmon, particularly on the lochs of the West Coast. In large sizes locate the hackle over the wing.

A variation using a hot orange seal's fur thorax is well thought of in certain areas as a sea-trout pattern.

Pheasant Tail Nymph (F. Sawyer)

PLATE 12

Hook: Partridge L2A or Kamasan B170, 10-16
Silk: Fine electrical copper wire (lacquered) is used instead of thread
Tail: Three or four cock pheasant tail fibres
Abdomen: Copper wire, with pheasant tail fibres wound over
Rib: Copper wire
Thorax: Build-up of copper wire
Thorax cover: Three or four cock pheasant tail fibres

This is Frank Sawyer's famous original dressing of the Pheasant Tail Nymph. It is hard to beat as a general impressionistic pattern for all sorts of aquatic lifeforms. Variations abound, but most notable amongst them are those tied with dyed black and claret pheasant tail fibres, and others with green, hot orange, pearly or silver thoraces.

This is not a fly to be fished fast or, generally, at great depths.

Poacher

PLATE 13

Hook: Partridge L2A/GRS2A, 8-14
Silk: Black
Tail: Slip of red feather, or bunch of red hackle fibres
Body: Flat silver
Rib: Very fine oval silver, or wire
Hackle: Black hen

Another name for this pattern could be the 'Wingless Butcher' which it is, to all intents and purpose. The Priest is a surprisingly effective hatching midge imitator when fished loch-style. The original dressing of this fly has a badger hackle and is a grayling fly, not highly rated for trout. For loch purposes, the above dressing is infinitely better. It gives of its best early and late in the season. (*see also* Butcher)

Professor

PLATE 13

Hook: Partridge L2A, 10-14, or SH2 12-16
Silk: Black
Tail: Red feather slip, or bunch of red hackle fibres
Body: Yellow floss silk or, alternatively, yellow seal's fur, or substitute
Rib: Fine oval gold
Hackle: Light ginger hen
Wing: Rolled grey barred mallard flank

The Professor is a real 'old stager', but I carry a couple in the corner of my fly box for difficult conditions on peat water lochs. A bright, windy day, with waves crashing on the rocks, might see the odd decent quality fish succumb to the charms of this pretty pattern.

It is still popular as a river wet fly, primarily for sea-trout on the East Coast rivers.

Qualifier (D. Chalmers)

PLATE 13

Hook: Partridge SH1 or Kamasan B175, 10
Silk: Black

Tail: Fluorescent orange floss (Glo-Brite, no.7), plus six strands of pearl Crystal hair over the top
Body: Flat silver
Rib: Very fine oval silver or wire
Hackle: Brown partridge, tied as a beard
Wing: Natural grey squirrel tail
Cheeks: Jungle cock eyes

The Qualifier is a mid to late season pattern from the Central belt, where it has done much damage to both brown and rainbow trout over the last six years or so. Fished quite quickly on the point during daylight hours, this pattern can prove itself to be a real winner.

Rainbow Attractor (D. Chalmers)

PLATE 13

Hook: Partridge SH3 or Kamasan B175, 10 & 12
Silk: Fluorescent white
Tail: Fluorescent scarlet floss (Glo-Brite no.4)
Body: Silver metallic chenille
Wing: White marabou
Cheeks: Fluorescent phosphor yellow floss (Glo-Brite, no.11)

This looks like an exercise in using modern synthetic materials to the exclusion of anything traditional. However, my own experience convinces me that patterns of this type can be extremely successful on their day, particularly for rainbow trout preoccupied with daphnia.

Ruthven Palmer (Jimmy Newlands)

PLATE 13

Hook: Partridge L2A or Kamasan B170, 10-14
Silk: Yellow
Tail: Fluorescent phosphor yellow floss (Glo-Brite, no.11)
Body: Invicta yellow seal's fur, or substitute
Body hackle: Red game cock hackle
Rib: Medium flat gold
Head hackle: Light furnace (Greenwell) hen

As soon as I saw this pattern I thought it looked the kind of fly that would be useful on daphnia-feeders, or where mayflies were hatching. This

might well be the case since Loch Ruthven, just outside Inverness, has a reliable mayfly hatch, but the basic bill of fare is daphnia. This pattern reminds me a bit of the Melvin Octopus, but is in a more traditional vein. (*see also* Ted's Olive)

Seal's Fur Palmer (Norman Irvine)

PLATE 13

Hook: Partridge J1A or Kamasan B175, 10 & 12
Silk: Red
Body: Scarlet seal's fur, well scrubbed out
Body hackle: Light ginger cock
Rib: Very fine oval gold or wire
Head hackle: Two turns of light ginger hen

This is a wonderful pattern for the wild trout of the Highlands and Islands, particularly in the hands of its inventor. I have witnessed some spectacular catches made with this fly in very difficult conditions, not the least of them during caenis hatches. This is one to reach for on evenings with a fiery red sunset and on peaty water in bright conditions. It is also very popular in larger sizes for loch salmon and sea-trout. (*see also* Soldier Palmer)

Sedgehog

PLATE 13

Hook: Partridge E1A or Kamasan B170, 12 & 14
Silk: Black or brown
Tail: Bunch of dark deer hair points
Body: Dubbed claret seal's fur wound over the roots of the wing bunches
Wing: Bunches of dark deer hair tied at intervals along the top of the hook shank
Hackle: Dark ginger hen, wound in front of the foremost wing clump and clipped flat underneath

This is an unashamed plagiarism on Sandy Nicholson's original Hedgehog, with only the hen hackle at the head to differentiate the two. Instead of being intended as a pulling, top dropper, wet pattern, this was designed as a dry fly to replicate the small dark sedges which abound locally. During the 1994 season, this proved to be my most successful 'dry' pattern. On two successive nights – one on Leven, the other on Coldingham – I had to use surgery to recover Sedgehogs from the gullets of rainbow trout, so greedily were they being taken. The fly should be thoroughly 'Ginked' and either inched back across the surface, or left static.

Other colour combinations are: dark deer hair and fiery brown seal's fur; dark deer hair and very dark hare's mask fur; light deer hair and pale hare's mask fur; light deer hair and dark hare's mask fur; light deer hair and green seal's fur. Hackle colour should vary accordingly.

The tying technique is simple once mastered and the secret to success is to maintain finger pressure on the bunches of deer hair until the dubbed thread has been wound over the hair roots. Don't allow the deer hair to flare and ensure that it stays on top of, rather than spinning around the hook shank.

Shellback, Goldhead (A. Murphy)

PLATE 13

Hook: Kamasan B830, 12
Silk: Fluorescent lime green Danville 'Flymaster'
Tail: Black marabou
Body: Gordon Griffiths sparkle chenille, black mix
Back: Lureflash black 'Shellback'
Rib: Nylon monofilament (about 3lb)
Collar: Lime green 'Cactus' chenille
Head: Gold bead

This is a fairly tricky pattern to tie, but worth the effort, according to Alastair Murphy of Kilwinning. He also states that it is best fished on a sinking line, with a 'mixed-up' retrieve. (see also Craftye)

Shipman's Buzzer, Claret (CDC variant)

PLATE 13

Hook: Partridge E1A, 10-14
Silk: Black
Tail & Head: Short tufts of cul de canard
Body: Claret seal's fur or substitute, well 'scrubbed'
Rib: Fine, clear monofilament

Were I restricted to just one CDC version of Dave Shipman's extraordinarily versatile design, this would be it. Whilst better for rainbows than browns, it does have its moments with wild trout. The beauty of this pattern is that there is never any requirement for floatant. The CDC tufts support the fly fore and aft, while the body sits awash in the surface film. This pattern will seduce the most suspicious of fish. It is one of those patterns that the more fish it has caught and the scruffier it becomes, the better it seems to fish. Some of mine are almost unrecognisable and they *still* slaughter trout. If your completed fly looks too neat and pretty, you haven't tied it properly!

Other useful versions are: black, hare's ear and olive green.

Shredge

PLATE 13

Hook: Partridge L2A, GRS2A or Kamasan B175, 8-12
Silk: Brown
Body: Tobacco coloured seal's fur, or substitute, wound to achieve a distinct fat cigar shape
Rib: Narrow flat gold
Wing: Paired slips of 'blae' duck, with the natural curvature downwards, tied fairly low over the back
Hackle: Longish palest ginger hen

Devised by Tony Knight to represent both shrimp and sedge (hence the name), this English reservoir pattern is a successful, if not widely used, taker of Scottish trout. It does very well early and late on my home waters, probably due to its resemblance in shape and colour to our gammarus species. A very good top dropper pattern, it deserves wider acclaim. (*see also* Shredge, Green).

Shredge, Green

PLATE 7

Hook: Partridge SH2, 12 & 14, or Kamasan B175, 10 & 12
Silk: Black
Body: Green olive seal's fur, or substitute

Rib: Narrow flat metallic gold
Wing: Slips of blae (greyish) mallard primary, tied low and arched over the body, against traditional rules
Hackle: Green olive hen, tied in front of the wing

Most green patterns are not particularly effective in poor light conditions, but this is a notable exception. I like to use this fly in mid position, with an Irishman's Claret on the top dropper, in the late evening or during the daytime when the light is very poor. Although it looks a bit like a freshwater shrimp imitation, it seems to work better as a vague representation of a hatching sedge. (*see* also Shredge)

Shuttlecock

PLATE 13

Hook: Kamasan B100, 10-14
Silk: Black
Body: One layer of tying thread
Rib: Very fine pearl
Thorax: Very fine black seal's fur, or substitute
Thorax cover & breathers: CDC plumes

This imitative semi-dry fly would seem to be the ultimate offering one could present to midge feeding trout. However, despite being remarkably effective for rainbows, at times, they are not reliable for wild brown trout and even fail sometimes with rainbows, for no apparent reason. Shuttlecocks are not as some would suggest, the final solution for trout feeding on hatching midge. They are, nevertheless, a valuable weapon in the surface fisher's armoury.

There are a few 'secrets', however, which will improve their strike-rate. Don't skimp on the CDC! A size 10 will take at least six feathers and you might be better off using eight. Patterns with dubbed bodies will pick up some of the natural oils from the CDC and, consequently, won't sit down properly into the surface film. Thread bodies are best, in this regard.

Vary dressing colours to suit local hatches and colour preferences.

Silver Cardinal

PLATE 13

Hook: Partridge SH2 10-14
Silk: Red
Tail: Slip of scarlet dyed duck or goose, or bunch of similarly dyed hackle fibres
Body: Flat silver
Rib: Very fine silver oval or wire
Hackle: Scarlet hen
Wing: Paired slips of scarlet dyed duck or goose

This is an old adaptation from the now virtually defunct Cardinal, which has some use for sea-trout and estuarine browns. It is very popular on Loch Stenness, in Orkney, which is a brackish water. The pattern is considered to be very much a bright day fly. (*see* also Cardineal)

Soldier Palmer

PLATE 14

Hook: Any wet fly hook, 8-14
Silk: Black or red
Tail: Tuft of red/scarlet wool
Body: Red/scarlet wool, wound
Body hackle: Light ginger cock
Rib: Very fine or fine oval gold, depending on size
Head hackle: Two turns of light ginger hen (optional)

The Soldier Palmer was once the king of traditional loch-style wet flies and a case can be made that it is, in essence, the oldest pattern in existence. It is still a useful fly, but its former popularity has been seriously dented by such modern usurpers as mini-Muddlers, Bumbles and Dabblers. In the truly wild waters of the North and West, where tradition dies hard, it is still rated very highly for brown trout, sea-trout and salmon in lochs.

Everyone has their own opinions on how to use this pattern. I prefer it for late evening work throughout the season and during the day from mid-July onwards.

Variations abound. (*see* also Fluorescent Palmer; and Seal Fur's Palmer)

PLATE 17
Adams, Badger & Red, Beacon Beige
Black & Red, Big Grey, Black Spider (Clyde style)
Black Gnat, Black Spider (Buchanan), Blae & Harelug
Broon Thing, CDC Midge, Claret Hen Blackie
Copper Nymph

PLATE 18

Cran Swallow, Crow & Black, Crow & Silver
Deer Hair Olive, Duck Tip, Easy Stone Nymph
Flashback Harelug, Gold-Ribbed Hare's Ear, Golden Olive
Grannom, Greenwell's Glory (dry), Greenwell's Glory (wet)
Greenwell's Glory (dry wingless), Grey Duster (parachute), Grey Hen & Rusty

PLATE 19
Hare's Ear Flashback, Hare's Ear Parachute, Harelug & Plover
Harelug Goldhead, Harelug Paradun, Hen Blackie
Hawthorn Fly (McPhail), Iron Blue Dun (dry), Iron Blue Dun (wet)
Kenny's Olive, Kenny's Sedge, Large Spring Olive
Lark & Grey, Light Olive, Linhouse Pheasant Tail Nymph

PLATE 20
Lureflush Nymph, Magpie Tail
Magpie Tail (night-time), March Brown (dry)
March Brown (dry wingless), March Brown (parachute), Silver March Brown, March Brown Spider
Medium Olive (dry), Medium Olive (wet), Medium Olive CDC (parachute)
Medwin Blue, Olive Dun, Olive Paradun
Olive Quill (dry), Olive Quill (wet)

Soldier Palmer, Fluorescent (1)

PLATE 5

Hook: Partridge SH2, 10-14
Silk: Red
Tail: Tuft of fluorescent fire red wool (eg Turrall's)
Body: Fluorescent fire red wool, as tail, wound or chopped and dubbed
Body hackle: Ginger cock
Rib: Fine or medium oval gold, dependent on hook size
Head hackle: Ginger hen

This very versatile pattern is effective for salmon, sea-trout, browns and rainbows. For brown trout I will use this pattern from mid-season onwards, particularly in very dull conditions or in the late evening. It is an excellent mid-fly for this kind of work. Also a very good loch pattern for salmon. On one well-remembered day on Loch Fada, in South Uist, a salmon savaged this fly with such violence that I almost dropped the rod and ran!

Soldier Palmer, Fluorescent (2)

PLATE 5

Hook: Partridge L2A, or GRS2A, 10 & 12
Silk: Red
Body: Fluorescent fire red seal's fur, or substitute
Body hackle: Ginger cock
Rib: Narrow flat gold (robust)
Head hackle: Ginger hen

This pattern should not to be considered as just an alternative dressing for the Fluorescent Soldier Palmer (1). It performs in totally different circumstances. During the doldrums of July and early August, this pattern is a safe bet for the middle dropper. Put it on there and leave it on! It will almost always take a few good fish and, on its day, will fill the boat.

In Scotland we are blessed with a sprinkling of highly productive waters in which swim some truly specimen wild trout. This is one of the best patterns with which one might take a really large wild trout.

Soldier Palmer, Fluorescent (Muddler version)

PLATE 5

Hook: Partridge SH2, 12-14
Silk: Red
Tail: Tuft of fluorescent fire red wool, (eg Turrall's)
Body: As for tail, wound or chopped and dubbed
Body hackle: Ginger cock
Rib: Fine oval gold
Head: Light coloured, natural deer hair – spun and clipped, leaving a few of the fine tips as a collar

This is a good general purpose pattern for use from mid-season until late in the year. It works well on daphnia feeders, or at times when the trout are being 'bloody-minded' and difficult, not taking much interest in anything vaguely imitative.

This one is also well worth trying for loch salmon and sea-trout.

Soldier Palmer Muddler

PLATE 14

Hook: Partridge SH2 or Kamasan B175, 10-14
Silk: Black or red
Tail: Tuft of red/scarlet wool
Body: Red/scarlet wool, wound
Body hackle: Light ginger cock
Rib: Very fine or fine oval gold, size dependent
Head: Fine, pale deer hair, spun and clipped

This version makes a great pulling fly for mid-summer daphnia and midge feeders. It is very popular on Central Belt waters with mixed populations of brown and rainbow trout. It works best in clear water free from algal tints. (see also Fluorescent Palmer Muddler)

Sooty Olive

PLATE 14

Hook: Partridge L2A or Kamasan B170, 10-14
Silk: Black
Tail: G.P. tippets

Body: Mix of green olive and black seal's fur, or substitute
Rib: Very fine oval silver or wire
Hackle: Short black hen
Wing: Bronze mallard

There are almost as many recipes for the 'Sooty' as there are days in the year! I like this one for general purpose loch work. Flies which are very dark, but not totally black, seem to be a major part of my armoury. I suspect this is probably because pitch black is quite a rare colour in nature. Most of the 'black' natural insects we attempt to imitate are often very dark browns, greys or greens.

This is a very good shrimp pattern, but will take any opportunist feeder, it seems.

Sooty Olive (Dermot O'Hara)

PLATE 14

Hook: Partridge SH2 or Kamasan B160, 10-14
Silk: Black
Body: Rear: black tying silk; fore: blended golden olive and brown seal's fur
Wing: Bronze mallard, slim and tied low over the back
Hackle: Black cock, longish and tied in front of the wing

This is a Lough Conn pattern which was introduced to the Orkney trout, when its creator visited here some years ago. It made quite an impact upon early season midge feeders and, I am sure, is worthy of wider use in this country.

A variation on this dressing using a claret seal's fur thorax and a claret hackle has done some good for me as a partner to the above.

Squirrel-Tailed Dunkeld (D. Chalmers)

PLATE 14

Hook: Drennan Carbon Lure or Partridge SH3, 10
Silk: Black
Tail: Fluorescent phosphor yellow floss (Glo-Brite, no.11)
Body: Flat silver

Rib: Very fine oval silver or wire
Throat: Short tuft of hot-orange marabou
Wing: Natural grey squirrel tail
Cheeks: Jungle cock eyes

A modern lure with a traditional look, this pattern mixes ancient and modern materials to good effect.

It is popular in the Central Belt, where it is often used for daytime fishing in deep water. (see also Deepwater Dunkeld)

Stick Fly

PLATE 14

Hook: Partridge SH2 or Kamasan B200, 12 & 14
Silk: Black or brown
Tail: Mixed fluorescent phosphor yellow and lime green floss (Glo-Brite, nos. 11 & 12)
Body: Two peacock herls, the first wound up the body in butting turns, the second wound down in slightly open turns
Rib: Two strands of pearl Crystal Hair, twisted together
Hackle: Shortish ginger hen

There are many versions of the ubiquitous Stick Fly, originally conceived – if memory serves – to imitate a cased caddis. In August 1990, I won the Scottish National on Loch Leven due, in great part, to this particular pattern. Since then, it has been invaluable for me on Leven and many other Scottish waters. This Stick will work on any line density and is particularly effective fished fast, just under the surface, when trout are feeding on daphnia in foul weather.

It is sometimes referred to as the Leven Stick. (see also Mini-Stick)

Suspender Nymph (B. Leadbetter)

PLATE 14

Hook: Partridge K14ST, 10-14
Silk: Olive
Tail: Short, slim bunch of pearl Crystal Hair
Body: Medium olive seal's fur, or substitute
Rib: Narrow, flat pearl Mylar, unstretched
Head: Ethafoam

This is Brian Leadbetter's version of the 'Suspender Buzzer', originally devised by the famous angler entomologist, John Goddard. It has antecedents that are far older. This style of buoyant fly has had quite an impact, particularly on the English reservoirs for stocked rainbows. It seems much less useful for wild browns which are, perhaps, not quite so gullible. It is, however, very popular on Loch Leven and other Central Belt waters.

There are a variety of ways of forming the head. My way is to start by tying in a thin strip of Ethafoam at the eye, then take the thread back to the point where the body is to end. I then fold the unstretched foam back to this point and tie it down with a lap or two of thread. I now take the thread forward to the eye again, under the hook. The foam is then folded forwards again and tied in and the process repeated so that there are four segments of foam involved. If one imagines that an 'orange' of four segments is being formed around the central core of the hook shank, then the process becomes easily understood. The body can now be dressed. This procedure ensures there is sufficient buoyancy to keep the fly afloat, and produces a neat head.

Body and head colours should match, if possible. Other popular colours include orange, red, scarlet, claret, hare's ear and black.

Teal & Black

PLATE 14

Hook: Partridge L2A or Kamasan B170, 8-14
Silk: Black
Tail: Slim bunch of G.P. tippets
Body: Black seal's fur, or substitute
Rib: Very fine or fine oval silver, sometimes wire
Hackle: Black hen (tied in front of the wing for best effect)
Wing: Strip of teal flank, rolled

The Teal series of flies rank with the Mallard series as the most popular and effective of the ancient and traditional loch flies. This example is still a firm favourite early in the season and particularly during a hatch of dark midge. (see also Teal, Blue & Silver [variant]; Teal & Green; Teal & Green [variants]; and Butcher, Teal-Winged)

Teal, Blue & Silver (variant)

PLATE 14

Hook: Partridge SH2 or Kamasan B170, 10 & 12
Silk: Black
Tail: Slim bunch of G.P. tippets
Body: Flat silver
Rib: Very fine oval silver or wire
Wing: Paired slips of blue dyed goose or duck, veiled on either side by strips of barred teal (substitute, widgeon)
Hackle: Blue dyed hen hackle, tied in front of the wing

The correct colour for the underwing and hackle of this pattern is referred to as 'teal blue' and any other shade is inferior.

A remarkably able sea-trout pattern, the Teal, Blue & Silver is also surprisingly effective for brown trout, particularly in peat-stained waters in bright conditions. In just such conditions, one afternoon on Orkney's Loch Hundland, this fly caught me 11 trout for a weight of 11lb.

A variation incorporating a tail of fluorescent yellow floss is popular in the Western Isles for sea-trout. It should also be noted that the usually prescribed dressing for this fly does not have the under-wing of dyed blue duck or goose. (see also Teal & Black; Teal & Green; Teal & Green (variants); and Butcher, Teal-Winged)

Teal & Green (1)

PLATE 14

Hook: Partridge L2A or Kamasan B170, 8-14
Silk: Black
Tail: Slim bunch of G.P. tippets
Body: Green seal's fur, or substitute
Rib: Very fine or fine oval gold
Hackle: Black hen
Wing: Strip of teal flank, rolled

Once again, getting the colour right is essential in this member of the Teal clan. The seal's fur for the body should be bottle green and is usually described by suppliers of flytying materials as 'bright green'.

Arguments rage as to whether a brown or black hackle is the most effective. I have come down in favour of black, which seems to be superior in the Northern and Western parts of the Britain, whilst the brown hackle is preferred in Southern regions.

This is a very good fly for trout. For those who restrict themselves to a simple and limited fly selection, this is one which should be considered essential equipment. (see also the following variants: Teal & Black; Teal, Blue & Silver (variant); and Butcher Teal-Winged)

Teal & Green (2)

PLATE 14

Hook: Partridge SH2 or Kamasan B170, 10 & 12
Silk: Black
Tail: Slim bunch of G.P. tippets
Body: Green Lurex
Rib: Very fine oval silver
Wing: Strip of teal flank, rolled
Hackle: Black hen, wound in front of the wing

Superior to the original on its day, this pattern has a much more defined usage. I like it in the early months, in very difficult conditions, as a point fly, frequently fished behind mini-Muddlers. Early in the season, fish are often taking dark midge pupae, many of which have a greenish cast to their intrinsic blackness and this may be why this fly is successful. During intense midge hatches, I would tend try more imitative patterns, but would always consider this pattern should such efforts fail. (see also Green Priest; and Teal & Black)

Teal & Green (3)

PLATE 14

Hook: Partridge SH2 or Kamasan B160, 12-16
Silk: Fluorescent lime green thread or floss
Tail: Slim bunch of G.P. tippets
Body: The tying silk, with an overlay of pearl Lurex
Rib: Very fine oval silver
Wing: Strip of teal flank, rolled
Hackle: Insect green hen hackle, wound in front of the wing

Whereas Teal & Green (2) is primarily an early season pattern, this one is best in mid-summer. It is very good for rainbows at any time. Browns prefer this pattern when they are feeding on green items and whenever subtlety and vaguely imitative patterns are required. At certain times of the year, trout can become totally preoccupied with hatches of small apple green midge. In such circumstances, this is a pattern that I use with great confidence. (see also Fluorescent Green Midge)

Technocat (B. Peterson)

PLATE 15

Hook: Drennan Carbon Lure, 8 & 10
Silk: Black
Tail: Long white marabou
Body: Fluorescent fire red chenille
Wing: White marabou, to extend as far back as tail
Eyes: Pair of silver bead chain eyes, painted fluorescent fire red

This is a real shocker of a lure which I find hard to believe any trout could ignore. It is primarily a small stillwater pattern to be fished singly on a long leader. It also has potential as a point fly fished on fast sinking lines for loch work in dire emergency.

Ted's Olive

PLATE 15

Hook: Partridge G3A or Kamasan B405, 10-14
Silk: Black
Butt: Fluorescent lime green floss (Glo-Brite, no.12)
Body: Light olive green seal's fur, or substitute
Body hackle: Red game cock hackle
Rib: Fine oval gold
Head hackle: Light furnace hen (Greenwell)

For some time, I knew of this pattern, but was unaware of its name. However, I do know that it works, because I filched an identical pattern from Charles Jardine's box many years ago and have used it to good effect ever since. Jimmy

Newlands, of Inverness, supplied the fly depicted and reckoned it to be essential for lochs in his area.

It is an early to mid-summer pattern which vaguely imitates a wide variety of trout food items. It is a good middle dropper pattern on a floating line for me and I have no hesitation in advising its inclusion in any fly box.

Treacle Parkin (variant)

PLATE 15

Hook: Partridge J1A, G3A or SH1, 10-14
Silk: Black
Tail: Fluorescent phosphor yellow floss (Glo-Brite, no.11)
Body: Peacock herl, tied bulky
Rib: Very fine oval gold or wire
Hackle: Longish dark furnace hen

Originally a grayling pattern from Yorkshire, I rate this variation on the traditional dressing a very useful 'second eleven' player in the earliest part of the season and whenever the water is discoloured or turbid. It can, and often does, prevent total disaster. Not by any means an imitative pattern, it does contain many features which are irresistible to trout.

Tup's Indispensable (variant)

PLATE 15

Hook: Partridge GRS2A or Kamasan B160, 12 & 14
Silk: Light yellow/primrose
Tail: Slim bunch of honey dun hackle fibres
Body: rear half: yellow seal's fur or substitute; front half: yellow and red seal's fur mixed, all very sparse
Rib: Very fine oval gold or wire
Hackle: Sparse honey dun hen

The Tup's Indispensable was devised by a professional tyer, R.S. Austin, of Tiverton, Devon, in about 1900. The great G.E.M. Skues, father of modern nymph fishing, is said to have given it its name.

Surely this is a strange pattern to be found in a collection of Scottish loch flies? Nevertheless,

this version of the old 'Tup' is popular when pale midge or caenis are on the menu. It can be fished dry in these circumstances, but is most often fished wet, high in the water and slowly amongst rising fish. This is not a general pattern to be used in a 'prospecting' style, but it can be very effective in specific circumstances, as mentioned. (see also Caenis Muddler)

Viva (variant)

PLATE 15

Hook: Partridge SH1 or Kamasan B175, 12 & 10
Silk: Black
Tail: Fluorescent green floss (I mix Glo-Brite, nos. 11 & 12)
Body: Originally black chenille, but black ostrich herl for a finer profile and in small sizes
Rib: Medium flat silver, or pearl mylar
Hackle: Black hen or henny-cock
Wing: Black marabou

Victor Furze's Viva was for a long time probably *the* most popular 'lure' used on the English reservoirs. Its popularity has waned only slightly and it is one of the few of this type of lure which works exceptionally well for wild brown trout throughout Scotland. In the early part of the season, when fish are sometimes loathe to come anywhere near the surface, this pattern on a sinking line can save the day. It is very popular in the Central Belt region for rainbows and browns all through the season.

If you were to limit your fly box to just one mini-lure, you could do a lot worse than make it a Viva. (see also Viva, Cactus Head; Viva, Gold; and Viva Spider)

Viva, Cactus Head (D. Chalmers)

Hook: Drennan Traditional, 8 & 10
Silk: Black
Tail: Glo-Brite floss, no.11
Body: Black chenille
Rib: Oval silver
Hackle: Blue guinea fowl, throat only
Wing: Black marabou
Head: Gold metallic or Cactus chenille, three turns

PLATE 21
Partridge & Brown, Partridge & Orange, Partridge & Orange (Glassford)
Pheasant Tail Nymph, Pheasant Tail Nymph (variant), Pheasant Tail Nymph (Glass)
Red Tag, Rough Olive (dry), Rough Olive (wet)
Red Sedge, Sam Slick, Sand Fly (dry)
Sand Fly (wet)

PLATE 22
Snipe & Purple, Sedge (Glass), Spent Red spinner
Stank Hen, Stewart's Black Spider, Teal & Black
Tup's Indispensable (variant), Wee Grey, Wee Silver Nymph
Woven Nymphs (x3)
Yellow May Dun (Miller), Yellow May Dun (Glass), Yellow May Dun Emerger

PLATE 23
Alistair, Black & Orange (Waddington)
Black & Red (Waddington)
Black Brahan, Brown Turkey
Blue Charm, Black Doctor (fully dressed)
Bourrach, Black & Yellow

PLATE 24
Chameleon, Black Silver & Yellow
Collie Dog (tube)
Collie Dog (Donaldson)
Silver Delphi, Comet (tube)
Blue Elver

PLATE 25
Executioner, Fast Eddie, General Practitioner (GP)
Findhorn Killer, Fast Eddie (Waddington)
Garry Dog [Gold] (tube)
Ghost, Garry Dog
Glow Fly (dibbler), Glow Fly (Waddington)

PLATE 26
Green Highlander (hairwing), Gordon's Fancy (variant), Grey Turkey (McPhail)
Green Highlander (fully dressed), Hairy Mary
Jamie's Fancy, Green Highlander (tube)
Greg's Glory, Green Mamba (Rattray)

PLATE 27
Jeannie (hairwing), Jeannie (featherwing)
Kerry Blue, Kenny's Killer
Kylie (Waddington), Kylie
Kylie Shrimp
Lady Ewe, Logie (feather wing)

A proliferation of effective patterns have emerged with heads constructed in this manner. This one is an excellent daytime pattern for Central Belt waters and it works well in bright conditions. Use it from mid to late season. (*see* also Black Kitten; Viva; Viva, Gold; and Viva Spider)

Viva, Gold (D. Chalmers)

PLATE 15

Hook: Drennan Traditional, 10 & 8
Silk: Black
Tail: Fluorescent yellow floss (Glo-Brite, no.10)
Body: Black seal's fur or sub
Rib: Oval silver
Hackle: Brown partridge
Underwing: Gold Flashabou
Overwing: Black marabou

This variation of the Viva is popular on Loch Leven, where gold is a popular colour for mid-summer trout. This version works best from June to September, particularly in bright conditions. (*see* also Viva; Viva, Cactus Head; and Viva Spider)

Viva, Jungle Cock

Hook: Partridge SH1 or Kamasan B175, 10 & 12
Silk: Black Tail: A mix of lime green and phosphor yellow fluorescent floss
Body: Short flued ostrich herl (clip if necessary)
Rib: Pearl Lurex, with an over-rib of fine oval silver
Hackle: Black cock or hen
Wing: Black marabou or dyed rabbit fur
Cheeks: Jungle cock eye feathers

This variation on Victor Furze's original Viva must be one of the most popular mini-lures throughout Scotland. It has achieved remarkable success with both brown trout and rainbows. Everyone seems to have his own version of the Viva, but this one has been my most successful.

Normally fished on sinking and fast sinking lines, this is *the* early season mini-lure. Indispensable!

Viva, Jungle Cock [Claret] (D. Malcolm)

Hook: Drennan Wet Fly Supreme, 10 & 12
Silk: Black
Tail: Lime green fluorescent floss
Body: Claret seal's fur
Rib: Flat pearl Mylar
Wing: Black marabou, with a short tuft of fire orange fluorescent floss (Glo-Brite, no.5) over the top
Cheeks: Jungle cock eyes

Davie Malcolm gave me a simplified version of this pattern some years ago, which had no fire orange over-wing or jungle cock eyes. I found it an excellent middle fly for 'desperation' sunk-line work. I am sure that this up-dated version will outperform the original. This is a highly effective fly on the difficult middle dropper position; as attractive to wild fish as it is for stocked browns and rainbows. (*see* also Viva; Viva, Gold; Viva, Goldhead and Viva, Spider)

Viva Spider (B. Peterson)

Hook: Partridge SH1 or Kamasan B175, 10 & 12
Silk: Black
Tail: Fluorescent phosphor yellow floss (Glo-Brite floss or yarn, no.11)
Body: Black seal's fur, or substitute
Body hackle: Black cock
Rib: Fine oval silver
Hackle: Black hen
Cheeks: Jungle cock eyes (optional)

Some anglers have trouble fishing traditional patterns on sinking lines alongside mini-lures. Take a Black Pennell, 'jazz' it up a bit and call it a Viva Spider, and the credibility gap fast disappears.

Sometimes deep-lying trout demand simple patterns and black is always a favoured colour. Under such circumstances, this fly works very well as a top dropper, fished on a sinking line and using the 'lift & hang' method of retrieve.

Watson's Fancy

PLATE 15

Hook: Partridge SH2 or Kamasan B170, 8-14
Silk: Black
Tail: G.P. crest
Body: Rear half – red seal's fur; front half – black seal's fur (or substitute)
Rib: Fine or medium oval silver, dependent on hook size
Hackle: Black hen
Wing: Paired slips of crow or mag.p.ie tail
Cheeks: Small jungle cock eyes

Watsons' Fancy is an ancient pattern that is not now as popular as once it was. It is still useful in small sizes when trout are feeding on dark midges. Perhaps the jungle cock eyes suggest wing buds, while the red thorax resembles the haemoglobin in the natural's blood.

It is a useful pattern in larger sizes for loch salmon and sea-trout, but for this use I prefer to wind the hackle in front of the wing and cheeks and would slightly increase the relative size of the jungle cock eyes.

Wee Man [dapping fly] (J. Millar)

PLATE 38

Hook: Partridge K12ST, 8 & 10
Silk: Black
Body: A slim bundle of dyed black deer hair formed into a detached body. A collar of Glo-Brite no.5 floss is wound at the junction of the detached body and the hook shank
Legs: Six pairs of knotted, black dyed cock pheasant tail fibres: three pairs on either side of the hook, tied to trail downwards
Wings: Two grizzle cock hackle points, tied 'spent'
Hackles: Blue peacock neck feather wound in front of a long fibred black cock hackle

In Scotland we have a tradition that to mention the real name of the 'Earl of Hell' brings bad luck. Another of his soubriquets is 'The Wee Man' and if he had invented a dapping fly, this would be it. It was in fact designed by Jimmy Millar, of Edinburgh, as a dapping fly for use in poor light conditions on Loch Lomond. In this role, it works very well for salmon and sea-trout and is, I believe, a pattern worthy of greater acclaim. (see also Dapping Daddy; and Yellow-Tailed Daddy [DAPP])

Wet Daddy

PLATE 15

Hook: Partridge SH3 or Kamasan B800, 10 & 12
Silk: Brown
Body: A thin strip of natural raffia, wetted and wound
Body hackle: A shortish ginger cock, palmered to halfway down the hook shank
Rib: Fine oval gold
Head hackle: A short G.P. tippet feather wound in front of a few turns of brown speckled partridge hackle

Crane flies, known to everyone as 'Daddy Longlegs', are terrestrial insects. They are relatively weak fliers and frequently get blown out onto the water, especially in late summer and autumn. Their arrival is usually welcomed by the trout. They are most often imitated with dry flies, but this pattern is fished as a wet fly and can be remarkably effective when the natural insects are being 'drowned' on very windy days and when fishing a dry fly conventionally is impossible.

This pattern is also very popular on the English reservoirs where, ironically, it seems to appeal to fry-feeding fish as well as to those feasting on daddies.

The tippet hackle should *not* be bound down so that it collapses along the **Hook:** it should flare at right angles to the hook shank, so that it has as much 'kick' and movement in the water as possible. The tippet fibres should slightly exceed the hook shank length.

White-Hackled Orangeman

PLATE 15

Hook: Partridge L2A or Kamasan B170, 8-12
Silk: Red
Tail: G.P. crest
Body: Invicta yellow seal's fur, or substitute
Body hackle: Hot-orange hen or cock

PLATE 28
Loser (Griffith), McCallan
Mar Lodge (fully dressed), Megan
Berthdee Munro, Gold Munro
Munro Killer
Munro Killer (dibbler), Munro Killer (long-tail)

PLATE 29
Mini-Tubes (a selection)
Northern Dog
Orange & Blue
Orange Bourrach, Orange Cuileag
Oykel GP, Pearly Muddler, Patsy Mary
Pearly Stoat, Purple McBain

Rib: Fine or medium oval gold, dependent on hook size
Wing: Paired slips of hen pheasant secondary
Hackle: Longish white hen, wound in front of the wing

On days of burning sun, when the glare from the water is blinding and I've almost given up hope, this is the pattern which can occasionally 'save the bacon'. I do not use it much except under such difficult conditions, but I am sure that further investigation would be rewarded.

Although I carry this pattern in my loch trout box, it has drawn some positive responses from salmon, again in the sort of difficult conditions outlined above. (*see* Orangeman; and White Hackled Invicta)

White Weazel (D. Wood)

PLATE 15

Hook: Drennan Wet Fly Supreme, 10 & 12
Silk: White
Tail: White marabou over a few strands of pearl Crystal Hair
Body: Pearl 'Cactus' chenille
Hackle: Longish grizzle soft cock hackle
Head: Two or three turns of the pearl Cactus chenille, wound in front of the hackle

This is a likely looking fry pattern from Davie Wood's stable. He advises that it is at its best at the back end of the season, fished on sinking or intermediate lines.

Wickham's Fancy (variant)

PLATE 15

Hook: Partridge J1A or L2A, or Kamasan B170, 8-14
Silk: Black
Body: Flat gold
Body hackle: Dark ginger cock
Rib: Very fine oval gold or wire
Wing: Paired slips of mallard primary, from the middle of the quill
Head hackle: Dark ginger hen, wound in front of the wing

A famous old pattern, the Wickham's Fancy was originally devised as a dry fly for the chalk stream trout of the River Test. The original had tail whisks and was tied without the hen hackle in front of the wing. This variant has no tail as it is intended to be fished as a wet fly and to imitate shrimp or sedges. Just as the Cinnamon & Gold is more successful without a tail, so is this – its first cousin.

Fish it early and late in the season as a tail fly or on the top dropper, on floating or intermediate lines. (*see also* Wingless Wickham's (1) and (2))

Wingless Wickham's (1)

PLATE 15

Hook: Partridge J1A or Kamasan B175, 10-14
Silk: Black or brown
Tail: Slim bunch of ginger cock hackle fibres
Body: Flat gold
Hackle: Ginger cock, two turns at head then palmered
Rib: Very fine oval gold or wire

Considering what has been said about the Wickham's Fancy(variant) and its *lack* of a tail, it seems ironic that this pattern is much better *with* a tail! Mind you, I would normally use the Wingless Wickham's under different circumstances. It has worked well in mid-summer, when trout are feeding on daphnia. It is one of those few patterns that excels on the difficult middle dropper, which on its own gives it a valid raison d'être.

Wingless Wickham's (2)

PLATE 15

Hook: Partridge SH2 or Kamasan B175, 10-14
Silk: Fluorescent white thread or floss
Tail: A tuft of fluorescent fire orange floss (Glo-Brite, no.5)
Body: Pearl Lurex over a layer of the tying silk
Hackle: Ginger cock, two turns at head, then palmered
Rib: Very fine oval silver or wire

There are many variations on the Wingless Wickham's theme: essentially tinsel bodied flies, palmered with a brown or ginger hackle. This one is very good and extremely useful in a variety of circumstances. The basics of the pattern were shown to me some years ago by Brian Leadbetter after he had had much success with it on Loch Leven. Since then I have used in a wide variety of circumstances and have been surprised by its versatility.

Woodcock & Green (variant)

PLATE 16

Hook: Partridge L2A or SH2, or Kamasan B170, 10-14
Silk: Black
Tail: A slim bunch of dyed hot-orange G.P. tippet fibres
Body: Bright green seal's fur, or substitute
Rib: Fine oval gold
Hackle: Dark ginger hen
Wing: Paired slips from golden pheasant wing secondaries

The original pattern had a woodcock wing, of course. It is a good fly, but I venture to suggest that this version is better. As a point fly in the difficult conditions of high summer, this will out-fish most other patterns and seems to select the better fish. I suspect it is taken either for a shrimp or a sedge pupa. But whatever, it is worth a place in anyone's collection.

Wormfly

PLATE 16

This fly is tied on a 'tandem' mount of two hooks, joined by a short length of braided monofilament, suitably whipped and 'superglued' to each hook. The dressing is the same for each hook.
Hooks: Partridge L2A or J1A, 10 or 12 (two in tandem)
Silk: Red or black
Tails: Fluorescent fire red wool (Turrall's)
Bodies: Two peacock herls: one tied up in butting turns, the other wound down over the first in open turns.
Ribs: Very fine oval gold

Hackles: Ginger hen (longer fibred for the front hook)

It is a great pity that this pattern has slipped from popularity, as it is a very successful fly on a wide variety of line densities. I like to use it as a bob fly on a floating line, where it seems to have the ability to 'bring up' the biggest brown trout in any water. On sinking lines, it is probably best fished on the point, though in this role I rather prefer the Wormfly (long shank variant).

It is also a good fly for sea-trout and salmon in lochs. (see also Wormfly, Black)

Wormfly (longshank variant)

PLATE 16

Hook: Partridge H1A or SH3, or Kamasan B800, 12
Silk: Red or black
Tail: Fluorescent fire-orange/red wool
Rear body (abdomen): Peacock herl, tied slim (one strand)
Rib: Fine oval gold
Mid-Hackle: Smallish ginger or dark ginger hen
Front body (thorax): Two peacock herls, tied fat
Rib: Very fine oval gold or wire
Head hackle: Longish ginger or dark ginger hen

This versatile pattern is a very firm favourite of mine. It is exceptional in the earliest days of the season fished over shallow, rocky ground. It takes fry feeders in the late evening when the big trout start hunting sticklebacks. It works very well late in the season as a top dropper pattern, fished in a decent wave. For sinking line work for wild brown trout, I rarely have it off my cast. Indispensable! (see also Wormfly, Black (longshank variant); and Wormfly, Orange)

Wormfly, Black

PLATE 16

Hook: Partridge L2A or J1A, or Kamasan B175, 10 or 12 – two hooks tied in tandem
Silk: Black or red
Link: Short length of braided monofilament
Tail: Short tuft of red, or fluorescent red, wool, on both bodies

PLATE 30
Rana, Sam's Badger
Rusty Rat
Sheila, Ally's Shrimp, Ally's Shrimp (Waddington), Yellow Ally's, Black Ally's
Magenta Ally's, Ayrshire Red Shrimp, Blue Shrimp, Brown Shrimp
Black Shrimp, Claret Shrimp

PLATE 31
Curry's Red Shrimp, Knockdolian Shrimp
Findhorn Shrimp
Sandy's Shrimp (Leventon), McClure Shrimp (McPhail)
Silver Garry (Waddington), Silk Cut Shrimp (Wren)

Body: Two strands of bronze peacock herl, one wound up the shank, the other down. Try to achieve a bulky but translucent effect.
Rib: Gold, fine oval or wire
Hackle: Black hen-medium length on tail fly, longer on front

In the early part of the season, I have found this pattern very effective in bringing good quality trout up to the surface. I prefer it for peat water lochs, but can also be useful on clearer waters in poor light conditions. However, for floating line work this fly always needs a good wave. Strangely, in some lochs, it seems to work best on the point, while in others it is more effective on the bob. My first ever salmon from a loch fell to this pattern and it has led more than the odd seatrout to its doom. A very old and traditional wet fly style, it is as effective now as it has ever been. (*see also* Wormfly, Black [longshank variation]; Wormfly)

Wormfly, Black (longshank variation)

PLATE 16

Hook: Partridge SH3 or Kamasan B800, 12
Silk: Black or red
Tail: Tuft of fluorescent red wool with four G.P. tippets over
Abdomen: One strand bronze peacock herl, wound once up the shank in butting turns, ribbed medium oval gold
Mid-Hackle: Shortish black hen
Thorax: A strand peacock herl, wound up and down the shank to give a fuller effect than the abdomen, ribbed fine oval gold
Head hackle: Longish black hen

In dressing this pattern, strive to achieve a 'nymphal' shape, with a bulky thorax and a slim abdomen. I came up with this variant about 18 years ago and I have never been without it since. I use it in the early season as a general purpose pattern and, later on in the year, in conditions of poor light and good wave. It can be fished slow or fast, both shallow and deep and usually on the point position. It has been successful in all types of lochs and for all major game species. (*see also* Wormfly, Black; Wormfly [longshank variant]; and Wormfly, Orange)

Wormfly, Orange

PLATE 16

Hook: Partridge SH3, or Drennan Traditional Wet, 12
Silk: Red
Tail: G.P. tippets dyed hot orange, over fluorescent red wool
Abdomen: A single peacock herl, wound in butting turns
Abdomen rib: Fine oval gold
Mid-hackle: Shortish hot-orange hen, sparse
Thorax: Two peacock herls, one wound up the shank in butting turns, the other wound down the hook in open turns
Thorax rib: Very fine oval gold, or wire
Head hackle: Longer hot orange hen, tied full

Tied in a vaguely nymphal style, this pattern is effective on both sunk and floating lines and for both stocked and wild salmonid species. It is really little more than two Orange Ke-Hes, stuffed in tandem onto one hook. I used to be very fond of this pattern for wild brown trout. I once watched it take three virtually identical trout, each of around two pounds, one early April day on Loch Harray. Of late, it seems less popular and quite why the fish's preference should change over the longer term in this way has always mystified me. This pattern is a very effective sunk fly for rainbow trout as an alternative to mini-lures of similar coloration. (*see also* Ke-He, Orange)

Xmas Tree

PLATE 16

Hook: Partridge SH2 or Kamasan B175, 10 & 12, or Kamasan Double B270, 10 & 12
Tail: Fluorescent pink floss (Glo-Brite, no.2)
Body: Short flued black ostrich herl (clip if necessary)
Rib: Medium flat silver (robust), or pearl Lurex over-ribbed with fine oval silver
Hackle: Black cock or hen, tied as a beard
Wing: Black marabou or dyed rabbit, with a short stub of fluorescent lime green floss (Glo-Brite, no.12) over the roots of the wing

Although mini-lures have a limited role for wild brown trout from Scottish lochs, this tying is one of the most successful for all waters and, on its day, can out-perform most other mini-lures, even the ubiquitous Vivaof which it can be considered a variant. Fish it on the point with standard wet flies above, either with floating, intermediate or full sinking lines.

It is, of course, a deadly pattern throughout the season for rainbow trout.

Yellow Owl

PLATE 16

Hook: Partridge L2A or Kamasan B170, 10-14
Silk: Black
Tail: Brown partridge hackle fibres
Body: Yellow floss silk (fluorescent optional)
Rib: Black silk
Hackle: Brown partridge
Wing: Paired slips of hen pheasant secondary

One of the most specific flies in current usage in Scotland in that it is almost totally restricted to the waters of Lock Leven, where it is considered essential. This fly is probably used only on Loch Leven. It is employed during hatches of buzzer (locally known as 'curly bums'), which occur in the evenings from June to August. As regards its imitative character, I would refer the reader to the notes on Ossie's Owl.

I have enjoyed great success with this pattern fished on the top dropper, with a floating line. On 'the Loch', it works well when skated across the surface amongst rising fish.

Yellow Owl Muddler

PLATE 16

Hook: Partridge K2B or Kamasan B420, 12
Silk: Black
Body: Bronze peacock herl
Rib: Fluorescent chrome yellow floss (Glo-Brite, no.9)
Hackle: Brown partridge
Head: Fine roe deer hair, spun and clipped to a bullet shape, retaining some fine points as a collar

This logical adaptation of the Yellow Owl is highly effective when trout are feeding on sedge and midge late in a summer evening. This is not a pattern for a turbo-charged retrieve. Rather, fish it gently, skate it or hang it in the region of fish activity and await results. I regard this as a 'must' for Leven and its associated waters during the summer. (see also Ossie's Owl; and Yellow Owl)

Yellow-Eyed Damsel
(A. Murphy)

PLATE 16

Hook: Kamasan B830, 12
Silk: Fluorescent yellow Danville 'Flymaster'
Tail: Golden olive marabou
Body: Golden olive SLF
Rib: Fine oval gold
Hackle: Fluorescent yellow dyed grey speckled partridge
Eyes: A pair of silver bead-chain eyes, painted fluorescent yellow

This is a very 'fishy' looking pattern from Alastair Murphy. Although yellow is not a terribly popular colour with wild brown trout, its effectiveness for stocked rainbows is unquestionable. During periods of turbidity or algal discolouration, yellow is one of the most distinguishable colours at depth.

Alastair advises painting the eyes in the following sequence: one coat of matt white Humbrol modeller's paint; one coat of gloss white; three coats of fluorescent yellow; finally, one coat of clear lacquer. He must consider all this trouble worthwhile, as he ties literally thousands of this pattern each season.

Yellow-Tailed Daddy [Dapping]
(J. Millar)

PLATE 38

Hook: Partridge D3ST or K12ST, 8 & 10
Silk: Yellow
Body: Dyed yellow deer hair, tied as a detached body
Legs: Six pairs of orange dyed cock pheasant tail

fibre, each pair knotted, with three pairs tied in on each side of the hook to trail downwards
Wing: Cree cock hackle points, tied spent
Hackle: Two long dark furnace cock hackles wound around the bases of the wings in figure-of-eight

This is an early season dapping pattern (May onwards) for Loch Lomond, devised by Jimmy Millar. It has been suggested that its success is in part due to the presence of mayfly on the loch at this time.

The construction is rather an unusual concept, but it is a very attractive and confidence inspiring pattern, nonetheless. (*see also* Dapping Daddy; and The Wee Man)

Zulu

PLATE 16

Hook: Partridge J1A or Kamasan B175, 8-14
Silk: Black
Tail: Fluorescent fire red wool (Turrall's), or plain red wool
Body: Black seal's fur
Body hackle: Black cock
Rib: Fine to medium flat silver, depending on size
Head hackle: Longish black hen

The Zulu is one of the few flies of its type ever to be banned!

On my local waters I much prefer the Gold Zulu, but I am not surprised by the loyalty to the original, which has all the characteristics of the quintessential killing fly. Although popular everywhere, there is little doubt that the Zulu's popularity increases the farther North and West one travels.

This pattern destroys the old adage of 'bright day, bright fly', as it is one of the best patterns in sunny conditions. In large sizes it is a very good fly for both salmon and sea-trout in lochs. (*see also* Zulu, Blue; Zulu, Orange; and Zulu, Red)

Zulu, Blue

PLATE 16

Hook: Partridge J1A or Kamasan B175, 8-12
Silk: Black

Tag: Red wool (fluorescent fire red, optional)
Body: Black seal's fur, or substitute
Rib: Robust flat silver tinsel (or gold, optional)
Body hackle: Black cock
Head hackle: Longish, kingfisher blue hen

Whilst this pattern is largely looked upon as a sea-trout fly, it can be very effective for brown trout. A new generation of sea-trout patterns may have dented its popularity somewhat, but it still makes the 'first eleven' in my view. In sea-trout sizes I would stick closely to the above, traditional dressing, but for browns I would substitute a flat gold rib and a fluorescent tail for a very effective fly in peat-stained waters.

Zulu, Brown (Stewart Leslie)

PLATE 16

Hook: Partridge J1A or Drennan Wet Fly Supreme, 10
Silk: Brown
Tail: Tuft of fluorescent scarlet floss (Glo-Brite, no.4)
Body: Dark fiery brown seal's fur
Rib: Narrow flat gold
Body hackle: Medium red/brown cock
Head hackle: Red/brown hen

I always keep a few of these in my fly box, since an occasion when Stewart gave me one immediately before a competition on Hundland Loch in Orkney. I stuck it on and had the competition sewn-up within 45 minutes. For the record, I was drifting very close in and chucking towards the shore and the fish were hitting it in inches of water. Nothing else would do on the day. Elsewhere it has proved to be a good general purpose loch-style wet fly.

Zulu, Gold

PLATE 16

Hook: Partridge SH1 or J1A, or Kamasan B175, 8-12
Silk: Black
Tail: A tuft of fire red fluorescent wool (Turrall's)
Body: Black seal's fur, or sub
Body hackle: Black cock

PLATE 32
Silver Stoat, Emerald Stoat
Bill's Stoat (McLennan)
Pearly Stoat (Waddington)
Thunder Stoat, Stoat's Tail (long-tail)
Stinchar Stoat, Stoat's Tail

Rib: Narrow, flat metallic gold tinsel
Head hackle: Longish black hen

Historically speaking, the 'Gold Zulu' is quite another fly, but as the pattern has become almost redundant I have filched the name for the above dressing. This is a better fly for wild browns than its silver ribbed ancestor. I rarely now use the standard dressing except for sea-trout and salmon. I was shown this pattern by the Welsh master angler, Gwynfor Jones, and have owed him a debt ever since. Most anglers consider flies of this style to be strictly bob flies, but this one regularly performs in any position on the cast. (*see also* Zulu; Zulu, Pearly; and Zulu, Coch)

Zulu, Orange (Kenny Smith)

PLATE 11

Hook: Partridge SH1, or Kamasan B175, 8-12
Silk: Black
Tail: Tuft of fluorescent fire red wool (Turrall's)
Body: Black seal's fur, or substitute
Rib: Narrow flat silver, or fine oval silver
Hackle: Longish hot orange hen, tied full

This pattern, like a few other successful concoctions, began its life as a mistake! The palmered hackle, which is a hallmark of the Zulu tribe, was omitted and the resultant fly proved more efficient without it.

Now a standard fly for the brackish water trout of Loch Stenness and elsewhere, it is also useful for back-end wild trout and daphnia feeders on southern waters. The Orange Zulu is a useful fly to have tucked away in a general purpose fly box.

Zulu, Pearly

PLATE 16

Hook: Partridge J1A/SH1 or Kamasan B175, 8-12
Silk: Black
Tail: Tuft of fluorescent red wool
Body: Black seal's fur, or substitute
Body rib: Narrow flat pearl Mylar
Body hackle: Black cock, over the pearl Mylar
Hackle rib: Very fine oval silver or wire, over the

hackle and following the turns of the pearl Mylar
Head hackle: Longish black hen

There are two problems in using pearl mylar as an over-rib for palmered hackles. Firstly, the flat Mylar tends trap and flatten the fibres of the body hackle, leaving unsightly gaps in the palmering. Secondly, pearl Mylar is rather susceptible to being cut by trout teeth, rendering the fly useless.

By winding the pearl Mylar rib *before* palmering the hackle, then using the fine oval/wire to secure the hackle, one avoids these problems and adds a dash of flash to the finished fly as well.

The popularity of this pattern is growing each season. Use it as top of-the-water pattern for wild trout, sea-trout and salmon all through the year. (see also Zulu, Bibio[variant])

Zulu, Red

PLATE 16

Hook: Partridge J1A or SH1, 8-12
Silk: Black
Tail: Red wool (fluorescent, for choice)
Body: Black seal's fur, or substitute
Rib: Flat silver
Body hackle: Black cock
Hackle rib: Very fine oval silver or wire
Head hackle: Scarlet or red hen

This is a popular and very successful pattern for the brackish water browns and sea-trout in Orkney's Loch Stenness. It is also favoured by some for more typical freshwater lochs, particularly very early and late in the season. Patterns of this type were very popular in the past and belonged to the 'fancy' rather than the imitative school of wet flies. Such patterns are fast losing popularity amongst today's anglers. No doubt the odd 'baby' will disappear with the 'bath water', if such trends continue.

Zulu, Slimline

PLATE 16

Hook: Partridge K14ST or L2A or Kamasan B160, 10 & 12
Silk: Black
Butt: Fluorescent fire orange floss (Glo-Brite, no.5)
Body: Black ostrich herl, clipped short if necessary
Rib: Narrow flat gold
Hackle: Longish, sparse black hen

Many years ago, prior to the stillwater dry fly revolution, this pattern was my first line of attack against trout feeding on dark midge in conditions of light wind. Put across the nose of a rising fish and retrieved as slowly as possible, it was 'death on a hook'. More recent and imitative patterns (emergers, semi-emergers, CDCs, etc.) pushed the Slimline Zulu into relegation, until I discovered that it proved very effective on sinking lines when midge pupae were active at deep levels. A 'lift & hang' method with this pattern on the bob and perhaps a small Mallard & Claret backing it up has accounted for many good quality wild brown trout.

It has usually fished best early and late in the season, but is occasionally successful in mid-season. (*see* also Zulu)

The River Flies

The story of river fishing for trout in Scotland is a strange one. Apart from some areas, notably in the South of Scotland, river fishing for trout was largely discouraged for many years. It was believed that it interfered with the more important business of salmon and sea-trout fishing.

In fact, until quite recent times, trout were considered vermin where they existed in important salmon waters. Their removal, by all and any means, was considered a vital and important part of salmon river management. On top of this, there seems to have existed an intense paranoia amongst the proprietors of prime salmon water: many riparian owners considered 'trout fishing' to be a synonym for salmon poaching! In all, this hardly created an atmosphere conducive to the development of river trout fishing. So, while loch fishing for trout was accepted, river trout fishing was actively opposed.

The fact that some of the country's best river trout habitat exists in the Tweed, Tay, Tummel, Don and Spey must have had aspirant river trout fishers of previous generations weeping with frustration.

In the past few decades, however, attitudes have softened somewhat and the desire by riparian owners to maximise any possible revenue from exploitable fish stocks has caused a population explosion amongst river trouters. However, the nucleus of expertise which grew up in Straththclyde and the Tweed valley has had the most profound influence on Scottish trout fishing. Almost all of the traditional patterns emanate from these areas and the modern patterns are very much products of the late 20th century. There is a gaping hole in the lists of Scottish river trout patterns. The flies are either over a hundred years old, or they were devised 'yesterday'. The interim had to be filled by imports from other parts of the British Isles.

Adams

PLATE 17

Hook: Partridge GRS3A or L4A, 14-18
Silk: Grey
Tail: Mixed grizzle and red game cock hackle fibres
Body: Blueish-grey dubbed fur, SLF Finesse or similar
Wings: Two grizzle cock hackle points, tied upright
Hackle: Mixed grizzle and red game hackles

Given that this import from the USA is possibly the World's most popular dry fly for trout, it is surprisingly low in the Scottish popularity ratings, with only one region having it in their top dozen 'dries'. Perhaps a little targeted publicity is what it needs, so here it is.

A general purpose, speculative pattern, also useful to represent hatches of early duns.

Badger & Red

PLATE 17

Hook: Partridge E6A or L3A, 14
Silk: Bright red
Tail: Slim bunch of badger cock hackle fibres
Body: The tying silk, un-ribbed
Hackle: Badger cock hackle

The River Tweed has spawned a number of dry patterns for trout, being one of the few Scottish 'salmon' rivers to have a long and strong reputation for its trout fishing.

This is an early spinner pattern which works best in late summer and is also very useful on rain-fed streams, in which situation a yellow bodied variation (Badger & Yellow) also finds favour. The badger hackle is preferred on the lower reaches of the Tweed, grizzle in the mid-reaches, and becomes the Grey Hen & Rusty on the upper Tweed.

Beacon Beige

PLATE 17

Hook: Mustad 79703 or Partridge L3A, 14-18
Silk: Brown
Tail: Grizzle cock hackle fibres
Body: Stripped peacock quill from 'eye' feather
Hackle: Cock hackles, grizzle over red game

The Beacon Beige was developed from an older pattern by Peter Deane, shortly after the Second World War. He named it after the Culmstock Beacon, in Devon, which overlooked his first workshop. Willie Miller of Uddingston, recommends this dry pattern for general purpose use on the Clyde. He admits it does not have the typical 'Clyde' look but, nonetheless, it does work remarkably well.

Strikingly similar in general appearance to the Adams and, not surprisingly, they fulfil similar roles.

Big Grey (Franz Grimley)

PLATE 17

Hook: Partridge L4A, 12
Silk: Black
Body: Dubbed dark hare's ear or black Super Poly
Hackle: Smokey grey grizzle, palmered then clipped flush underneath

A fly that has been in use for over thirty years, Franz says that it is "... very useful for most of the season, especially during Large Olive and March Brown hatches and a superb fly for 'prospecting' during the warm summer months when fish lie in the fast, well oxygenated water at the head of streams." It has proved itself on all the major Scottish trout rivers as well as English and Welsh waters. A general purpose, utility pattern. A lighter bodied version uses primrose tying silk and either primrose yellow, or light olive dubbing.

Black & Red

PLATE 17

Hook: Partridge L4A or Drennan Buzzer, 14 & 16
Silk: Primrose
Body: Tying silk or dark hare's ear
Hackle: A poor quality cock hackle which has a red game tip & black towards the base

Franz Grimley, who supplied this pattern, advises that the hackle should be palmered so that the part of the hackle which extends down the body should be red game and the part wound at the head should incorporate the black portion of the hackle. In theory, at any rate, two hackles – one a black and one a red game – could be used to achieve the same ends.

Originating in Ayrshire, this pattern is an excellent general olive imitator and doubles as a Cow Dung representation. Franz also appreciates its worth as a stillwater dry. Also has good visibility features for poor light conditions. Works throughout the region.

Black Gnat

PLATE 17

Hook: Partridge L4A, 14-18
Silk: Black
Body: Black dubbing
Wing: Bunch of white hackle fibres, or a modern synthetic
Hackle: Black cock

Either a very precise imitation of a variety of naturally occurring insects, or a speculative pattern which is always likely to bring up a good fish when nothing much is happening. Particularly useful under trees or any shaded area where its hard silhouette will help to seduce suspicious or opportunistic trout. In its smallest sizes it will serve to imitate the dreaded reed smut. (see also Hawthorn Fly)

Black Spider [1] (W.C. Stewart)

PLATE 22

Hook: Partridge GRS3A or L4A, 12-18
Silk: Brown Pearsall's Gossamer (waxed)
Body: Tying silk
Hackle: Cock starling neck feather

W.C. Stewart, was by all accounts a dauntingly good angler. This simple pattern was his favourite wet fly, which he actually attributed to one James Baillie. In Stewart's much re-issued book, *The Practical Angler* (1857), he gives precise details for dressing this fly. The starling hackle is tied in halfway down the body, then twisted together with the tying silk, before both are wound forward to the hook eye. Not only does this technique produce a peculiar 'half-palmered' effect, it greatly enhances the durability of the otherwise rather fragile starling feather. (see also other Black Spiders; Harelug & Plover; Partridge & Brown; Partridge & Orange; Partridge & Orange [variant]; and Snipe & Purple)

Black Spider [2] (Paul Buchanan)

PLATE 17

Hook: Partridge GRS3A or L4A, 12-18
Silk: Black
Body: A layer of the tying silk tied just a short way down the shank
Hackle: Cock starling neck feather, retaining some of the blue/grey flue at the base of the feather

Paul uses Stewart's semi-palmering technique: tying the hackle by its tip, about half-way along body, and winding up to the eye. The retention of the blue/grey flue gives an attractive touch of contrast.

Most anglers are aware that small black patterns can often be devastatingly effective and I have little doubt that this version is well worth a place in any river fisher's box.

Paul advises that this fly can be used throughout the season: larger sizes early and late and smaller sizes in mid-summer hot, dry spells.

Black Spider (Clyde style)

PLATE 17

Hook: Partridge L3A or E6A, 14-18
Silk: Black or brown
Tail: Black cock hackle fibres
Body: Well-marked peacock quill from 'eye' feather
Hackle: Two black cock

As with many Clyde-style dry flies, this pattern incorporates two 'head' hackles. Normally these two hackles are of differing colours: one to match the body, the other to give a degree of contrast. In this case, however, we have a simple black dry fly for general purpose use, or for when smuts, black gnats, etc., are being taken.

Blae & Harelug

PLATE 17

Hook: Partridge L3A or E6A, 14 & 16
Silk: Yellow or olive gossamer
Tag: Three or four turns of narrow flat gold
Body: Hare's ear dubbed lightly, with the tying silk appearing through the dubbing
Wing: Starling secondary, rolled and set upright
Hackle: Two turns of tying silk more thickly dubbed with hare's ear fur, which is then picked out to give a suggestion of thorax and legs

This is a venerable and essential wet fly, tied in the distinctive Clyde style by Ian Glassford. Ian considers it an excellent 'emerger' pattern and in the early part of the season would fish it on the middle dropper, with a Pheasant Tail Nymph on the point and a Dark Olive on the top.

Broon Thing (Davie McPhail)

PLATE 17

Hook: Partridge E6A, 12-20
Silk: Primrose
Tail: Three grey 'Microfibbets'
Body: Cream SLF Finesse
Wing: Coastal deer hair, tied in a 'fan' shape

Davie McPhail, of Ayrshire, is a first-class dresser of flies. Surprisingly, perhaps, he rates this uncomplicated little pattern as one of his most reliable fish takers throughout the season. It was actually intended to represent the pale watery dun.

Davie ties a number of other dressings to the same format. One is the same as the above, but has a body of dubbed hare's ear fur. Another version uses bleached deer hair and has a body of plain yellow tying silk. These are functional, generally representative, dry flies in the modern idiom.

CDC Midge (Paul Buchanan)

PLATE 17

Hook: Partridge GRS3A, 14-18
Silk: Black
Body: Stripped quill from a peacock 'eye' feather
Wing: Two small CDC plumes, tied to reach just beyond the hook bend
Head: Two turns of thread, sparsely dubbed with hare's ear

Paul advises that this pattern be used in glides and slacks where the surface is smooth and 'thick' and trout are dimpling to small insects. He says that if very small sizes are being used, it often pays to fish this pattern *downstream* to the rising fish.

The body length should extend to just above the hook point and extra durability can be given to the quill body by winding it over wet varnish. If doing this, allow the varnish to dry before completing the fly, otherwise the CDC wing gets gummed up.

Claret Hen Blackie

PLATE 17

Hook: Partridge GRS3A, 14 & 16
Silk: Pearsall's claret Gossamer, waxed
Body: Tying thread, short
Wing: Hen blackbird substitute (starling), tied low over the body
Hackle: Cock starling neck, one turn in front of wing

This minor variation of the Hen Blackie is reckoned by Paul Buchanan to be a great evening fly from early June to the end of the season. Claret bodied flies are very popular with loch fishermen for conditions of poor light, though the practice does not seem so common for river work.

Copper Nymph (Jimmy Fairgrieve)

PLATE 17

Hook: Kamasan B170, 10-14
Underbody: Lead wire
Silk: Black
Tail: Three brown goose biots
Abdomen: Copper wire, medium gauge
Thorax cover: Brown Flexibody
Thorax: Brown SLF dubbing

Jimmy Fairgrieve, an accomplished and dedicated river fisherman, has produced a range of modern Scottish patterns that are both attractive and effective. They have a 'fishy' look about them which engenders that all-important component: confidence.

This pattern is fished singly on a long leader, or as a point fly in a team. It is particularly useful for slow deep pools where it is best fished with a jerky, figure-of-eight retrieve.

Cran Swallow (John Reid)

PLATE 18

Hook: Partridge GRS3A, 14 & 16
Silk: Primrose Pearsall's Gossamer (waxed)
Body: Of tying silk, kept short
Wing: Originally, swift. For substitute use starling (dyed iron blue), or coot, or crow. The wing should be tied to lie low over the body
Hackle: Starling, one turn in front of wing

Paul Buchanan supplied the example for the illustration. He advises that it is a top performing evening pattern for use from June to the end of season.

In its form and use of materials, this is typical of so many of the old Clyde patterns. There is probably not much profit in pondering too long on exactly what some of these old river patterns are supposed to represent ...just so long as they continue to be reliable.

Crow & Black (Jimmy Hislop)

PLATE 18

Hook: Partridge L3A, 10 & 12, occasionally 8
Silk: Black
Tail: Red floss, sparse
Body: Tying silk
Rib: Narrow flat silver
Wing: Crow secondary, rolled and set low over the back
Hackle: Four turns of black cock hackle, wound in front of the wing

To those in the know, this is obviously a member of 'The Big Flee' tribe: a night pattern for the Clyde. Ian Glassford, who supplied the example shown, obtained one from its originator some thirty years ago. He has used the pattern ever since. (see also Crow & Silver; Kenny's Sedge; Magpie Tail; and Stank Hen)

Crow & Silver (Willie Miller)

PLATE 18

Hook: Mustad 9143 or Partridge L2A, 10
Silk: Black
Body: Flat silver
Wing: Crow primary or secondary, tied low and sloping downwards
Hackle: Black cock or hen

This is another night pattern for the Clyde, in the typical colours for the job. (see also Crow & Black; Kenny's Sedge; Magpie Tail; and Stank Hen)

Deer Hair Olive (Jimmy Fairgrieve)

PLATE 18

Hook: Mustad 79703, 10-16
Silk: Yellow Uni-Thread
Tail: A few fibres from a grizzle cock hackle
Body: Tying silk
Wing: Deer hair, set upright
Hackle: Grizzle cock, wound both behind and in front of the wing

Jimmy claims that this is his 'first choice dry fly, anywhere, all through the season'. It can be tied in a range of sizes and material densities, to suit conditions of water and weather.

The under-part of the hackle can be trimmed flush with the body to allow the fly to sit down in the surface film, but it is at its best as a high floating, fast water fly. It can be fished confidently either to rising fish or used as a 'search' pattern. This pattern is also known by some as Jimmy's Deer Hair.

Duck Tip

PLATE 18

Hook: Partridge L3A, 12 & 14
Silk: Black

Butt: Three turns of narrow flat silver
Body: Tying silk
Wing: Paired slips from the white-tipped section of a mallard blue speculum feather
Hackle: Three turns of black cock

This venerable Clyde night-time pattern has lost little of its popularity and is still recommended by all the authorities of the region. (*see also* Crow & Black; Crow & Silver; Kenny's Sedge; Magpie Tail; and Stank Hen)

Easy Stone Nymph
(Franz Grimley)

PLATE 18

Hook: Partridge K12ST, 14 & 16
Silk: Black or yellow
Underbody: Lead wire
Body: Brown or black mole fur, dubbed onto the thread and wound, with strands of yellow Translucent Lureflash along and under the hook shank
Rib: Copper wire
Hackle: Brown or black hen, optional

Heavily weighted large nymphs, of this kind, are becoming ever more important for the upstream style fishing that is gaining so much favour these days. Many of the patterns – especially those imported from the USA – are extremely tricky and time-consuming to tie. Franz assures me that this one is not, hence its name. Here are his tying instructions:
1. Weight the hook shank with the lead wire, adding extra turns in the thorax area.
2. Using the tying thread, tie in the ribbing wire at the bend of the hook.
3. Take 10 or 12 filaments of yellow Translucent Lureflash about two inches long and tie them in *under* the body at the bend of the hook. Catch in the bundle half way along its length, effectively *doubling* the number of filaments. Pull the filaments out of the way to the rear of the hook, for the time being.
4. Dub the mole fur on to the thread and wind a body up to the thorax.
5. Now, draw the bunch of Lureflash filaments under the body and tie it in securely at the point

that will be the rear of the 'thorax'. Do not trim the excess.
6. With the copper wire, rib the body from bend to rear of thorax; tie off the wire securely and remove the excess.
7. Dub more mole on to the thread and wind a thorax up to head of fly, leaving enough room for the hackle (if one is intended).
8. Pull the remnants of the Lureflash filaments under the thorax towards the head and secure, removing any excess.
9. If a hackle is required, tie this in now.
10. Whip finish and varnish, as usual.
(*see also* Woven Nymph)

Flashback Harelug Nymph
(Franz Grimley)

PLATE 18

Hook: Mustad 79703, 12-16
Silk: Black
Underbody: Lead wire, with extra turns in the thoracic region
Tail: Three or four fibres of teal or mallard flank
Body: Well-mixed hares mask, medium to dark
Rib: Fine oval silver
Thorax cover: Pearly or holographic strip, cut to size
Legs: Two or three teal or mallard flank fibres each side, tied in at the head

This is a general, vague imitator of all sorts of underwater food items which interest trout. The addition of the 'flashback' may increase its effectiveness, if only by catching the fish's attention as the nymph is tumbled along in the swirling current of fast streams. In any event, this pattern has proved especially effective in the powerful currents of the larger, deeper rivers such as the Tay and the Tummel. (*see also* Hare's Ear Flashback)

Gold-Ribbed Hare's Ear (GRHE)

PLATE 18

Hook: Partridge GRS3A, 12-16
Silk: Primrose
Body: Well-mixed hare's mask with guard hairs
Rib: Fine flat gold

Hackle: Picked-out hare's ear fibres
Wing: Starling or grey duck, tied low over the body

There is a clutch of very old, traditional patterns which defy the modern tendency to replace them with 'souped-up' innovations. The Gold Ribbed Hare's Ear is a prime example. It remains one of the most effective representations of the nymph-cum-emerger stage of a whole range of insects: small ephemerids, sedges and chironomid midges. In stillwater, incidentally, it can be used to represent corixae and shrimps. Quite why this fly remains so devastatingly and generally effective is hard to ascribe. Perhaps it is its very vagueness? Whatever the reason, the Gold Ribbed Hare's Ear works well in fast, medium or slow water and particularly well when fish are 'up' and visibly taking hatching olives. A wingless version probably represents the nymph stage better.

Grannom (Davie McPhail)

PLATE 18

Hook: Partridge GRS3A, 14 & 16
Silk: Black
Egg Sack: Green Ethafoam
Body: Mole
Wing: Coastal deer hair, tied 'sedge' style, i.e., low over the body and splayed
Hackle: Blue dun cock, trimmed underneath

The Grannom (*Brachycentrus subnubilus*) is a small, early season sedge (caddis) fly, that is active during the day-time. Where it occurs, it can be of great importance to the angler. Sadly, there is evidence that its range is decreasing and that it is a lot less common now than in the past. However, where it is still found, the hatches can be immense and there is no doubt that trout love this insect, particularly the egg-bearing females.

The egg-sack is a slightly blueish green and this feature has been extraordinarily well mimicked by Davie McPhail by his use of green Ethafoam. This is a very 'fishy' looking pattern.

Greenwell's Glory

PLATE 7

Hook: Partridge L4A, 14-18

Silk: Yellow Pearsall's Gossamer, darkened with cobbler's wax
Tail: Medium dark furnace cock hackle fibres
Body: Tying silk
Rib: Fine gold wire (optional)
Hackle: A medium dark furnace cock hackle
Wing: Starling (originally, hen blackbird, but this is protected)

Canon William Greenwell's fly, originally tied by James Wright, of Sprouston on the Tweed, in 1854, is probably the most famous trout fly of all. It is the quintessential Scottish river pattern and it is a patriotic necessity to show it here in all its 'glory', as dressed by Davie McPhail.

The Greenwell is a good taker of fish in the early and late months, or at any time when olives are hatching. It is also, unusually, one of the few, traditional, river dry patterns to be very useful on stillwaters.

Greenwell's Glory (dry)

PLATE 18

Hook: Partridge L4A, 14-18
Silk: Yellow Gossamer, darkened with cobbler's wax
Tail: Medium dark furnace cock hackle fibres
Body: Tying silk
Rib: Fine gold wire (optional)
Hackle: Two medium dark furnace cock hackles

This is the dressing of a dry Greenwell that is now preferred by most anglers on the Clyde. It functions both as a general purpose representation of ephemerids and more specifically in imitation of the light olives.

As with all the wingless dry flies from this region, the hackles should occupy a substantial amount of hook shank.

Greenwell's Glory (wet)

PLATE 18

Hook: Partridge GRS3A or L3A, 12-16
Silk: Pearsall's primrose Gossamer, waxed with cobbler's wax
Body: Tying silk
Rib: Fine gold wire

Hackle: Medium furnace hen
Wing: Dark starling slips, concave to concave

By all accounts, the original pattern had no rib. However, a ribbing of fine gold wire crept into the recipe a long time ago and it seems that no-one would be happy without one these days. A common mistake is for tyers to dress the fly paler than it should be. Some waxes hardly darken the silk and cobbler's wax is advised. A good dark wing is best, split as shown, except in exceptional circumstances.

As with the dry version, the Greenwell is an exceptional wet fly for general imitation of the olives and other medium sized ephemerids. It can be reliably expected to take fish throughout the season. The 'correct' dark renderings of the pattern – as illustrated here – are often referred to as 'Border Greenwell's'.

Grey Duster [parachute]
(Davie McPhail)

PLATE 18

Hook: Partridge GRS3A or E6A, 10-16
Silk: Brown
Tail: Grey Microfibbets, splayed
Body: Mixed rabbit fur, with a good proportion of the 'blue' underfur
Wing: Coastal deer hair
Hackle: Badger cock, tied parachute style

The Grey Duster is something of an enigma. It can often beat more precise imitations of particular ephemerids when trout are being selective, although it imitates nothing in particular itself. In very small sizes, it can catch fish in caenis hatches and plenty of trout have been taken on a large 'Duster' at mayfly time. Some anglers will fish with nothing else and leave the water if it fails.

The original pattern, which was Courteney Williams's favourite fly, had no tail or wing. Davie McPhail offers this variation on the theme. He says that fish take the parachute style more confidently. The Microfibbets are an added aid to floatation, but at times Davie will actually bite them off to allow the fly to sit well-down in the water. Truly, a great river dry fly patterns.

Grey Hen & Rusty

PLATE 18

Hook: Partridge L3A or E6A, 14-18
Silk: Brown
Body: Orangey brown dubbing
Hackle: Two turns of grizzle cock

This very simple little dry pattern originates from the South East of Scotland. It should be regarded as a speculative pattern, which imitates nothing in particular. (see also Badger & Red)

Hare's Ear Flashback
(Jimmy Fairgrieve)

PLATE 19

Hook: Kamasan B170, 10-14
Underbody: Lead wire
Silk: Black
Tail: A few fibres from a grey partridge hackle
Abdomen: Light hare's ear
Abdomen rib: Fine silver wire
Thorax cover: Veniard's pearl film
Thorax: Brown SLF dubbing

Jimmy offers this pattern as an alternative to his Copper Nymph. He advises its use in slow, deep pools, fished with a jerky, figure-of-eight retrieve. Other anglers fish it upstream in heavy currents and report that it is remarkably effective. It is clearly one of those generally useful patterns that can be used in a wide variety of locations and conditions, when one needs a fly with some ballast to get down to the fish. (see also Flashback Harelug Nymph)

Hare's Ear Parachute
(Alberto Laidlaw)

PLATE 19

Hook: Kamasan B170 or Partridge E6A, 12-16
Silk: Black or yellow
Tail: Four or five dun coloured Microfibbets
Body: Pale hare's ear
Rib: Tying silk (optional)
Wing: A bundle of natural brown coastal deer hair, approx. the thickness of a cocktail stick

Hackle: Grizzle or blue dun cock, five or six turns tied parachute style

Alberto Laidlaw, of Renfrewshire, is a very successful river fisherman and this pattern of his is an excellent general purpose representation of a wide range of natural insects. Slight variations of the dressing allow it to mimic particular insects more specifically.

The killing qualities of this style of fly may be due to its sitting well down in the surface film. Perhaps this gives the appearance of an emerging or crippled fly and thus an easier target than a fully eclosed insect about to fly away?! (*see also* Jimmy's Deer Hair)

Harelug & Plover

PLATE 19

Hook: Partridge GRS3A & L4A, 12-16
Silk: Primrose
Body: Lightly dubbed hare's ear, allowing tying silk to shine through
Hackle: Pale brown feather with a yellow tip from the coverts of a Golden Plover's wing

This traditional pattern is one of the family of North Country wet 'spider' patterns. Paul Buchanan, of Livingston, rates it as one of the best summer spider patterns, alongside Stewart's Black Spider. He fishes it in every imaginable river style: down & across; upstream; to rising fish; twitched through the slacks; etc. Paul reports that this little fly markedly outfishes winged wet flies in bright, clear conditions.

Harelug Goldhead

PLATE 19

Hook: Kamasan B100, 10-14
Silk: Primrose
Body: Fawn/red fur from base of hare's ear, with guard hairs added
Rib: Medium flat gold
Bead: Gold bead (3mm)

Sometimes referred to as a Golden Nugget Hare's Ear, this is a widely acclaimed heavy nymph for upstream work on all types of rivers.

Few, if any, knowledgeable river anglers will be without this excellent, general purpose pattern. There are very many variations on this and other 'Goldhead' themes. They more or less all fulfil the small 'depth charge' role for fast and/or deep water.

Hawthorn Fly (Davie McPhail)

PLATE 19

Hook: Kamasan B100, 16
Silk: Black
Legs: Dyed black cock pheasant tail fibres, knotted and trailing
Body: Black Ethafoam
Wing: Two CDC feather tips, tied more along the sides of the body rather than over
Thorax cover: Black Ethafoam
Thorax: Black dubbing
Hackle: Black cock, palmered through thorax and trimmed underneath

This is a realistic imitation of the natural hawthorn fly (*Bibio marci*), a great favourite of trout. Breezy days in April and May can see quantities of these relatively weak fliers being deposited on the water, much to the delight of the awaiting fish. To be without a suitable imitation in such circumstances would be unforgivable. This is one of the best I have seen. (*see also* Black Gnat)

Hen Blackie

PLATE 19

Hook: Partridge L2A or L3A, 14
Silk: Yellow gossamer
Tag: Two turns of flat gold
Body: Tying silk
Wing: Originally, hen blackbird secondary. Use starling as a substitute
Hackle: Black hen, sparse

The delicacy and finesse of the Clyde wet fly is shown in this perfect little fly. Rather like a dark Greenwell's Glory, it is popular as a tail fly for the middle part of the season. (*see* Claret Hen Blackie)

Iron Blue Dun (dry)

PLATE 19

Hook: Mustad 79703 or Partridge L3A 16 & 18
Silk: Brown
Tail: Dark grey or brown hackle fibres
Body: Dyed brown stripped peacock quill
Hackle: Two cock hackles: dark blue dun in front of red game

This somewhat variant pattern is recommended for the Clyde by Willie Miller. He states that the natural is most common in April and May and later on, in September. They appear in large numbers even in blustery weather and the trout really seem to relish these little dark ephemerids. On occasions, a successful imitation is a must.

Iron Blue Dun (wet)

PLATE 19

Hook: Partridge L3A, 16
Silk: Purple or claret
Body: Mole fur
Wing: Cock Blackbird substitute, here tied in the classic Scottish style (optional)
Hackle: Black hen (or feather from a Jackdaw's throat)

The wingless version is known as The Infallible and has a blue dun hen hackle and uses scarlet or claret silk. It usually features a few turns of the bare thread as a butt, behind the dubbed bodying. The dressing in the illustration is the classic original. It offers a vague representation of the iron blue (*Baetis muticus* and *baetis niger*) in any of its juvenile or adult (drowned) forms. The pattern is useful from day one until the middle of the season and again in September.

Kenny's Olive (Kenny Miller)

PLATE 19

Hook: Partridge L3A, 14 & 16
Silk: Brown Pearsall's Gossamer
Body: Tying silk
Rib: Narrow flat gold
Wing: Thrush (substitute) secondary, rolled and

set upright (the correct winging material should be slightly brownish grey)
Hackle: Dark olive, one turn behind wing and one in front

Ian Glassford, who supplied this pretty pattern, says that it is probably the best general olive pattern he has come across. He reports that he usually fishes it on the middle dropper: in which position it provides total confidence.

Kenny's Sedge (Kenny Miller)

PLATE 19

Hook: Partridge L3A, 10 & 12
Silk: Orange Gossamer
Tag: Two or three turns flat gold
Body: Light dubbing of hare's ear, with tying silk showing through
Rib: Narrow flat gold
Wing: Woodcock secondary, rolled and set low over the back, with the dull side of the feather showing
Hackle: Three or four turns of ginger cock

Night patterns for the Clyde are typified by long, slim profiles with 'rolled' wings, swept back low over the body. The above is a typical example. This is a very pretty fly which must give much confidence to those who use it. It would usually be fished on the top dropper, from mid to late season. It is sometimes referred to as a Woodcock & Harelug. (*see* Crow & Black; Crow & Silver; Duck Magpie Tip; Magpie Tail and Stank Hen)

Large Spring Olive (Willie Miller)

PLATE 19

Hook: Mustad 79703 or Partridge L3A, 12
Silk: Olive
Tail: Olive cock hackle fibres
Body: Stripped, or semi-stripped, peacock quill dyed olive
Hackle: Dark blue-dun over dark or medium olive cock hackles. Alternatively, dark or medium olive over ginger

One glorious May morning on the Burnbane beat of the Tay, I witnessed a phenomenal hatch of large dark olives (*Baetis rhodani*). The resultant rise of river trout was as impressive as I have ever seen. These insects are common on rivers throughout Scotland and a good, high-riding, imitation is essential. Willie Miller's pattern should serve as well as most.

Lark & Grey

PLATE 19

Hook: Partridge GRS3A or L4A, 14-18
Silk: Primrose
Tail: Grizzle hackle fibres
Body: Cream or primrose dubbing
Hackle: Grizzle cock hackle
Wing: Originally lark; now, teal secondary or starling (optional)

I must admit that I thought I was being 'sold a pup' when I received this pattern from Davie McPhail. After a great deal of research, I could find no mention of it in any of the reference books. But I am assured that it is genuinely an old Clyde pattern, designed to represent the pale watery dun. The hackled version is popular early in the season, with the winged pattern finding favour later in the year.

Light Olive (Willie Miller)

PLATE 19

Hook: Mustad 79703 or Partridge L3A, 16-18
Silk: Light olive (waxed to darken)
Tail: Very pale yellow cock hackle fibres
Body: Tying silk
Hackle: Two cock hackles: blue dun in front of very pale yellow

Willie Miller tells me that the above is a very successful representation of the pale evening dun (*Procloeon rufulum*) which, I am also led to believe, is a great favourite of trout. These duns emerge, often after hot weather, in the evenings from July through to September. Their coloration is extremely light, hence the name.

Linhouse Pheasant Tail Nymph (Paul Buchanan)

PLATE 19

Hook: Kamasan B170, 12-16
Underbody: Tapered under-layer of fine lead foil, with a little hump in the thoracic region using very fine copper wire
Silk: Pearsall's Gossamer, slate grey
Tail: Sparse bunch of pale blue dun hen hackle fibres
Abdomen: Cock pheasant tail fibres dyed brown olive (Veniard's shade)
Abdomen rib: Fine copper wire
Thorax cover: Pale grey mallard wing quill fibres
Thorax: Rabbit fur, retaining some blue underfur
Hackle: Small blue dun hen, wound (not a beard)

Paul advises that he usually fishes this pattern as a point fly, with two spider patterns above. He says it excels in fast, rocky, broken water fished down and across, but that it also produces fish when twitched through 'fishless' slacks and eddies. Use the smaller sizes in shallow water and the larger dressings in deeper pools.

For durability, add very dilute cellulose varnish to the thorax and thorax cover. (*see also* Medwin Blue; Pheasant Tail Nymph; and Pheasant Tail Nymph [Olive])

Lureflash Nymph (Franz Grimley)

PLATE 20

Hook: Mustad 79703, 12-18
Underbody: Lead wire
Silk: Yellow cobweb, waxed
Tail: Three or four fibres of red game cock hackle
Body: Tying silk
Back/Thorax cover: Dark brown Translucent Lureflash filaments
Throat hackle: Red game cock fibres, tied as a beard

Franz gives this realistic and successful pattern as a useful tool for all Scottish rivers.
Tie in the Translucent Lureflash filaments at the bend of the hook; shape a tapered abdomen with the tying thread, then tension the Lureflash

filaments over the back and rib them with tying thread to give the segmented effect shown. Build up the thoracic region with tying thread and bring the filaments over to form a thorax cover. Simple and effective. An alternative dressing incorporates olive hackle fibres and green Translucent Lureflash filaments.

Magpie Tail (Bert Sharp)

PLATE 20

Hook: Partridge L3A, 14 & 16
Silk: Black Pearsall's Gossamer
Tag: Two turns of narrow flat silver
Body: Tying silk
Wing: Paired slips of magpie tail, tied low over the back
Hackle: One or two turns (depending on hackle quality) of black hen, wound in front of the wing

The importance of slim, black patterns for the Clyde cannot be overstated. I am advised, from a variety of sources, that this reliable pattern should always be fished as a point fly. It is successful throughout the season and some anglers *always* have it on their casts, which must be a pretty strong recommendation.

Tied on a 10 or 12 hook and given a peacock herl body, with a fine silver wire rib and a somewhat heavier application of hackle, it becomes a superb night pattern for the same river. (see also Crow & Black; Crow & Silver; Kenny's Sedge; and Stank Hen)

March Brown

PLATE 20

Hook: Partridge L4A, 10-14
Silk: Yellow
Tail: Brown partridge hackle fibres or bronze mallard
Body: Dark hare's ear
Wing: Well-marked darkish hen pheasant secondary
Hackle: A brown partridge hackle, mixed with a red game cock hackle

The march brown (*Rhithrogena germanica*) is an indicator of good water quality and, thankfully, we have many rivers in Scotland that still support this ephemerid insect. It hatches in the early part of the season, when it brings the trout up with gay abandon. Unfortunately, these spring hatches are often fitful and of short duration, so the angler has to be on his toes to make the most of them. The early spring angler should always have a good imitation, such as this one, at the ready. (see also, March Brown [wet] in the Loch Fly section)

March Brown (parachute)

PLATE 20

The ingredients for this pattern are the same as for the preceding entry, except that the hackles are wound around the base of the wings, parachute style.

The traditional style of dressing dry flies – with upright split wings, etc.– is certainly aesthetically pleasing. These are the flies much loved by Halford, et al. However, this is not always the optimum design for catching fish. In recent times, we have discovered that parachute dressings, that allow the fly to sit well down in the surface film, are often dramatically more effective. The same applies to a whole host of emerger and 'cripple' dun designs that have been introduced in the past few years.

March Brown [dry wingless] (Willie Miller)

PLATE 20

Hook: Mustad 79703 or Partridge L3A, 12 & 14
Silk: Brown
Tail: Dark ginger cock hackle fibres
Body: Reddish-brown cock pheasant tail fibres, twisted
Rib: Gold wire
Hackle: Brown partridge, in front of dark ginger cock hackle

The march brown is one of the prettiest Ephemeropteran insects and possibly the most frustrating. Every time I experience a hatch, it seems to be over by the time I have managed to find a representation, tied it on my leader and am ready to cast!

Willie Miller's version follows a typical Clyde-style dry fly format, with a significant proportion of the hook shank occupied by the hackle. He says he uses this pattern not only in the Spring as an imitation of the natural march brown, but also on summer evenings as a vague representation of a variety of small sedges.

March Brown, Silver

PLATE 20

Hook: Partridge GRS2A, 10 & 12
Silk: Black
Tail: Fibres of brown partridge (optional)
Body: Medium flat silver
Rib: Fine oval gold
Hackle: Brown partridge, tied as a beard
Wing: Well marked hen pheasant secondary slips, tied low over body

Paul Buchanan proffers this pattern as 'a top quality attractor for cold, early/late season days when fish are on minnows, or in high but reasonably clear water'.

I must admit to being slightly surprised by the gold rib, expecting a silver one, but I won't argue the point. A slim and sleek effect is essential. (see also Invicta, Silver)

March Brown Spider
(Willie Miller)

PLATE 20

Hook: Mustad 9143 or Partridge L2A, 10 & 12
Silk: Brown
Tail: Cock pheasant tail fibres
Body: Reddish/brown cock pheasant tail fibres
Rib: Gold wire
Hackle: Brown partridge

Many wet fly patterns styled 'March Brown' are now rarely used to imitate the natural insect, which, sadly, is declining throughout its range. Willie Miller designed this fly, which he finds very successful when trout are feeding on the ascending nymph during a march brown hatch on the Clyde.

An alternative dressing uses a hare's ear body and a tail of partridge hackle fibres and is closer to the more traditional patterns.

Medium Olive [dry] (Willie Miller)

PLATE 20

Hook: Mustad 79703 or Partridge L3A, 14
Silk: Olive
Tail: Dirty yellow (or perhaps golden olive) cock hackle fibres
Body: Stripped quill from olive dyed ostrich herl
Hackle: Two cock hackles: blue dun in front of medium olive

This is a good, wingless alternative to all the more widely known dressings to imitate *Baëtis tenax*, such as the Olive Quill or Greenwell's Glory. Willie Miller, who invented this particular dressing, says that it is very useful in May and June.

Medium Olive (wet)

PLATE 20

Hook: Partridge L3A, 14
Silk: Olive
Tail: Medium olive hackle fibres
Body: Peacock quill, dyed yellow
Wing: Slips of snipe secondary feather
Hackle: Medium olive cock

This medium olive imitation is usually prescribed as a dropper pattern for the classic 'down & across' style of wet fly fishing. This method of tackling insect imitation is still popular in the strongholds of traditional fishing in Scotland. But for how much longer? Anglers are increasingly embracing more modern (effective?) techniques and patterns.

Medium Olive, CDC parachute
(Davie McPhail)

PLATE 20

Hook: Partridge GRS3A or L4A, 14 & 16
Silk: Primrose
Body: Medium olive seal's fur, or sub.

Wing: Two cul de canard plumes, tied upright
Hackle: Medium olive cock hackle, wound around the root of the CDC wings, parachute fashion

The smoky grey/brown of CDC plumes very closely matches the wing colour of many of the duns, particularly those at the beginning of hatches. It is for this, more than its floating qualities, that CDC was chosen in this pattern. The parachute hackle design allows the fly to sit well down in the water: mimicking either an emerging fly filling its wings, or perhaps a crippled individual trapped in the surface film.

Medwin Blue (Paul Buchanan)

PLATE 20

Hook: Kamasan B170, 12-16
Underbody: Tapered underbody of fine lead foil, with a slight hump in the thoracic region using fine copper wire
Silk: Cobweb fluorescent yellow, waxed
Tail: Slim bunch of blue dun hen hackle fibres, splayed
Abdomen: A fine dubbing of muskrat underfur allowing the tying thread to show through
Thorax cover: Pale mallard wing quill fibres
Thorax: Muskrat underfur
Hackle: A small blue dun hen, wound (not a beard)

Another Paul Buchanan pattern for fast, broken water, fished as a point fly below a team of spider patterns (*see* Linhouse Pheasant Tail Nymph).

It is important that the dubbing is not too thick, or the effect of using the fluorescent tying silk will be lost.

Olive Dun

PLATE 20

Hook: Partridge L3A or E6A, 12-18
Silk: Olive
Tail: Olive dun cock hackle fibres
Body: Olive dun dubbing, seal's fur in larger sizes, mole or rabbit for smaller dressings
Rib: Fine copper, or gold wire (often omitted)

Wing: Starling
Hackle: Olive dun cock

The quintessential river dry fly to imitate the early and late olives on all types of rivers. The one shown is from Ron Glass of the Lower Tweed, who rates it very highly for his waters.

Olive Paradun (Jimmy Millar)

PLATE 20

Hook: Kamasan B170 or Partridge E6A, 14 & 16
Silk: Olive
Tail: Blue dun Microfibbets
Body: A 50/50 mix of pale hare's ear and yellow dyed squirrel body fur
Wing: Dun coloured siliconized polypropylene yarn
Hackle: Pale blue dun, tied parachute-style

Jimmy Millar does almost all his fishing on the Water of Leith, in Edinburgh, where, I am reliably informed, the trout have a degree of sophistication second to none. Jimmy says that these fish are very 'surface oriented' and rarely refuse this pattern. It is particularly effective when fish are on aphids, on which occasions the fishing can be most frustrating.

Olive Quill (dry)

PLATE 20

Hook: Partridge E6A, 12-18
Silk Primrose
Tail: Three Microfibbets (olive or grey) splayed
Body: A well marked peacock quill, stripped
Wing: Starling
Hackle: Medium olive cock

The Olive Quill is a time-served standard pattern for all rivers, principally for the early and latter parts of the season.

Olive Quill (wet)

PLATE 20

Hook: Partridge GRS3A, 12-16
Silk: Olive

Body: Stripped peacock quill, laid over wet varnished tying silk
Wing: Hen blackbird (substitute)
Hackle: Yellowy-olive hen, wound in front of the wing

This ubiquitous wet fly pattern has many variations in its dressing: no two authorities seem to agree on a definitive formula.

Paul Buchanan offers this dressing as an essential tool when finding it difficult to match exactly the shade of hatching olives.

Partridge & Brown

PLATE 21

Hook: Partridge or Drennan Wet Fly Supreme, 12-16
Silk: Brown
Body: Tying silk or medium brown floss
Rib: Fine gold wire (optional)
Hackle: Dark brown speckled partridge hackle

Sometimes known as the Partridge Glory, this pattern is recommended by Willie Miller for the Clyde. He also has a dry version tied fuller and with a palmered red game cock hackle. (*see also* Partridge & Orange; Partridge & Orange [variant]; and Partridge & Yellow)

Partridge & Orange

PLATE 21

Hook: Partridge L2A, 12-16
Silk: Orange Pearsall's Gossamer (shade no.6a)
Rib: Fine gold wire (optional)
Hackle: Longish, sparse brown partridge

Also known as the Orange Partridge, this is one of the best known of the North of England 'spider' patterns. Whilst most Scottish river authorities list this pattern, the traditional river wet flies seem to be giving way to the upstream leaded nymphs.

Primarily an early season pattern for rough streams, the Partridge & Orange is also one of the few Spiders to be accepted for contemporary loch work. Some Clyde pundits actually recommend a dry version, which incorporates a red game cock hackle wound before (i.e., behind) the partridge. (*see also* Black Spiders; Partridge & Yellow; Plover & Harelug; Snipe & Purple)

Partridge & Orange [variant] (Ian Glassford)

PLATE 21

Hook: Partridge L3A, 14 & 16
Silk: Orange Gossamer (shade no.6a)
Tag: Two turns of narrow flat gold
Body: Tying silk, or orange floss
Hackle: Brown partridge

I had never before come across a variant of this pattern, so I have included this because you may relish a chance to try something a bit different.

If Ian Glassford says that he prefers this pattern dressed in this way, then that is good enough for me.

Partridge & Yellow

Hook: Partridge GRS2A, GRS3A or L4A 12-16
Silk: Primrose Pearsall's Gossamer
Body: A layer of the waxed tying silk, tied very short
Hackle: Shortish grey partridge hackle

This is another old North-country wet pattern, only slightly less well known than its orange cousin. Those in the know admire its qualities, but it is not widely accepted. This would seem surprising, given that a waxed yellow silk body seems to be the base line from which pattern choice for river fishing starts. Standard down and across fishing style is advised, but almost any other technique will work on its day.

I have heard of this pattern, tied 'buzz', fished dry. (*see* Partridge & Brown; Partridge & Orange; and Partridge & Orange [variant])

Pheasant Tail Nymph [1] (Franz Grimley)

PLATE 21

Hook: Mustad 79703, 10-18

Underbody: Lead or copper wire, built up in thoracic region
Silk: Yellow
Tail: Three or four cock pheasant tail fibres
Abdomen: As tail, wound
Abdomen rib: Copper wire, red or brown
Thorax cover: As tail, doubled, or pearl strip
Thorax: Dark hare's ear
Hackle: As tail tied beard style or divided each side (optional)

The versions we use here in Scotland tend to differ somewhat from the simple dressing made famous by the originator, the late Frank Sawyer. Franz Grimley's variation on the Sawyer's theme has a somewhat darker hue which seems to suit the Scottish trout. Useful when the nymphs of iron blue dun, large dark olive and small dark olive are on the menu. Effective on all rivers.

Pheasant Tail Nymph [2]

PLATE 21

Hook: Partridge L2A or Kamasan B175, 12-16
Silk: Black or brown
Tail: Three or four cock pheasant tail fibres
Underbody: A layer of fine copper wire, built up under thorax
Abdomen: Cock pheasant tail fibres, wound
Abdomen rib: Fine copper wire
Thorax cover: Cock pheasant tail fibres
Thorax: Copper wire build up, or dubbing. The Scottish preference is for a dubbed hare's ear thorax
Legs: These are distinctly optional: pheasant tail tips in larger sizes, or picked out hare's ear guard hairs from the thorax dubbing

Another variation on the Sawyer original. Some form of the Pheasant Tail Nymph must be regarded as an essential inclusion in the fly box, particularly in the early months when *Baëtis* nymphs are active and being hunted by the trout. I recently discovered Highland browns susceptible to this pattern while feeding on cased-Caddis in clearing floods.

Pheasant Tail Nymph [3]
(Ron Glass)

PLATE 21

Hook: Partridge L2A or Kamasan B175, 10-16
Silk: Black
Tail: Cock pheasant tail fibres
Body: Mixed natural & olive-dyed cock pheasant tail fibres
Rib: Fine gold wire
Thorax: Olive dubbing (mole, hare's ear or synthetic)
Thorax cover: Melanistic cock pheasant tail fibres

Ron Glass's pattern is a general purpose imitation of Ephemeropteran nymphs, but is particularly good for those of the olive tribe. Ron recommends this for the Tweed and all other Scottish rivers.

Red Sedge

PLATE 21

Hook: Partridge L3A or E6A, 12-16
Silk: Orange
Body: Dark hare's ear
Rib: Fine gold wire
Wing: Red-brown/cinnamon slip from a partridge tail feather, rolled and tied to lie low over the body
Hackle: Longish red game cock
Outside of Scotland, this pattern would probably more usually be called a Little Red Sedge. Whatever name one gives it, it is a very good taker of fish from May to September. Obviously, it can be used when small brown sedges are active, but it is a particularly good fly when little or nothing is hatching, or as a distracting pattern when fish are 'locked-on' food items that are difficult to imitate.

Red Tag

PLATE 21

Hook: Partridge L3A or Kamasan B170, 14 & 16
Silk: Olive
Tail: A short tuft of red wool (fluorescent red, optional)

PLATE 33
Tana (Waddington), Tadpole (Waddington)
Thunderflash (Rattray)

Body: One strand of bronze peacock herl
Rib: Fine gold wire
Hackle: Dark ginger hen

Known primarily for its ability to take grayling, the Red Tag does catch its fair share of trout. In some regions, particularly Strathclyde, it really is rated as a pattern for brown trout.

Rough Olive (dry)

PLATE 21

Hook: Partridge L3A or E6A, 14 & 16
Silk: Yellow
Tail: Medium olive cock hackle fibres
Body: Olive mole
Rib: Fine gold wire
Hackle: Two badger cock hackles dyed medium olive, or two olive cock hackles with a shorter black cock in between

This well-known pattern is shown 'Clyde-style', in which a noticeably large proportion of the hook shank is occupied by hackle (cf. the hackling style used in other regions). Useful for large olive hatches in the Spring.

Rough Olive (wet)

PLATE 21

Hook: Partridge L3A or E6A, 14 & 16
Silk: Yellow
Tail: Medium olive cock hackle fibres
Body: Olive mole
Rib: Fine gold wire
Hackle: One badger hen dyed olive, or medium olive hen with a shorter black hen hackle behind

A very popular fly on the rivers of the Grampian area, the wet version of the Rough Olive is used in the early part of the season to represent large dark olive nymphs ascending to hatch.

Sam Slick

PLATE 21

Hook: Partridge L2A or Drennan Wet Fly Supreme, 12 & 14

Silk: Brown
Tail: Slim bunch of golden pheasant tippet fibres
Body: Rear third – yellow floss; remainder – dark hare's ear
Rib: Fine oval gold
Hackle: Brown partridge
Wing: Speckled partridge tail

This fly is recommended for the Tweed and its tributaries. Surprisingly, all works of reference state that it is a loch or even a sea-trout pattern. However, the colours and materials are all shared by other successful river patterns and it isn't far away from a March Brown (wet). A Borders' pattern. They do things differently down there!

Sand Fly [dry] (Willie Miller)

PLATE 21

Hook: Mustad 79073, 14 & 16
Silk: Black
Body: Very lightly dubbed mole fur
Hackle: Brown partridge over a longish black cock hackle

The natural sand fly, or 'gravel bed' (*Hexatoma fuscipennis*), as it is widely known, is an insect with a limited range. It hatches in vast quantities on the Clyde, mostly in May and June. The rise of trout to this insect can be spectacular. As is often the case with such frenetic 'rises', it can be very difficult to interest the fish in artificial imitations. Willie Miller recommends the above dressing as a representation of the adult. The insect is a leggy creature, related to the crane flies and therefore, the imitation should be straggly and unkempt.

NB this is not the same insect as the sand fly sedge (*Rhyacophila dorsalis*).

Sand Fly [wet] (Willie Miller)

PLATE 21

Hook: Mustad 79703, 14 & 16
Silk: Black
Body: Very lightly dubbed mole fur
Wing: Small brown partridge hackle, tied flat and low over body

Hackle: Longish sparse black hen, wound in front of the wing

This dressing is given by its designer as a representation of the drowned gravel bed insect, or one that has become trapped in the surface film.

Sedge (Ron Glass)

PLATE 22

Hook: Partridge E6A or Kamasan B170, 10-14
Silk: Black
Body: Well mixed hare's mask, including guard hairs
Body hackle: Palmered ginger cock
Wing: Fine roe deer hair, well splayed out
Head: Roots of wing (in the manner of the Elk Hair Caddis)
Head hackle: Ginger cock, wound through head

From mid to late summer, sedge hatches can be important on those rivers still supporting enough of these insects to elicit a response from trout. This is the pattern Ron Glass likes for evening work on the Tweed.

It is also worth mentioning that sedge patterns can often work used in a speculative role, even when the naturals are not about. A sedge skated across a quiet pool or glide can often seduce quality brown and sea-trout at the right times – particularly late at night.

Snipe & Purple

PLATE 22

Hook: Partridge L2A, 14-18
Silk: Purple Pearsall's Gossamer
Body: Tying silk
Hackle: Jack snipe under covert feather, sparse

The Snipe & Purple (also known as the Dark Snipe) is one of the best known of all North-country spider patterns. Some authorities maintain that the correct hackle comes from the jack snipe, rather than the common snipe, which has a faint fawnish mottling on the dark feather. The jack snipe is now a protected species, and an

acceptable substitute can be obtained from the common starling.

Reckoned to be indispensable on all Scottish rivers, it seems to be best in the early spring through to May. Fish it in the traditional spider manner and as part of a team. (*see* Black Spider; Partridge & Orange; Plover & Harelug; and Partridge & Yellow)

Spent Red Spinner (Ron Glass)

PLATE 22

Hook: Kamasan B400 or Partridge E6A, 12-16
Silk: Red
Tail: Six ginger cock hackle fibres, divided into two well splayed parts
Body: Seal's fur, or sub., dyed 'red spinner'
Rib: Fine gold wire
Hackle: Blue dun cock

This is an excellent general purpose Red Spinner pattern for use when female olive spinners are drifting downstream after egg laying. Ron Glass likes this pattern for mid-summer work on the Tweed, when the reduced flow means that the river is best treated as if it were a chalk stream.

Stank Hen (Willie Miller)

PLATE 22

Hook: Mustad 9143 or Partridge L2A, 10
Silk: Black, brown or dark olive
Tag: Two turns of flat gold
Body: Bronze peacock herl
Rib: Gold wire
Wing: Waterhen (moorhen) primary or, alternatively, dark 'blae' duck
Hackle: Dark ginger cock or hen, tied in front of the wing

In the Strathclyde region, fly fishers refer to patterns of this type as 'The Big Flee' and they are almost invariably reserved for night use. This fly is almost identical to the Lead-Winged Coachman (well known in the USA, if not in Britain), that I have used to good effect in different circumstances.

PLATE 34
Thunder & Lightning (fully dressed)
Thunder & Lightning (hairwing)
Thvera Blue (variant)
Salscraggie

PLATE 35
Tosh (tube)
Tosh
Tosh (gold bodied variant), Weasel (Rattray)
White Muddler, Whitewing (fully dressed)
Whitewing (Waddington)

Stank Hen is an old Scottish name for the waterhen, or moorhen. (*see* also Crow & Silver; Crow & Black; Duck Tip; and Magpie Tail)

Teal & Black

PLATE 22

Hook: Partridge L3A, 14 & 16
Silk: Black
Body: Tying silk
Rib: Fine silver wire
Wing: Well marked teal, tied low over back
Hackle: Black hen, sparse

A general purpose pattern for early and late in the season on any river, this pattern is generally fished 'down & across'. Ian Glassford, who likes this for the Clyde, tells me that he will replace it with a similarly dressed Teal & Red in the summer months.

Tup's Indispensable (variant)

PLATE 22

Hook: Partridge L3A or Drennan Buzzer, 14-18
Silk: Yellow
Tail: Pale honey-dun cock hackle fibres
Body: A mixture primarily of cream and yellow dubbing, with a trace of crimson added
Hackle: Pale honey-dun cock

This version strays slightly from the original Austin dressing, which specified materials for the body dubbing mixture that are rather hard to obtain. Lemon coloured spaniels are not too thick on the ground, while harvesting the correct shade of wool from the dangly bits of a ram might be regarded a dodgy enterprise.

Even in its emasculated form, the 'Tup' is a very good pattern for high-summer days, when reduced flows and high temperatures can make trout very pernickety, or when pale watery spinners are on the water. Ron Glass, who supplied the pattern for the illustration, advises that the finished fly should look very pale and washed-out: not like some of the brash and colourful commercially tied offerings.

Wee Grey (Franz Grimley)

PLATE 22

Hook: Drennan Buzzer or Partridge E6A, 16
Silk: Black
Body: Black Super Poly dubbing
Hackle: Well marked grizzle cock, preferably from a genetic saddle, palmered but not clipped

Unlike its relative, the Big Grey, the hackle is not clipped underneath and the fly therefore rides higher and more buoyantly. This pattern is better suited to fast, streamy water in which it excels. It fishes best in the late Spring and summer and is very effective on Tweed, Tay, Tummel and Clyde. It has, incidentally, also proved its worth against high-summer, stillwater rainbows.

Wee Silver Nymph (Franz Grimley)

PLATE 22

Hook: Mustad 7780C, 14 & 16
Silk: Black
Underbody: Small, tapered piece of lead, laid over the back/top of hook shank. This helps produce the distinctive hump-backed appearance.
Body: Butting turns of fine oval silver
Hackle: Black hen or starling, two turns only

Grimley says that this unlikely looking offering is his most effective river wet fly, bar none.

The lead underbody is vital, ensuring that the fly gets down to its fishing depth quickly and swims up-side down. If this improves its efficiency, who are we to argue? Franz fishes it singly on a long leader and takes brown trout, grayling and sea-trout with it wherever he goes.

Woven Nymph (Jimmy Fairgrieve)

PLATE 22

Hook: Kamasan B100, 10-14
Underbody: Lead wire
Silk: Yellow or black
Abdomen: Ultra-Lace, woven in various colour combinations

Thorax: Sparse dubbing of SLF to match and/or compliment abdomen colour
Legs: Goose biots to match and/or compliment

There is no room here to describe weaving techniques, but they have been well covered in many modern books on flytying (e.g., Oliver Edwards' *Flytyers Masterclass*, Merlin Unwin Books 1994).

These patterns are designed to be fished deep, at or near the bottom of fast to medium paced runs. They work best in the continental style of 'rolled nymph', which involves relatively short upstream casts and a 'controlled lift' as the flies approach the caster and drift past him downstream. A great proportion of fish are taken on the 'lift'. Jimmy reckons that pattern colour or conformity is not of great importance, but that the method of fishing them and the swimming depth are critical to success. (*see* also Easy Stone Nymph)

Yellow May Dun (Ron Glass)

PLATE 22

Hook: Partridge L3A or E6A, 12-16
Silk: Primrose
Tail: Pale yellow cock hackle fibres
Body: Washed-out yellow dubbing
Rib: Fine gold wire
Wing: Very pale blae
Hackle: Pale yellow cock hackle

Ron Glass tells me that with the changes in Tweed fly populations, the Yellow May Dun has 'gone from being an oddity, ignored by trout, to being a major hatch for much of late May and through June'. He offers the above pattern as a successful imitation of the natural dun. Surprisingly, it is much paler than most other dressings I have come across, but this may have to do with some sort of regional variation in the natural insect, a not uncommon phenomenon. (*see* also Yellow May Dun Emerger; and Yellow May Dun [Willie Miller])

Yellow May Dun (Willie Miller)

PLATE 22

Hook: Mustad 79703 or Partridge L3A, 14
Silk: Yellow
Tail: Yellow cock hackle fibres
Body: Stripped quill from a dyed yellow ostrich herl
Hackle: Dyed yellow cock hackles

I can do no better than quote Willie's notes on this pattern: 'The natural is commonly found on stretches of the Clyde below Lanark, from mid May to end of June and I have had best results with the artificial in the evenings.' (*see* Yellow May Dun Emerger; and Yellow May Dun [Glass])

Yellow May Dun Emerger (Jimmy Fairgrieve)

PLATE 22

Hook: Mustad 80050 BR, 12-16
Silk: Yellow
Body: Soft flue from the base of a yellow hackle, dubbed
Rib: Fine gold wire
Thorax: Dark olive and brown SLF dubbing, 50/50 mix
Plume: Three olive CDC feathers

The yellow may dun (*Heptagenia sulphurea*) is a source of much confusion.

Many anglers state categorically that trout find it inedible. They are wrong. It is also often erroneously called a 'yellow sally', but this name properly applies to certain small stoneflies (Plecoptera), eg *Isoperla grammatica*.

Jimmy Fairgrieve seems to have hit the nail on the head with this clever pattern, as many authorities are convinced that it is the emerging dun stage of this insect that is of primary interest to trout. The hackle-less construction, with the CDC plumes, allows the fly to sit three parts below and one part above the surface, thus mimicking the ecloding insect.

Jimmy advises fishing it singly on a long (12-14 foot) leader and casting to cover individual rising fish.

The Salmon & Sea-Trout Flies

Nothing in God's creation is as perfect as an Atlantic salmon, fresh off the tide. Months later, when the silver has tarnished and they are spending their last efforts in the act of procreation, we still feel intense admiration for these extraordinary fish. It follows, therefore, that the flies used to tempt this wondrous beast are almost mystical creations themselves, reflecting the respect and love that is felt for the King of Fish.

Scotland's part in the history of salmon flies is indelible. The complex built-winged patterns of the 19th century, with such evocative names as Mar Lodge, Jock Scott, Lady of Mertoun, Green Highlander and Childers, are considered the zenith of the flytyer's art. Collections of them are hoarded for their sheer beauty by people who never wish to stand by the riverside or wield a fly rod. That these complex patterns no longer play an active part in today's salmon fishing is an irrelevance. Their place in the history of angling is secure, for many of the complicated techniques developed in that era still impact upon all kinds of fly dressing today and resonate, especially, in many contemporary salmon fly patterns. Scotland's pre-eminent importance in this history is reflected in the number of classic patterns which originate from the 'auld country'.

In the past ninety-odd years, the 'fly' patterns used for practical salmon fishing have evolved considerably. The hair-wing patterns and the articulated flies – Waddingtons and tubes – have made the greatest impact, while shrimp and prawn patterns, long-wing, dibbling and even 'dry' flies are also part of this evolution. The numbers of anglers tying their own flies has increased dramatically in the last few years, while the burgeoning angling press has hugely amplified the flux of information. Doubtless this will all contribute to an even greater rate of innovation and change.

In my research of contemporary patterns, conducted in every region of Scotland, I have noticed that there is a fundamental difference between flies of very recent times and those of the past. Up-to-the-moment patterns increasingly use materials more commonly associated with stillwater trout flies. This must in part be due to the trends in modern flytying that have accompanied the 'stillwater revolution' in trout fishing. Inevitably, many of these trout anglers are eventually drawn to try their skills against Salmo salar. Now trout fishermen have always considered that pattern choice is vital for success. Until lately, few salmon fishermen shared this belief, but things appear to be changing.

The increased use of synthetic materials for wings and bodies has been an important trend in modern salmon patterns. They have brought irrevocable changes to the way we think about luring salmon. Modern salmon patterns are very effective and the use of synthetic materials is no mere

PLATE 36
Willie Gunn (tube)
Willie Gunn (long-wing)
Willie Gunn (Waddington)
Willie Gunn (purple haired variant)
Willie Gunn [Gold] (tube)

passing fashion. To ignore this you would have to have your head buried deep in the sand. The modern salmon 'fly' is brighter and more extrovert. Flytyers and anglers are willing to experiment and there is far less of the rigid conformity to pattern that was seen in the past.

As I have stated elsewhere, the only arbiter of a fly's effectiveness is the fish, not the angler, nor the flytyer. It is commonly held that a 'taking' fish will accept almost any old fly. Personally, I have always been unconvinced by this argument, except in rare circumstances. In the past, when vast numbers of fish ran into our rivers, perhaps pattern choice was less important. Statistically, the sheer numbers of fish meant that some of them were likely to find a particular lure attractive, at any particular time, under reasonable conditions. Moreover, it is quite possible that salmon are more aggressive and competitive when in a large crowd and, therefore, more likely to seize a lure. Hopefully, we may yet see a recovery in the populations of the Atlantic salmon. Sadly, the current reality is that runs, generally, are declining. I am convinced that salmon in isolation, or in small groups, are harder to tempt. I believe that they are far more wary and critical of the lures offered to them.

The days when an angler could take to the river bank with a couple of patterns in various sizes and reasonably expect success may be gone forever. In the face of reduced salmon numbers, today's salmon anglers need to be better equipped than their forefathers. Modern tackle and equipment has helped, but I believe that intelligent use of the best that modern flytying has to offer can also load the dice a little in the angler's favour. I hope that the following pages will provide you with something to boost your expectations and improve your results.

Alistair

PLATE 23

Hook: Doubles & trebles, sizes 6-12
Silk: Black
Body: Flat gold
Rib: Medium oval gold
Wing: Dirty yellow bucktail from the back of a tail, tied all-round on tubes or Waddington shanks; or under and over on doubles and trebles

The flies originating in the far North are poor travellers and though the above pattern, devised by a Mr. Chamberlain of Alness, is very popular in Caithness and Sutherland, it is not much used on rivers outside this region. Donald Sutherland, a gillie for the Suisgill estate on the Helmsdale, fishes this pattern – and little else – throughout the year. In the Spring, it is fished in Waddington or tube format and in the summer, it is often fished greased, or on a riffling hitch.

Berthdee Munro (Cormack & Davies)

PLATE 28

Hook: Doubles, 6-12
Silk: Black
Tag: Fine oval gold
Butt: Yellow floss
Tail: Orange cock fibres or squirrel
Body: Unribbed black floss
Throat: Black cock
Wing: Yellow dyed squirrel, with a few of the throat fibres over

Sometimes, one can look at a new pattern and *know* that it is a guaranteed killer. This is one of those flies. It was devised by a Mrs Cormack and her brother Mr Davies and named after the Cormack's residence in Wales. The above is a phonetic rendering.

I foresee a great future for this pattern. It combines elements of two hugely successful patterns: the Tosh and the Munro Killer.

Bill's Stoat

PLATE 32

Hook: Doubles, sizes 6-12
Silk: Black
Tail: Unbleached squirrel dyed red, not too long
Body: Flat silver
Rib: Silver wire or fine oval
Hackle: Bleached squirrel, dyed blue
Wing: Black dyed squirrel
Head: Red varnish

Bill McLennan is a professional fly dresser, from Elgin, who produces many innovative patterns for the rivers of the Buchan coast. This dressing has that Findhorn/Spey look, where the use of unbleached and dyed squirrel tail is very popular and a bulkier dressing is favoured than elsewhere. He advises that this fly is very effective for fresh fish, just off the tide. It is best as a point fly and useful for sea-trout as well.

Black & Orange

PLATE 23

Style: Tube or Waddington
Silk: Red
Tail: Shortish tuft of orange bucktail or squirrel on hook (optional)
Tag: Two turns flat gold
Body: Black floss
Rib: Medium oval gold
Wing: Sparse bunch of orange Crystal Hair filaments, under hot orange bucktail, under black bucktail

One of the essential Spring patterns for the northern rivers and a year-round offering for southern waters. I prefer to use it on my favoured northern rivers in clear and cold conditions, or immediately after a spate, as it may be a touch inconspicuous in even slightly discoloured water. A variation for discoloured water would have the wing tied in alternating bunches of orange and black bucktail.

PLATE 37
Nameless Shrimp
Yabbie (Bett), Yellow Dolly (Knowles)

PLATE 38
Yellow-Tailed Daddy (dapping), Dry Daddy
Wee Man (dapping)
Dapping Daddy, Detached-Body Daddy

Black & Red

PLATE 23

Style: Tube or Waddington
Silk: Black
Tag: A number of turns of medium oval silver
Body: Black floss
Rib: Medium oval silver
Wing: Red and black bucktail tied in bunches (in Waddington format: black above the shank and red under)

A Spring pattern for the Morayshire rivers, where red is strongly favoured. Doubtless this pattern could find a use on any other river, particularly at the back-end of the season when salmon seem to show a predilection for red. If one dresses this fly with a gold tag and rib and with silver Flashabou incorporated into a *mixed* wing of red and black bucktail, the fly becomes a 'Moody Brag'.

Black & Yellow

PLATE 23

Style: Tube or Waddington
Silk: Black
Body: Black floss
Rib: Silver, either medium oval or flat embossed
Wing: In two equal bunches of yellow and black (in Waddington format, the yellow below the shank and the black above)

Strikingly similar to the Tosh (and often wrongly identified as such), this pattern is more like the standard dressing of Gordon's Fancy, which has identical components but four distinct colour bunches in the wing, as opposed to two.

This is a very popular and effective early Spring pattern for northern rivers, where such runs exist. Elsewhere, it is considered a year-round pattern, where it is fished in a range of sizes and seems to work in all water conditions.

Black Brahan

PLATE 23

Hook: Doubles, sizes 6-12
Silk: Black

Tag: A number of turns of oval silver
Tail: Yellow squirrel or fine bucktail (optional)
Body: Red Lurex
Rib: Oval or flat embossed silver
Hackle: Black
Wing: Black dyed squirrel or fine bucktail

During my research for this book, the most noticeable trend in modern salmon patterns was the use of tinsel bodies. For the greater part of the 20th century, black floss bodies, finely ribbed with tinsel, were the predominant fashion: anything else was likely to be regarded as a flight of fancy. In the past few years, however, tinsel bodies have been sweeping the board.

This pattern is immensely popular, particularly north of the Highland Boundary Line and is regarded by some as a 'must' for grilse and even occasional sea-trout, when the rivers are down at summer levels. Alan Donaldson supplied the pattern for the illustration and advises that it is a fly whose popularity fluctuates: some years it is almost indispensable, while in others it is virtually ignored!

A variation using green Lurex is often referred to as a Green Brahan, but I have listed it here as an Emerald Stoat, which seems a more widespread and popular name.

Black Doctor (fully dressed)

PLATE 23

Hook: Singles, Doubles or trebles, sizes 4-10
Silk: Black or red
Tag: Fine oval silver and yellow floss
Tail: GP crest with Indian crow sub. over
Butt: Scarlet wool
Body: Black floss
Rib: Oval silver
Hackle: Claret cock
Throat: Guinea fowl
Wing: G.P. tippet in strips; sections of red, blue and yellow goose; pintail/teal; light mottled peacock and dark mottled turkey; wood duck and bronze mallard
Topping: G.P. crest feather
Head: Red

The use of fully-dressed salmon flies on large single hooks has dwindled, but they still enjoy popularity in Northern Europe, particularly in Norway. Some anglers who use them over there feel impelled to give them a wetting on this side of the North Sea and the Black Doctor is one that is useful for Scottish salmon.

The dressing of these complex old patterns demands the highest skills and any detailed description of the processes involved falls outwith the scope of this book. However, any competent dresser should have little difficulty in interpreting the traditional patterns as simplified hairwing versions. I am sure that the fish would find them just as acceptable. (see also Blue Charm; Jeannie; Logie; Mar Lodge; Salscraggie; Thunder & Lightning; and Whitewing)

Black, Silver & Yellow
[Waddington] (Robert Rattray)

PLATE 24

Style: Waddington
Silk: Black
Body: Flat silver
Rib: Fine oval silver
Hackle: Yellow cock hackle, set under shank
Underwing: Sparse bunch of pearl Crystal Hair
Overwing: Black bucktail

This strongly resembles the very popular, Kenny's Killer. Robert recommends this as a reliable year-round pattern for all migratory fish. Interestingly, he states that in large sizes it makes a particularly effective late evening pattern for Spring fish – a valuable weapon to have in one's armoury.

Blue Charm

PLATE 23

Hook: Singles & doubles, sizes 6-10
Silk: Black
Tag: Fine oval silver
Tail: Yellow cock hackle fibres, or G.P. crest
Butt: Yellow floss over the hackle fibre roots, followed by black ostrich herl
Body: Black floss
Rib: Oval silver
Throat: Pale blue cock

Wing: Bronze mallard, with a thin strip of barred teal over
Head: Black

The Blue Charm is one of only a handful of feather-winged salmon flies to retain its popularity. It is still widely used as a summer pattern on all rivers, but it is most strongly associated with the Dee. This little fly clearly has all the hallmarks of a fine sea-trout pattern. (see also Black Doctor; Jeannie; Logie; Mar Lodge Salscraggie; Thunder & Lightning; and Whitewing)

Blue Elver

PLATE 24

Hook: Singles or doubles, 8 & 10
Silk: Red
Body: Black floss or silver
Rib: Flat silver
Hackle: Cobalt blue vulturine guinea fowl feather, or long-fibred light blue hen hackle, wound as a collar in front of the wings
Cheeks: Jungle cock (optional)
Wing: Two long striped vulturine guinea fowl neck feathers, tied in 'streamer' fashion along either side of the hook
Head: Red

This most interesting pattern was devised by Arthur Ransome. He designed it to imitate the elver of the common eel, which he believed was part of the diet of Atlantic salmon. We now know that it is unlikely that elvers form any part of the salmon's staple food.

Nonetheless, this pattern is effective primarily for extremely fresh fish, just off the tide. Surprisingly, it is also popular as a loch fly in the Western Isles.

Bourrach

PLATE 23

Hook: Doubles & trebles, 6-12
Silk: Black
Tail: Dyed blue hackle point
Tag: Oval silver
Body: Flat silver

Rib: Oval silver
Hackle: Dyed blue cock, longish
Wing: Yellow bucktail (squirrel in small sizes), twice the body length

The literal translation of the name from the Gaelic would be 'mess' or, perhaps, untidiness'. I can think of many patterns which deserve the name more, as this is quite a neat and pretty little fly. It works very well on grilse and summer salmon in fast, streamy water. I have seen it take Spring salmon from the Thurso, but on its home waters of the Spey, it is really only regarded as a summer pattern for streamy runs. (see also Orange Bourrach)

Bourrach, Orange

PLATE 29

Hook: Doubles, 6-12
Silk: Black
Tag: Fine oval silver
Tail: Yellow hackle fibres
Body: Flat silver
Rib: Oval silver
Throat: Blue hackle fibres
Wing: Orange bucktail, or dyed squirrel (bleached), tied long
Head: Black

This modern variation seems to be becoming more popular than the original Bourrach. It is a fly that is well-respected by certain Spey gillies for grilse and summer salmon work.

It reminds me of Keyser's Findhorn Fly, although it lacks the characteristic 'tear-drop' outline of Peter's patterns.

Brown Turkey

PLATE 23

Hook: Singles & doubles, 6-10
Silk: Black
Tag: Oval gold
Tail: G.P. crest, with tippet fibres over
Body: In three parts: rear – yellow seal's fur; mid – red seal's fur; front – black seal's fur (or subs.)
Rib: Oval gold

Hackle: Black cock or hen
Wing: Brown mottled turkey, or peacock quill

This venerable pattern undoubtedly pre-dates the garish butterfly imitations of the 19th century. It has close affinities with the earliest recorded salmon patterns, which favoured drab rather than gaudy materials. The Brown Turkey is still a popular fly used on the Ayrshire rivers of Ayr and Girvan. It is also used on Loch Lomond for salmon and sea-trout. (see also Grey Turkey)

Butcher, Kingfisher (wee double)

PLATE 9

See page 13 in the section on Loch Flies.
This old pattern is popular for river sea-trout in the West and I know of a few anglers who like to use it in the estuaries of East Coast rivers.

Chameleon (Robert Rattray)

PLATE 24

Style: Waddington (one to three inches)
Silk: Red
Body: Rear half – yellow floss; front half – black floss
Rib: Oval gold (occasionally flat gold)
Wing: Black, yellow and red bucktail, mixed, with a few strands of pearl Crystal Hair over
Head: Red

Robert advises that this is an excellent general pattern for use throughout Scotland and in all types of water: clear or peat-stained, high or low. It combines the most popular traditional colours with a bit of modern 'flash'. I can't see how it could fail!

Collie Dog

PLATE 24

Style: Tube (plastic or aluminium, rarely brass)
Silk: Black
Hackle: Sparse black cock (optional)
Wing: Long black goat, calf tail, or monkey hair, with a few strands of pearl Crystal Hair over (optional)

Of all the recent additions to the range of salmon flies, this is, I believe, the most exciting and innovative. A properly dressed and fished Collie is the epitome of suggestion and movement. Its ability to 'move' salmon when all else has failed is phenomenal. Even Spring salmon in cold water will come up to it like the most naive and over-enthusiastic trout. Some authorities recommend that it is fished in streamy water, but I have witnessed it taking fish from the slowest of slow water. It can also be an excellent fly for sea-trout when skated across the tail of a pool on a floating line and the fish are in confident mood. Small versions 'dibbled' in the fast water at the head of pools can provide welcome sport in the evenings during dry, low water periods.

Collie Dog (Alan Donaldson)

PLATE 24

Style: Plastic tube
Body: Rear third – left undressed; mid third – lilac Lurex; front third – flat copper Lurex (after ribbing, varnish the body to protect the fragile Lurex)
Rib: Silver wire over the Lurex body
Wing: Two sum bunches of goat hair, with a few strands of fluorescent pink 'Twinkle' sandwiched in between
Head: Black

Alan Donaldson, of the Amat Estate on the Sutherland Carron, is a master of the Collie Dog. His catch rate with this variant pattern is enviable. He tells me that, hand-lined smartly cross a pool on a slow-sinking or intermediate line, the Collie Dog is the best late Spring pattern available on the Sutherland rivers. He also maintains that anyone who has difficulty moving fish to this pattern is simply fishing it *too* slowly. Surely this is quality advice and simple enough to follow?

Comet

PLATE 24

Style: Tube or Waddington
Silk: Black
Tail: Yellow bucktail, tied right around the tube or shank and extending just beyond the hook-bend
Body: In two parts: rear – red floss; front – black floss
Mid 'Wing': Red bucktail, tied right around the shank/tube and cloaking the 'tail'
Rib: Oval gold
Forewing: Black bucktail, cloaking both the mid 'wing' and the tail.
Head: Black

The Comet is a heavily dressed tube or Waddington, strongly associated with the Tweed and its tributaries. It is remarkably similar in construction and colouring to that mainstay of Northern early Spring fishing, the Tadpole. It is normally dressed on large brass tubes and is popular for the autumn runs.

Dark Mackerel

PLATE 4

See page 27 in the section on Loch Flies.

The Dark Mackerel is an effective salmon and sea-trout fly on rivers and lochs, particularly in the North and West. The efficiency of claret flies is not perhaps widely appreciated. Charlie McLaren, icon of Scottish salmon and sea-trout fishers, had a self-imposed ban on claret flies when after river sea-trout, because he believed that they attracted *too many* salmon.

Delphi Silver

PLATE 8

Hook: Longshank singles & doubles, 8-12
Silk: Black
Tail: Two jungle cock 'eyes', back to back, tied in a vertical plane
Body: Flat silver, in two equal parts
Rib: Fine oval silver
Mid-hackle: Black cock or hen
Head hackle: Longer black cock or hen

Named after the famous Delphi fishery, in Ireland's Co. Mayo, the Delphi Silver's reputation has spread to wherever sea-trout are fished for. Black and silver flies are a indispensable for sea-trout and although this is primarily a lough fly in its country of origin, it is very popular in the West of Scotland for river work. Double hackled patterns, such as this, make good night-time flies and are useful in the transition period when anglers are contemplating changing from a floating to a sunk line: what Hugh Falkus called 'half time'.

Dunkeld

PLATE 5

See p. ??? in the section on Loch Flies

The Dunkeld is a relatively popular sea-trout pattern for river work, good in clearing water during daylight hours. A fully-dressed salmon pattern exists which was the pre-cursor of this trout fly, but it is rarely, if ever, used nowadays. There is a similar steelhead pattern of North American/New Zealand origin, popularized by Zane Grey, referred to as a Golden Demon, which has a strong if declining reputation for Thurso salmon. The original was indistinguishable from our Dunkeld, but the favoured dressing now has brown squirrel wing.

Emerald Stoat

PLATE 32

Hook: Doubles & trebles, 6-12
Silk: Black
Tag: Fine oval silver
Tail: Yellow cock fibres with sparse addition of lime Crystal Hair
Body: Green Lurex (or pearl Mylar over black silk)
Rib: Oval silver followed, by fluorescent lime green floss (Glo-Brite, no.12)
Hackle: Black cock
Wing: Black squirrel
Head: Black

Sometime referred to as a Green Brahan, this is a very popular pattern for summer salmon and grilse in the North and East of Scotland. It is at its best fished in the smallest sizes, during periods of restricted flow.

Executioner

PLATE 25

Hook: Doubles & trebles, 8-12
Silk: Red
Tag: Fine oval silver
Tail: Yellow cock
Body: First quarter: Glo-Brite no.4 fluorescent floss; remainder: flat silver
Rib: Fine oval silver
Hackle: Black cock
Wing: Black squirrel
Cheeks: Jungle cock
Head: Red (use either fluorescent floss and clear varnish, or fluorescent red head enamel)

Although this pattern is popular and widely used in all the regions of Scotland, it is not widely publicised. I first saw a dressing for this fly in a *Trout & Salmon* article by Alastair Gowans. As he stated there, it is an excellent grilse pattern, but it is also a very useful tool when salmon are the main target, with the chance of a sea-trout.

Fast Eddie

PLATE 25

Hook: Doubles & trebles, 6-12
Silk: Red
Tag: Two turns flat gold
Body: Flat gold
Rib: Fine or medium oval gold (not over the tag)
Hackle: Hot orange hackle fibres or squirrel
Wing: Green hair over yellow, squirrel or bucktail
Head: Red

I devised the original following a conversation with Eddie McCarthy, River Superintendant on the Thurso. He insisted that the best colours on his river were gold, orange, yellow and green and this is was what I came up with. It has proved itself, in this format, as a late Spring and summer fly for this river and I feel some pride that it is now a firm favourite there.

Like claret, green, has never been a very popular colour for Scottish salmon flies, but this state of affairs is changing slowly.

Fast Eddie (Waddington)

PLATE 25

Hook: Doubles & trebles, 6-12
Silk: Red
Tail: Fine yellow bucktail, bound to the treble with Glo-Brite no.5 fluorescent floss, varnished
Body: Flat gold
Rib: Oval gold
Wing: Bucktail: yellow, under orange, under green
Head: Red

Findhorn Killer

PLATE 25

Style: Tube or Waddington
Body: Black floss
Rib: Oval gold
Wing: Bucktail: yellow under orange
Head: Black

I have little difficulty believing that this is a favourite on the Findhorn, where orange is such strong medicine. Bill McLennan, a professional tyer from the region, supplied this and other Buchan Coast patterns.

It has strong similarities to a Garry Dog.

Garry Dog

PLATE 25

Hook: Doubles & trebles, 6-12, also tubes & Waddingtons
Silk: Black
Tag: Fine oval silver
Butt: Yellow floss
Tail: G.P. crest
Body: Black floss
Rib: Oval silver
Throat: Dyed dark blue guinea fowl
Wing: Yellow hair over red: bucktail in large sizes; dyed bleached squirrel for smaller dressings
Head: Black

One of Scotland's most popular flies, the Garry Dog is rated in all the regions but particularly in those where rivers carry a peat stain. In tube format, the blue guinea fowl is frequently omitted and the tail is always dispensed with. The Waddington and tube versions are probably the North's most popular Spring flies. (see also Garry Dog (golden); Northern Dog; and Silver Garry)

Garry Dog (golden)

PLATE 25

Hook: Tube or Waddington
Silk: Black
Body: Flat gold
Rib: Embossed silver
Wing: Red bucktail under red Crystal Hair, under yellow bucktail
Head: Black

Alan Donaldson, from the Sutherland Carron, supplied this pattern and states that it is a very good heavy water Spring fly. It will work in a variety of sizes throughout the year, given adequate flow of water.

Tinsel bodied variants of standard, time-served patterns are becoming increasingly important and popular. This is in direct contrast to the aversion previous generations of salmon anglers seemed to have had towards tinsel bodied flies. It is just a thought, but has the advent of light-weight, non-tarnishing Mylar tinsels had something to do with this change in opinion? (see also Gold Munro; Silver Garry; and Willie Gunn [Gold])

General Practitioner (G.P.)

PLATE 25

Hook: Almost always on Esmond Drury trebles, or similar, 6-12
Silk: Red
Long Whiskers: A sparse bunch of long orange bucktail fibres from base of tail
Shrimp's Head: Two Golden Pheasant red body feathers, concave to concave
Body: Orange seal's fur
Rib: Oval gold
Hackle: Orange cock, palmered
Wing/Back: Two or three whole G.P. tippet feathers, tied in stages up the body, with a G.P. red body feather over all

Esmond Drury's prawn fly can be alarmingly successful at times (usually in the hands of others), but it can also disappoint. There is no such thing as a fail-me-never fly! As a floating line fly for summer months and low levels, it has a longer and better track record than most. Some circumspection should be used at the end of the season when it seems to drive 'tartan' cock fish absolutely crazy. (see also Oykel G.P.)

Ghost

PLATE 25

Hook: Low water singles, 10 & 12
Silk: Yellow
Tag: Flat silver
Butt: Fine oval silver
Tail: G.P. crest
Body: White chenille
Rib: Fine oval silver
Hackle: White cock or hen
Wing: White goose

All-white patterns have always been popular for night fishing for sea-trout. This one hails from the River Ewe. David Mateer, who supplied the pattern, says that it is indispensable on the Ewe and always seems to select out a better class of fish. It has also taken salmon from this river. (see also White Muddler)

Glow Fly (dibbler)

PLATE 25

Hook: Doubles or trebles, 8 & 10
Silk: Black
Tag: Fine oval silver
Tail: Fibres of magenta cock; two strands pink Crystal Hair, plus a few fibres of G.P. red body feather (not over long)
Body: Flat lilac Lurex
Body **Hackle:** Magenta cock
Rib: Fine oval silver
Collar hackle: Orange cock
Head: Black

Salmon in Northern rivers are very susceptible to 'dibbled' flies during periods when they are lying well up in the necks of pools. They will, of course,

take dibbled and skated patterns when spread out through the pools, but are less easily located and worked over. To see the open-mouthed head of a fish appear and engulf a well presented fly in the rushing waters is one of the great thrills of salmon fishing.

This pattern is popular and effective for this style of fishing, as its bright colours help the angler locate his fly in the dim light of late evening when this technique is at its most productive. (see also Munro and Sam's Badger)

Glow Fly (Tube)

PLATE 25

Hook: Tube or Waddington
Silk: Black
Body: Veniard's Colour Glow Pearl Mylar piping – red
Wing: Orange bucktail, under sparse pink Crystal Hair, under magenta bucktail

This pattern is referred to by some as the Barbara Cartland, for obvious reasons. It is another one from Alan Donaldson in the North East. He says that despite extreme suspicion and reticence from the anglers, this fly has developed a strong band of faithful fans who fish it all year round, given enough water. It works very well on the Carron and Upper Shin.

Garish patterns of this type often work best in very bright conditions in the Spring, or in poor light or coloured water at other times of the year. This is one of those flies that is worth trying when all else has failed.

Gold Munro (Alan Donaldson)

PLATE 28

Hook: Doubles & trebles, 6-12
Silk: Black
Tag: Fine oval gold
Tail: Orange hackle fibres
Body: Flat gold
Rib: Oval gold
Throat: Orange cock with fibres of blue guinea fowl over
Wing: Grey squirrel dyed yellow
Head: Black

One of the prettiest and most effective of the modern pattern variants, the Gold Munro reinforces my belief that there is a marked swing in favour of tinsel bodied salmon flies in Scotland.

Alan says that it is extremely popular on his home river, the Carron, but it has taken fish for him all over Scotland. (*see also* Munro, Berthdee; Munro Killer; Munro Killer [dibbler]; and Munro Killer [longtail])

Gordon's Fancy (variant)

PLATE 26

Hook: Tube or Waddington, large sizes
Silk: Black
Body: Gold Mylar piping
Wing: In two bunches – black & yellow. On a Waddington, the black should be above the shank and the yellow below

The accepted dressing of Gordon's Fancy has a silver ribbed black floss body, with a quartered wing of black and yellow, but the pattern given here is the one I am more familiar with. It is a very popular Spring fly in the North. (*see also* Black & Yellow Tube; and Tosh)

Green Brahan *see* Emerald Stoat

Green Highlander

PLATE 26

Hook: Doubles & trebles, 6-12
Silk: Black
Tag: Fine oval silver
Body: In two parts: rear third – yellow floss; front two-thirds – green floss
Rib: Oval silver
Throat: Green & yellow cock hackle fibres, mixed
Wing: orange hackle fibres under sparse fluorescent. lime Twinkle, under brown squirrel
Head: Black

This pattern refuses to die. Originally one of the built-wing beauties of the late 19th century , it has evolved into a hairwing that still sees some use. The Green Highlander is notable, given the almost total Scottish refusal to accept green salmon flies. Its popularity is restricted to the peat-stained

waters of the North, which is surprising since it is regarded as an essential pattern in Norway where rivers tend to run gin-clear! (*see also* Fast Eddie)

Green Highlander [tube]
(Alan Donaldson)

PLATE 26

Silk: Black
Body: Green Colour Glow pearl Mylar piping
Wing: Green bucktail under sparse strands of lime Crystal Hair, under yellow then orange bucktail

This is Alan Donaldson's treatment of the venerable old pattern, turning it into a popular and reliable Spring pattern for Northern rivers. The use of Glow Colour Mylar tubing, Crystal Hair and other modern synthetics, is a hallmark of Alan's Spring tubes. This is a modern trend which is being followed almost everywhere in the country. (*see also* Fast Eddie [Waddington])

Green Mamba [Waddington]
(Robert Rattray)

PLATE 26

Silk: Black
Body: Three layers of pearl Lurex
Rib: Medium oval silver
Underwing: Silver Flashabou
Overwing: Quartered – yellow above and below; green at the sides
Head: Black

In my comments regarding the Green Highlander I drew attention to the fact that green flies have some popularity in the peat-stained waters of the North of Scotland, whereas they were greatly favoured for the gin-clear waters of Norway. Robert tells me that the above is a very good early season fly in rivers that run clear, and are *not* peat-stained. It does make me wonder what real justification there has been for the harsh treatment of green salmon flies by the majority of Scottish anglers.

Green Peter

PLATE 7

See page 37 in the section on Loch Flies.

Given as a sea-trout pattern for the Beauly by Willie Mathieson, this Irish lough fly is an unlikely choice for river work at first view. However, in its home country, patterns adapted for use outside their originally intended duties are important in certain areas for river fish. The Green Peter may well be a river sea-trout pattern worthy of more attention.

Greg's Glory [Waddington] (Willie Mathieson)

PLATE 26

Style: Waddington
Silk: Black
Body: Black floss
Rib: Flat embossed silver
Wing: Black bucktail
Cheeks: Jungle cock (large & prominent)

Willie Mathieson is a prolific tyer and produces specific patterns for the Beauly, the river on which he gillies. The above is a very successful sea-trout pattern best employed skated across the surface of pools in the last of the evening light. Willie tells me that it is good for salmon and grilse.

Grey Turkey (Davie McPhail)

PLATE 26

Hook: Singles & doubles, 6-10
Silk: Black
Tag: Silver
Tail: G.P. crest with tippet over
Body: In three parts: rear – yellow; mid – red; front – black
Rib: Oval silver
Hackle: Badger cock or hen
Wing: Grey squirrel

An up-dated version of the Brown Turkey, by Davie McPhail, this lighter, hair-wing variant is more acceptable to modern anglers and flytyers. The

traditional feather slip wing is fast falling from general favour in salmon flies: at least for those that are actually 'used', as opposed to put in frames for hanging on the wall.

Hairy Mary

PLATE 26

Hook: Singles & doubles, 6-12
Silk: Black
Tag: Fine oval gold
Tail: G.P. crest, or yellow hackle fibres (in big sizes)
Body: Black floss
Rib: Oval gold
Throat: Mid-blue cock
Wing: Barred brown squirrel, or fine brown bucktail in large sizes
Head: Black

The Hairy Mary was one of the first hair-wing patterns, but it is still an important and much-used pattern all over Scotland. It is mainly a summer pattern, in which context it is dressed slim and sparse. It is also often used as a dropper pattern in larger sizes for late Spring fish, in northern rivers.

Invicta, Silver

PLATE 8

See page 48 in the section on Loch Flies.

The Silver Invicta is a good river pattern for sea-trout and is recommended for the Beauly by Willie Mathieson. Many experienced anglers like it for use in the brackish water of estuaries and sea lochs.

Jamie's Fancy [Waddington] (Willie Mathieson)

PLATE 26

Silk: Black
Body: Black floss
Rib: Flat embossed silver
Wing: Yellow bucktail, under sky blue, under black
Head: Black

This variation on the Willie Gunn theme was suggested to the originator by his eldest son, who thought that replacing orange bucktail with blue would produce a more attractive fly. It turned out to be a pretty good hunch: in the 1995 season, this pattern took 35 fish from February to May on the lower Beauly. What stronger recommendation is required?

Jeannie

PLATE 27

Hook: Singles & doubles, 6-10
Silk: Black
Tag: Fine oval silver
Tail: G.P. crest, or yellow hackle fibres in large sizes
Body: In two parts: rear – yellow floss; fore – black floss
Rib: Oval silver
Throat: Black cock
Wing: Brown squirrel
Cheeks: Jungle cock
Head: Black

The original Jeannie had a wing of bronze mallard but, that aside, little has changed for this pattern. It retains much of its popularity as a late spring to summer fly for reduced flows.

Kenny's Killer

PLATE 27

Hook: Singles, doubles & trebles, 8-12
Silk: Black
Tag: Fine oval silver
Tail: G.P. tippet or yellow hackle fibres
Body: Flat silver
Rib: Oval silver
Hackle: Yellow cock
Wing: Black squirrel

This is one of the best grilse and sea-trout patterns and is noticeably at its most popular in areas where runs of these fish coincide. There is a gold variation listed by Buckland and Oglesby in *A Guide to Salmon Flies* and attributed to Crawford Little, but it is so similar to that well known trout pattern, the Goldie (*see* Loch Flies section), that

to refer to it as a Gold Kenny's Killer is verging on the spurious.

Kerry Blue *(Harry Davis)*

PLATE 27

Hook: Low-water doubles, 4-10
Silk: Black
Tag: Flat silver
Tail: G.P. crest
Butt: Black ostrich herl
Body: In two halves: rear.– blue Lurex; front – red Lurex
Rib: Oval silver
Hackle: Fine black bucktail, extending to hook points
Wing: Black squirrel, twice body length
Topping: G.P. crest over the wing
Head: Black

Another very popular pattern, which shows the increasing use of modern synthetic materials and/or tinsel bodies.

Devised by Harry Davis – formerly of Glasgow Rangers F.C. – for use on the River Ewe, it is now a standard for that system. A simplified dressing, given to me by David Mateer, lacks the tail, butt and topping, but none of the appeal. A very pretty fly for summer salmon, grilse and sea-trout. (*see* also Lady Ewe

Kylie *(Alan Donaldson)*

PLATE 27

Hook: Doubles, 6-12
Silk: Black
Tag: Silver wire
Tail: Longish orange hackle fibres
Butt: Black floss
Body: In two halves: rear – flat copper: fore – black floss
Rib: Silver wire over copper only
Hackle: Orange cock
Throat: Sparse dyed blue guinea fowl
Wing: Orange hackle fibres under black squirrel

I have rarely been so impressed with the strike rate of a fly pattern as I have with the Kylie. Alan has certainly found an effective colour combination for peat-stained rivers. Alan's own catches with his Kylie patterns only serve to underline their effectiveness – 102 fish in three seasons. Beat that!

The name has nothing to do with Australian 'soap' stars, past or present, but refers to the Kyle of Sutherland, the estuary that unloads the waters of the Carron, Oykel, Shin and Cassley into the North Sea. (see also Kylie (Waddington & tube); and Kylie Shrimp)

Kylie (Waddington & Tube)

PLATE 27

Tag: Flat silver
Butt: Black floss
Body: In two halves: rear – flat copper: fore – black floss
Rib: Silver wire over the copper half only
Wing: Fluorescent. orange Twinkle under orange bucktail, with sparse bunches of black bucktail above and below
Hackle: Sparse dyed blue guinea fowl (Waddington only)
Head: Black

This is Alan Donaldson's version of his fly for Spring, back-end and heavy water fishing.

Kylie Shrimp (Alan Donaldson)

PLATE 27

Hook: Doubles & trebles, 6-12
Silk: Black
Tag: Silver wire
Tail: A few orange bucktail fibres, plus sparse strands of orange Twinkle, with a shortish G.P. red body feather over, *not* wound.
Butt: Black floss
Body: In two halves: rear – flat copper: fore – black floss
Rib: Silver wire over the copper half only
Mid-hackle: orange cock
Head hackle: orange cock tied false, above & below, plus a few fibres of dyed blue guinea fowl

Wing: Pair of jungle cock eyes, back to back and long
Overwing: Bunch of orange cock hackle fibres
Head: Red varnish

If you have a winning combination, why not stick with it? The shrimp version of the Kylie is a very successful pattern in the tidal waters of the Kyle of Sutherland. It has also established a sound reputation as a river pattern throughout the North.

One evening in August 1996, Alan and I fished the Long Pool on the Amat Beat of the Carron, using this pattern. It hooked eight fish for us in two and a half hours. Alan was not surprised, but I was virtually speechless: an uncommon experience for me! Tie some up and carry them everywhere.

Lady Ewe (Dave Mateer)

PLATE 27

Hook: Low water doubles, 4-10
Silk: Black
Tag: Flat silver
Tail: G.P. crest
Body: In two parts: rear – blue Lurex; fore – silver Lurex
Rib: Fine oval silver
Throat: Dyed blue guinea fowl
Wing: Twice body length, white Twinkle under black bucktail
Head: Black

Influenced by Harry Davis's Kerry Blue, this was designed for the salmon and sea-trout runs of the Ewe. It looks a pretty fly which should travel well. Dave has a shrimp variation which replaces the G.P. crest tail with black bucktail.
NB Almost all recent salmon flies have tinsel bodies and synthetic winging materials. These patterns seem to be springing up spontaneously from tyers who have little or no contact with each other. This would seem to indicate that the motivating force is purely the success of this style of pattern.

Logie (featherwing)

PLATE 27

Hook: Singles & doubles, 4-12
Silk: Yellow
Tag: Fine oval silver
Tail: G.P. crest
Body: In two parts: first two fifths – yellow floss; remainder – red floss
Rib: Oval silver
Throat: Light blue cock
Wing: Yellow swan or goose veiled with bronze mallard
Head: Black

The Logie is another of a small band of feather-wing salmon patterns which retain their popularity. It still sees a surprising amount of use, particularly in the reduced flows of high summer. A Dee pattern devised by W. Brown, it is sometimes varied by the use of claret instead of red in the body and the addition of jungle cock 'eyes'. It is easily adapted to a hair-wing, using brown squirrel tail, with a little yellow underneath.

The fly in the illustration was tied for me by Jim Smail, a boatman on the Lower Floors beat on the Duke of Roxburgh's Tweed estate.

Loser (Niki Griffith)

PLATE 28

Hook: Doubles, 6-12
Silk: Black
Tail: G.P. yellow body feather fibres
Body: Flat copper
Rib: Oval gold
Throat: Hot orange cock, with a G.P. crest over
Wing: Hot orange hackle fibres, under brown hackle fibres, under a long G.P. crest/topping
Head: Black

Niki Griffith, whose family owns the Braelangwell Estate, tied this pattern many years ago and has fished it successfully on the Sutherland rivers. It remained un-named until May 1996 when, whilst playing a fish in the Miller's Pool, she tripped and dropped her rod. Whilst attempting to retrieve the rod, she plunged head-long into the river. Upon finally retrieving herself and her equipment, she discovered – not surprisingly – that the fish was gone. It is sad and distressing tale, but at least the fly she was using had at last been given a name.

The Loser is not unlike a Copper King, an obscure pattern that some like for northern rivers.

McCallan

PLATE 28

Hook: Doubles, 6-12
Silk: Black
Tag: Oval gold
Tail: G.P. crest
Butt: Black ostrich herl
Body: Yellow floss
Rib: Oval gold
Throat: Dark blue or cobalt cock hackle fibres
Wing: Unbleached grey squirrel, dyed yellow
Cheeks: Jungle cock
Head: Black

This is a modern pattern with a traditional look. It has become a very popular summer pattern on the Morayshire rivers, Findhorn and Spey and takes its name from a fine single malt whisky distilled in the region.

Megan

PLATE 28

Hook: Doubles, 6-12
Silk: Black
Tag: Silver wire
Tail: G.P. crest or yellow hackle fibres
Body: Black floss
Rib: Oval silver
Throat: Blue hackle fibres
Wing: Black bucktail or squirrel in small sizes
Overwing: Blue hackle fibres

Although not widely used, I have included this pattern as a tribute to Megan Boyd, of Kintradwell, that famous dresser of salmon flies.

Similar in construction and coloration to the Sweep, I should imagine that it makes a more than adequate hair-wing alternative.

Mini-Tubes

PLATE 29

Dressings: usually of standard patterns, such as Stoat's Tail, Ally's Shrimp, Willie Gunn, etc., adapted and simplified to suit the minuscule size.

I must admit to never having fished such offerings, but Davie McPhail of Ayr was good enough to supply me with a selection, which he uses on his Ayrshire rivers. I was once asked to tie some extremely simple Stoat's Tail mini-tubes for a friend a few years back. He used them to good effect during extremely low water conditions on the Halladale. If I have learned anything about these little scraps of flies, it is that it is almost impossible to incorporate *too little* material.

Davie, on the other hand, has dressed these patterns quite heavily and to stop them from 'skating' has tied them on tiny brass and copper tubes. Interesting! He tells me that he likes to fish them on a floating line and strip them quite fast.

Muddler, Minnow

PLATE 11

See page 63 in the section on Loch Flies

Muddlers are often pressed into service as functional 'surface lures' for sea-trout fishing at night. For this purpose, the dressing should have plenty of deer hair in the head and be treated with floatant. It is also useful for salmon in the low-water, high temperature conditions of Summer, when it can replace the Yellow Doggy as a last ditch offering. Muddler headed patterns are growing in popularity for general purpose use on small spate rivers. In the far North, for example, the Halladale sees quite a few of its summer fish caught on this type of fly.

Muddler, White

PLATE 35

Hook: Singles & doubles, 6-10
Silk: Fluorescent white
Tail: Slim slips of white feather, swan or goose
Body: Flat silver
Rib: Fine oval silver
Wing: Paired slips of white feather, swan or goose
Head: White deer hair, from the rump of the animal, spun and clipped in Muddler style, retaining some fine points as a collar, or false hackle

The White Muddler is a very useful floating line pattern for sea-trout in the earliest part of the evening session. Greased-up and skated across the runs, it will occasionally provoke a positive response from sulky salmon that are getting a bit stale and aren't showing much interest in more usual offerings.

Munro Killer

PLATE 28

Hook: Doubles & trebles, 4-12
Silk: Black
Tag: Fine oval gold
Tail: Optional, but in the North – orange hackle fibres
Body: Black floss
Rib: Oval gold
Throat: Orange cock with blue guinea fowl over
Wing: Unbleached grey squirrel dyed yellow

The Munro Killer is a strong candidate for the title of 'Best Scottish Salmon Fly'. Variations abound, but this dressing, using unbleached grey barred squirrel tail, dyed yellow, is regarded by many as being superior to the alternative, with a wing of yellow dyed *bleached* squirrel under black. Jim Mitchell, of Findhorn, once told me that the very first version had a wing – brown bucktail dyed yellow. He should know, as he once owned the shop in which the first Munro was tied.

Most fishers regard the Munro as a summer and autumn pattern, but I have had good results with it as a size 8 dropper fly as early as March on the Thurso. In such circumstances, I like to fish it above a Northern Dog or a Silver Garry, which combination gives the fish a choice of colour and shade.

Southern dressed Munros tend to be darker and dispense with the tail and under-hackle of orange hackle fibres. Again, this reflects the tendency to find brighter and brasher dressings the further north one travels. A great fly which many would regard as indispensable.

Munro Killer (dibbler)

PLATE 28

Hook: Doubles, 8 & 10
Tail: Orange cock hackle point
Body: Black seal's fur
Rib: Oval gold
Wing: Unbleached grey squirrel dyed yellow
Collar hackle: Hot orange hen, tied full and long
Throat: Cobalt blue guinea fowl, tied in front of the hackle but under the shank only
Head: Black

Dressed quite heavily to give a harder and more pronounced silhouette, this is a very effective 'dibbling' fly for the Northern rivers. (see also Glow Fly [dibbler]; and Sam's Fly[(dibbler])

Munro Killer [longtail] (Robert Rattray)

PLATE 28

Hook: Esmond Drury longshank treble, 10-14
Silk: Black
Tail: Yellow, red and black bucktail, plus four strands of pearl Crystal Hair, extending 1"–1 1/2" depending on hook size
Body: Black floss
Rib: Oval gold
Throat: Sparse orange cock, with blue guinea fowl over
Wing: Very short black calf
Cheeks: Jungle cock
Head: Black

Tiny flies of this type can bring sport when all else fails and particularly when one uses proven colour combinations adapted from existing 'killing' patterns. When tying in this scale, it is important to use suitably heavy irons to offset the buoyancy of the materials, otherwise the finished fly will tend to skate.

Northern Dog (Waddington)

PLATE 29

Hook dressing: Short, fine yellow bucktail, secured by varnished Glo-Brite no.5 fluorescent floss
Silk: Red
Tag: Flat silver
Body: Black floss
Rib: Oval silver
Underwing: Four strands of pearl Crystal Hair, pulled through the eye of the Waddington shank and divided either side
Wing: Orange under yellow bucktail
Head: Red with black central band (optional)

When the Spring waters of the northern rivers come down black and thick, this is my first choice pattern. Basically, it is a Garry Dog dressing, but with added flash and an orange, rather than red, wing component. The altered colour and extra flash are suitable adaptations for the heavy, peat-stained rivers of this region.

Orange & Blue (Waddington)

PLATE 29

Silk: Black
Body: Black floss or wool
Rib: Flat silver
Wing: Orange bucktail under blue
Head: Black

This is back-end fly with a difference. One can't fail to notice the horrific colour combination, but David Mateer assures me that it can work wonders when the river is cursed with autumn leaves floating down. He feels that it probably shows up rather better than the normal oranges and reds, which possibly get lost in all of that russet autumn splendour. He says that he once saw a fellow rod take five fish in an afternoon with this fly. It is sometimes called a Frank's Fancy. All I can say is 'poor Frank'.

Orange Cuileag (Frank Durdle)

PLATE 29

Hook: Doubles, 6-12
Silk: Black
Tag: Fine oval gold
Tail: Orange dyed bleached squirrel
Body: Black floss
Rib: Orange floss, with oval gold following
Hackle: Orange dyed bleached squirrel
Wing: Black squirrel, long
Head: Black varnish

Cuileag (pronounced 'coolack') is Gaelic for fly. The rest is self-explanatory. It is a good colour combination for late Spring, summer and autumn fish in Invernesshire and surrounding areas, to which Frank caters his professional fly tying services. This pattern reminds me of a fly which had a moment of glory on the Gledfield Beat of the Carron. The river was full of April 'springers' and the only colour combination they would look at was black, orange and copper.

There is a yellow version, which replaces all the orange elements with yellow.

Oykel G.P.

PLATE 29

Hook: Doubles, 4-10
Silk: Red
Tail: Orange bucktail, at least twice the body length, with a G.P. red body feather over
Body: Orange floss silk
Body **Hackle:** Orange cock, palmered
Rib: Oval gold
Wing: G.P. red body feather over G.P. tippet feather
Head: Red varnish

A marrying of the General Practitioner and Ally's Shrimp characteristics has – not surprisingly – produced this very effective shrimp pattern. A very large percentage of the Oykel's annual catch falls to this fly. Although not as popular anywhere else, it will rival any shrimp pattern on its day.

Patsy Mary

PLATE 29

Hook: Doubles (singles & trebles occasionally), 6-12
Silk: Red
Tag: Silver wire or fine oval
Tail: G.P. crest or yellow hackle fibres
Body: Flat silver
Rib: Oval silver
Hackle: Black cock
Wing: Unbleached grey squirrel dyed blue
Head: Red varnish

Many of the new generation salmon flies, of which this is one, have a basic simplicity and show trout or sea-trout influences. Perhaps this is because most modern salmon flytyers come through a trout flytying apprenticeship. Rumoured to have originated on the Ness, this pattern's popularity has spread wide and far. In small sizes, it is very effective for sea-trout in both fresh and brackish water.

Pearly Muddler (Robert Rattray)

PLATE 29

Hook: Low-water singles, 6-10
Silk: Black
Body: Medium oval silver in butting turns, well varnished
Underwing: Four or five fibres of silver Flashabou, or similar
Wing: Sparse black squirrel
Head: Roe deer hair tied Muddler-style, retaining plenty of fine points as a collar

Robert says that this is an excellent dropper pattern, either fished conventionally on a floating line, cutting the surface, or dibbled, in the heads of pools. Wake flies and surface-cutters of this general type have established themselves well as back-up patterns for salmon and sea-trout river work. It is an interesting branch of summer fishing which can either produce spectacular sessions in its own right, or prove to be a last ditch blank saver, when nothing else works. The technique really needs low water and/or summer temperatures.

This pattern is also very good for migratory fish in lochs.

Pennell, Black

PLATE 12

See page 69 in the section on Loch Flies

This is a perennially popular sea-trout pattern for late evening and night fishing. It also takes significant numbers of salmon and grilse. Its similarity to the indispensable Stoat's Tail must be obvious to anyone.

Peter Ross

PLATE 12

See page 70 in the section on Loch Flies

Almost every authority on sea-trout river patterns lists this as an essential, particularly for fresh fish. The Peter Ross is also very popular in large sizes for grilse in the North.

Purple McBain (Gordon McBain)

PLATE 29

Hook: Doubles, 6-10 (also tube & Waddington)
Silk: Black
Tag: Gold wire or fine oval
Body: Purple floss
Rib: Oval gold
Hackle: Purple cock
Wing: Black squirrel over bleached squirrel dyed yellow
Head: Black

This pattern has a well-deserved reputation in the North for use throughout the Spring. Its inventor, Gordon McBain, is an Aberdonian and, not surprisingly, he rates it for the Dee. Alan Donaldson, who supplied the fly in the illustration, says that he tailed-out Gordon's 100th fish to this pattern, from the McKenzie Pool on the Cornhill Beat of the Carron in September 1995.

Rana

PLATE 30

Hook: Doubles, 6-10
Silk: Black
Tail: G.P. crest, of a deep golden coloration
Body: Black floss
Rib: Oval gold
Hackle: Grey heron, with natural speckled guinea fowl in front
Wing: Black squirrel, over unbleached grey squirrel tail, dyed red and orange
Cheeks: Jungle cock
Head: Black

I have included this Norwegian pattern because while many Scottish flies are established over there, we seem to have had a very poor return on our investment: comparatively few Scandinavian patterns have made it westwards across the North Sea.

The Rana has been fished with success on the Braelangwell Beat on the Carron and it has the look of a good early and mid-summer pattern. (*see also* Tana)

Rusty Rat

PLATE 30

Hook: Low water singles, 8-12
Silk: Red
Tag: Flat or oval gold
Tail: Sparse bunch of peacock sword fibres, tied short
Body: In two halves: rear – fluorescent. orange floss: front – bronze peacock herl, with a veiling of fluorescent orange floss over the rear half of the body only
Rib: Oval gold
Wing: Guard hairs of grey fox or grey squirrel
Collar: Grizzle, or mixed black and white hen
Head: Red

I picked up this slight variation on the original from *A Guide to Salmon Flies*, by John Buckland and Arthur Oglesby. I have found it an excellent fly for salmon and sea-trout in spate water rivers. It is popular amongst those who use it, but not widely known in the British Isles. All the

Canadian Rat patterns are worthy of trial by those looking for alternative weapons.

Salscraggie (or Standard Torrish)

PLATE 34

A Helmsdale fly named after the bridge. It shows the transition between the tough, shiny Snow Fly and the subsequent Victorian fashion for more eleaborately built flies.

Sam's Badger (Sam Bremner)

PLATE 30

Hook: Doubles & trebles, 6-12
Silk: Optional, usually black
Tail: Yellow bucktail, long
Body: Two halves: rear – flat gold; front – flat copper
Rib: Over flat gold – oval copper; over flat copper – oval gold
Mid-hackle: Orange cock
Wing: Badger, above and below, not sides
Head: White varnish

This pretty pattern was devised by Sam Bremner, gillie on the Wester Elchies Beat of the Spey, and very popular it has become It gives the general impression of a shrimp fly in profile and looks a winner. Tied fuller and on trebles, it makes a very good dibbling pattern for low-water summer conditions.

Sheila (Willie Mathieson)

PLATE 30

Hook: Doubles & trebles, 6-12
Silk: Black
Body: Flat gold
Rib: Oval gold
Throat: Hot orange hackle fibres
Wing: Black squirrel or fine bucktail
Head: Black

Willie's wife, Sheila, was the source of inspiration for this very successful and popular pattern from the Beauly. Anywhere in the North-East it is rare not to hear mention of this pattern. It is an excellent summer and autumn long-wing pattern for grilse and salmon.

Shrimp, Ally's (variant)

PLATE 30

Hook: Doubles and trebles, sizes 6-12
Silk: Red
Tag: Two turns of flat silver
Tail: Long slim bunch of orange bucktail
Body: In two parts: rear – red floss or seal's fur; front – black silk or seal's fur
Underwing: Natural grey squirrel
Overwing: G.P. tippet feather, tied horizontal
Beard hackle: Natural grey squirrel
Hackle: Long hot orange hen hackle
Head: Varnished red

At the time of writing, this pattern is arguably the most successful Scottish salmon fly for all rivers and all seasons. Whilst we must allow that there are fashions in these things, there is no doubt that Alastair Gowans's little shrimp is one of the great patterns of all time.

It has spawned a multitude of variants and, strictly, the above pattern is one of them as it contains a silver tag, which the originator deemed unnecessary.

A correctly dressed Ally's will have a tail at least as long as the body, and often half as long again. Modern variations often contain a sparse addition of pearl or orange Crystal hair. The underwing should extend beyond the overwing and the hackle should cloak the full length of the body. (see also Ally's Black Shrimp, Claret; Ally's Magenta; Silk Cut Prawn; and Ally's Yellow)

Shrimp, Ally's (Waddington)

PLATE 30

Ally's Dressing as for the standard version, but suitably adjusted for a Waddington shank.

Many of the notes for the double or treble dressing apply to this style of dressing. Although there is no obvious reason to limit size, smaller patterns in this style are the most common. Dressed on 25mm shanks and sometimes even smaller, this makes an excellent summer spate fly. Rarely seen in anything but the original basic orange colour.

Shrimp, Ally's Black
(Alan Donaldson)

PLATE 30

Hook: Doubles & trebles, sizes 6-12
Silk: Red
Tail: Black bucktail with sparse addition of black Crystal Hair
Body: Flat silver
Rib: Medium oval silver, followed by Glo-Brite no.12 fluorescent lime-green floss
Underwing: Bleached squirrel, dyed yellow
Underwing: Black cock hackle fibres
Wing: G.P. tippet feather
Hackle: Black cock

This variation on the Ally's Shrimp, by Alan Donaldson, is gaining in popularity, particularly in the Kyle of Sutherland region.

Most of the modern variants of Ally's Shrimp include some form of sparkly/flashy synthetic addition to the tail. Apart from a few intransigent reactionaries, acceptance of these new synthetic materials is now almost universal. (*see also* Shrimp, Claret; Ally's Magenta ; Silk Cut Prawn; and Ally's Yellow)

Shrimp, Ally's Magenta

PLATE 30

Hook: Doubles & trebles, 6-12
Silk: Red
Tail: Magenta bucktail, mixed with sparse strands of pink Twinkle
Body: In two halves: rear – lilac Lurex; front – Glo-Brite no.4 fluorescent. floss
Rib: Fine oval silver
Underwing: Grey squirrel
Hackle: Magenta cock
Wing: G.P. tippet, with magenta cock hackle fibres over
Head: Red varnish

Ally's Magenta Shrimp is a fly with a rapidly expanding reputation. There are many slight variations in the dressing, but this is Alan

Donaldson's, that prolific and expert tyer from Strathcarron. If the fluorescent and synthetic materials offend some people, substitutes are easily found. I would, however, suggest giving this excellent dressing a chance before discarding it. It works very well indeed.

Shrimp, Ally's Yellow

PLATE 30

Hook: Doubles & trebles, 6-12
Silk: Red
Tail: Yellow bucktail, plus strands of fluorescent lime Twinkle
Body: Flat silver
Rib: Oval silver
Underwing: Grey squirrel
Hackle: Yellow cock
Wing: G.P. tippet feather, with yellow cock hackle fibres over
Head: Red

Another variation on Alastair Gowan's Ally's Shrimp which gains in popularity with each succeeding season. This version is a good late Spring pattern, effective during the grilse runs.

John Buckland gave me an alternative dressing for this fly, which he found exceptionally good on the rivers of Russia's Kola Peninsula. It lacked the Twinkle in the tail and had a flat gold body, instead of silver. Perhaps we should carry both.

Shrimp, Ayrshire Red

PLATE 30

Hook: Doubles & trebles, sizes 6-12
Silk: Red
Tag: Silver
Tail: G.P. red body feather, wound
Rib: Fine or medium oval silver
Body: In two parts: rear – red floss; front – primrose yellow floss
Mid-hackle: Red cock hackle, dividing the body
Cheeks/Wing: Jungle cock
Hackle: Badger cock
Head: Red

Davie McPhail, who supplied the dressing shown,

says that if he was limited to just one pattern for Ayrshire rivers, it would be this or a Willie Gunn.

Shrimp patterns are often characterised by a 'tail hackle' of wound G.P. red body feather. The long mobile fibres of the G.P. hackle give plenty of 'kick' in the water and I am sure that this is one of the most important features in the success of this style of dressing. By comparison, most 'hairwings' are rather slick and streamlined in the water. (see also Shrimp, Black; Shrimp, Curry's Red; Shrimp, Kylie; Oykel G.P.; and Shrimp, Sandy's)

Shrimp, Black

PLATE 30

Hook: Doubles & trebles, 6-12
Silk: Red
Tail: Black squirrel
Body: Rear: yellow floss; front: black floss
Rib: Fine oval silver
Mid-hackle: Orange cock
Head hackle: Black cock
Wing: Jungle cock
Head: Red

There are dozens of Black Shrimp patterns: every tyer having his own, it seems. This one contains most of the generally accepted attracting features and colours and is a popular alternative to an Ally's Shrimp for those who prefer some jungle cock in the recipe. This pattern is successful in late Spring and summer, in clear water conditions.

Shrimp, Blue (Davie McPhail)

PLATE 30

Hook: Doubles, sizes 6-12
Silk: Red
Tag: Oval silver
Tail: G.P. red body feather, wound
Rear Body: Glo-Brite no.14, fluorescent blue floss
Fore Body: Red floss
Middle Hackle: Dyed blue cock
Rib: Oval silver
Wing: Jungle cock

Head hackle: Badger cock
Head: Red

On one occasion, a guest on the Ayrshire Doon was succeeding in almost impossible conditions of low water and bright sunny skies using a blue shrimp pattern. Davie adapted the original and came up with the above dressing, which he uses under similar difficult conditions, but also when the weather is more favourable. It would seem to be worth including in any summer fly box, given that low water and mediterranean temperatures now seem to be the norm in a typical Scottish summer.

Peter O'Reilly gives a similar dressing in his *Trout & Salmon Flies of Ireland* (Merlin Unwin Books 1995), differing only in the colour of the rear body. Is it only my imagination, or do shrimp patterns of this type become more effective the further West one travels? (see also Ayrshire Red Shrimp; Knockdolian Shrimp; and McClure Shrimp)

Shrimp, Brown

PLATE 30

Hook: Doubles & trebles, 6-12
Silk: Red
Tag: Fine oval silver
Tail: G.P. red body feather
Rear body: Yellow floss
Fore body: Black floss
Mid-hackle: Orange cock
Head hackle: Brown henny-cock
Wing: Jungle cock
Head: Red

Brown Shrimps seem to be peculiarly favoured in the region between Bonar Bridge and Inverness, as there seems to be little or no mention of them from elsewhere. Be that as it may, the above dressing is very popular and effective in this area and Alan Donaldson, who supplied the pattern and fly for the illustration, states that it also well favoured on the Kyle of Sutherland. This stretch of tidal/estuarial water carries the waters of the Oykel, Carron, Cassley and Shin out to the Dornoch Firth and the North Sea. (see also Shrimp, Black; Curry's Red; and Shrimp, Kylie)

Shrimp, Claret

PLATE 30

Hook: Double or treble, 6-12
Silk: Red
Tag: Two turns flat silver
Tail: A slim bunch of red bucktail mixed with a few strands of red Crystal Hair, twice the length of the body
Body: Dark claret seal's fur
Rib: Medium oval silver
Underwing: Dyed red unbleached squirrel, extending beyond the hook-bend
Throat: Red unbleached squirrel, *not* extending beyond hook-bend
Wing: Dyed red G.P. tippet feather, tied horizontal, not extending beyond hook-bend
Hackle: Dark claret hen, not extending beyond hook-bend

The design of this fly owes much to Alastair Gowan's superb Ally's Shrimp. I originally tied it at the request of *Trout & Salmon* editor, Sandy Leventon, who required a shrimp selection for a salmon-fishing trip to Northern Ireland. Knowing of the Irish passion for claret seal's fur and shrimp patterns, the above seemed obvious. It was successful on that excursion and has since proved itself in a wide variety of locations and circumstances in this country.

For some strange reason, claret is not a particularly popular colour in Scottish salmon flies. However, the strike rate of claret *trout* flies when used against salmon is remarkable. Surely it is time for a re-think? (see also Ally's Black; Ally's Magenta; and Ally's Yellow)

Shrimp, Curry's Red

PLATE 31

Hook: Doubles & trebles, sizes 6-12
Silk: Red
Tag: Fine oval or flat silver
Tail: G.P. red body feather, wound
Body: In two parts: rear – red floss: front – black floss
Mid-hackle: Badger cock
Rib: Fine oval silver
Veilings: Indian Crow sub.

Wing: Jungle cock
Hackle: Badger cock (longer than mid-hackle)

The older shrimp patterns refuse to be totally superseded by more modern shrimp designs and still make a valid contribution. Curry's Red Shrimp is a founder member of its class, but its popularity is waning slightly. I think that this has less to do with any lack of effectiveness, but is rather more a problem of over familiarity. I list it here because it has worked for me as a dropper fly in late Spring and summer and also because it is still very popular in Ireland and abroad. (see also Shrimp, Ayrshire Red; Shrimp, Black; Shrimp, Blue; Shrimp, Knockdolian; Shrimp, Kylie; and Shrimp, McClure)

Shrimp, Findhorn

PLATE 31

Hook: Doubles & trebles, sizes 6-12
Silk: Black
Tail: Orange bucktail and orange Crystal Hair, tied long and sparse
Body: Red Lurex
Rib: Silver wire
Wing: Grey squirrel under a whole G.P. tippet feather
Head: Black

The significant aspect of this pattern is the marrying of elements from the ubiquitous Ally's Shrimp with the tinsel body and sparkling tail filaments. This seems to be the hall-mark of 1990s salmon patterns.

This pattern has become very popular in the Morayshire area for summer and autumn fishing.

Shrimp, Knockdolian

PLATE 31

Hook: Doubles & trebles, 6-12
Silk: Red
Tag: Fine oval silver
Tail: A long-fibred G.P. red body feather, wound
Body: Flat silver
Rib: Oval silver
Hackle: Hot-orange cock or hen, long enough to reach bend of hook

Cheeks: Jungle cock
Head: Red varnish

Davie McPhail, who supplied this pattern, received the original dressing from Lord Richard of Knockdolian Estates. It is extremely effective on all the Ayrshire rivers, but is not well known outside this area.

Shrimp, McClure *(Davie McPhail)*

PLATE 31

Hook: Doubles, 6-12
Silk: Black
Tag: Fine oval gold
Tail: G.P. red body feather
Body: In two halves: rear – flat gold; fore – black floss
Mid-hackle: Hot orange cock or hen
Rib: Gold wire over the rear half of the body; oval gold over the front half
Throat: Yellow calf
Wing: Black squirrel
Head hackle: Badger cock
Head: Black

This pattern has undergone a somewhat tortuous evolution to arrive at its present form. The black squirrel wing was a substitute for jungle cock, which Davie lacked at the time and the yellow calf was added to achieve a Willie Gunn coloration. Through a lucky combination of circumstances, he has produced a very effective fly for the South-West in all summer and autumn water conditions.

Shrimp, Nameless

PLATE 37

Silk: Red
Tag: Red floss, ribbed with fine oval silver
Tail: G..P crest, curving downwards
Butt: Black ostrich herl
Body: Rear half – red floss, ribbed fine oval silver
Centre wing: Slim bunch of tippet fibres, with two grizzle or cree cock hackles back to back, facing outward and a small jungle cock eye on either side
Body: Front half – yellow floss, ribbed fine oval silver

Throat: slim bunch of brown hackle fibres with natural guinea fowl over
Wing: Brown mallard
Head: Red varnish

At first sight this pattern looks either like a joke, or one devised by a committee! It contains almost everything in the flytying cabinet and certainly lacks the uncluttered sparsity normally associated with the successful modern salmon fly.

But this mysterious pattern is remarkably effective and comes well recommended from several disparate sources. There is a suggestion that the dressing appeared in a *Trout & Salmon* article some years back, but I have been unable to locate it. However, it is a good fly, if somewhat of a bind to tie. Those who use it strongly recommend it for summer work, nationwide.

Shrimp, Purple see Silk Cut Shrimp

Shrimp, Sandy's *(Sandy Leventon)*

PLATE 31

Hook: Doubles & trebles, 6-12
Silk: Black
Tail: Long black marabou, not overly thick
Body: Orange marabou, wound
Rib: Oval gold
Hackle: Longish black hen, tied full
Cheeks: Jungle cock (optional)

Devised by Sandy Leventon, editor of *Trout & Salmon*, this is an unusual pattern (for a salmon fly) in its use of marabou, such a common feature of so many reservoir trout lures. It is a favourite of mine. I have found it a good summer pattern, both for grilse and salmon. On one memorable afternoon on the private beat of the Thurso, a fining spate saw a major run of grilse and salmon running through the Sauce Pool. Were it not for the fact that my Sandy's Shrimps had been tied on very light-wire trebles, which kept straightening or breaking, I would have had a phenomenal day. Since then, it has rarely failed (on more robust hooks). With the mobility of the marabou, it is a good pattern for slack flows

Silk Cut Shrimp (Andy Wren)

PLATE 31

Hook: Doubles or trebles, 4-10
Silk: Black
Tail: Long purple bucktail, with a sparse addition of Crystal Hair
Body: Flat pearl Lurex over wet-varnished tying silk, with varnish over the completed body for protection
Wing: G.P. tippet feather dyed purple, tied to lie horizontal
Collar: Purple hen or cock, long and full
Head: Black

Purple prawn/shrimp patterns tied in this and more traditional styles have become very common and popular. Although purple is often regarded as a summer and autumn colour, I have witnessed the originator of this pattern take a succession of late Spring fish with it.

This pattern originated from the phenomenal Ally's Shrimp: a format which allows great variation in colour.

Silver Garry (Waddington)

PLATE 31

Hook Dressing: Short fine yellow bucktail, secured with Glo-Brite no.5 fluorescent floss, varnished
Silk: Red
Body: Flat silver
Rib: Oval silver
Wing: Yellow bucktail over orange, over sparse pearl Crystal Hair
Head: Red, with a black central band (optional)

Fresh fish love silver bodied flies and this has been one of my most effective patterns for early 'springers', when they are filtering quietly and unheralded into the pools. Although a first choice for all conditions at this time of year, it seems best in bright weather or, surprisingly, in the fading light of late afternoons. My good friend, Eddie Maudling, dresses this fly with a pearl body and reckons it even better in similar circumstances.

Dressed with long trailing wings on doubles and trebles, it makes a good dropper pattern fished above a Black & Orange(Waddington), or a Willie Gunn. This is a technique which is favoured on the northern rivers.

Stoat, Pearly (Stuart Topp & Davie Wood)

PLATE 32

Hook: Doubles & trebles, 6-12 (also tubes & Waddingtons)
Silk: Black
Body: Pearl Lurex over wet-varnished tying silk and varnished over for protection
Wing: Very sparse stoat's tail or black squirrel over pearl Crystal Hair (dressed more heavily in tube or Waddington form)
Head: Black

This is a modern variation on the extremely popular salmon and sea-trout pattern, the Silver Stoat. It is most popular on clear water rivers in the East and South, where very sparse patterns are required for low water levels. It is a very efficient night-time sea-trout pattern.

Stoat, Silver

PLATE 32

Hook: Singles, doubles & trebles, 6-12 and in 'mini-tubes'
Silk: Black
Tail: G.P. crest or yellow hackle fibres (optional)
Tag: Fine oval silver
Body: Flat silver
Hackle: Sparse black cock
Wing: Stoat's tail or similar

There can be few, if any, rivers where the Silver Stoat is not considered almost essential equipment for both salmon and sea-trout. A tremendously successful pattern from May through to the end of the season, it is very useful on resident fish in low water situations.

It is also very popular as a point fly for salmon and sea-trout in lochs.

Stoat, Stinchar

PLATE 32

Hook: Doubles & trebles, 4-12
Silk: Black
Body: None
Rib: None
Wing: Stoat's tail or black dyed squirrel, cloaking the hook shank
Hackle: Hot orange hen, tied full and in front of the wing
Head: Black

I am assured by Davie McPhail that this – the fly in the illustration – is the original dressing of this controversial pattern. The wing 'cloaks' the bare shank of the hook (there is no body dressing, as such). As Davie gillies on the Stinchar, I consider him to be a more than creditable authority on its patterns. Some authorities claim that a dressing similar to that of a Thunder Stoat is correct. This is a mistake, but a perfectly understandable one.

The Stinchar Stoat is a simple and effective dressing. Davie also gives variations with plain gold and copper bodies that he rates highly.

Stoat, Thunder

PLATE 32

Hook: Doubles & trebles, 8-12
Silk: Black
Tag: Two or three turns of ribbing
Body: Black floss
Rib: Oval gold
Hackle: Hot orange cock or hen
Wing: Stoat's tail, or black dyed squirrel
Head: Black

This pattern is much varied and seems to have no firm standard. Tied as above, sparse and spare, it is an indispensable summer and low water pattern for grilse and salmon.

Tied, as it often is, with tail of G.P. crest, hackle addition of blue dyed guinea fowl and jungle cock cheeks and it almost becomes a totally different pattern: much more like a Thunder & Lightning or Munro Killer.

Stoat's Tail

PLATE 32

Hook: Singles, doubles & trebles, 6-12 and 'mini-tubes
Silk: Black
Tag: Oval silver
Tail: G.P. crest (optional)
Body: Black floss (sometimes, black seal's fur)
Hackle: Black cock
Wing: Stoat's tail, or black squirrel

The quintessential 'little black speck', which at times can be irresistible to salmon, grilse and sea-trout in the difficult summer conditions of high water temperatures and low levels. The 'Stoat' is a fly that will take both stale and fresh fish, in all hook sizes and in all weather conditions. It is most popular in the big, clear water rivers of the South and East, but is also considered a top player in virtually all regions.

The addition of small jungle cock eyes seems to improve its acceptability to sea-trout.

Stoat's Tail [longtailed variant] (Robert Rattray)

PLATE 32

Hook: Esmond Drury longshank treble, 10-14
Silk: Black
Tail: Black calf, with four strands of pearl Krystal Flash and black bucktail over
Body: Black floss
Rib: Oval silver
Throat: Orange cock with blue guinea fowl over
Wing: Black calf with fibres of peacock sword over
Head: Black

I can't remember where I read it, but I am sure that I have seen mention of very early Stoat's Tails having peacock sword in the wing. If this is not just my imagination, then Robert may have good reason for including this feature in his variant. The short wing and long tail avoid the irritation of the wing getting caught up in the hook-bend, whilst still allowing a long, trailing flow of material behind the hook. This seems such a strongly attracting feature in modern salmon flies.

158

This is an excellent floating and intermediate line pattern for midsummer use against salmon, grilse and sea-trout.

Tadpole [tube & Waddington]
(Neil Graesser)

PLATE 33

Silk: Red
Body: In two halves: rear – flat silver; front – red floss
Mid-wing: Stemming from the body joint: yellow squirrel or bucktail, tied long
Rib: Oval or embossed gold
Wing: Black bucktail, long on top, short below (none at sides), with a few strands of pearl Crystal Hair under.
Head: Red varnish

I am a 'sucker' for new patterns and I seized on the original version of the Tadpole (yellow and red body) when I first heard of it. I expected it to work wonders – but it did nothing for me! This slight variation, with silver and red body looks more promising for the dark, peat-stained waters I fish in the Spring. Alan Donaldson recommends it for all the Kyle of Sutherland rivers and further afield.

A close cousin of the Collie Dog, it works earlier in the year than that pattern and in colder, heavier water.

Tana (tube & Waddington)

PLATE 33

Silk: Black
Tag: Flat gold
Butt: Black floss
Body: Flat silver
Rib: Embossed silver
Wing: Yellow bucktail under white bucktail, with natural guinea fowl over all
Head: Black

Alan Sutherland sent me a copy of this pattern for Spring work and I immediately liked the look of it. I asked him about it and he said it is his adaptation of a pattern from the very far North of Norway. It has established itself in the North-East of Scotland and is growing in popularity with

each succeeding year. It is an interesting fly for those who search for the new and esoteric and like to have something a bit different in their fly boxes. (*see also* Rana)

Thunder & Lightning
(featherwing)

PLATE 34

Hook: Singles & doubles, 4-10
Silk: Black
Tag: Fine oval silver and golden yellow floss
Tail: G.P. crest/topping and Indian crow
Butt: Black ostrich herl
Body: Black floss
Rib: Oval gold
Hackle: Orange cock
Throat: Blue jay, or dyed blue guinea fowl
Wing: Bronze mallard, with a topping over (optional)
Cheeks: Jungle cock
Horns (optional): Blue & yellow macaw

I can't look at this fly but I want to tie it on and go fishing. It is one of the few feather-wing patterns that I do still fish with: perhaps more out of respect for its beauty, rather than in any great expectation of fish. Many still fish it successfully, however, particularly on the bigger rivers such as Tweed and Spey. The usual advice is to fish it in clearing spates.

The fly has traditionally been attributed to James Wright, of Sprouston (who first tied the Greenwell's Glory), but there are some who hotly contend that Wright filched it from an Irish fly dresser, one Pat Hearns. Whoever the originator was, it is one of the great enduring patterns. I asked Jim Smail, of Tweedside, to tie the fly for the illustration, which he has done beautifully.

Thunder & Lightning (hairwing)

PLATE 34

Hook: Singles & doubles, 4-10
Silk: Black
Tag: Gold wire
Tail: Yellow and red cock hackle fibres
Butt: Yellow floss

Body: Black floss
Rib: Oval gold
Throat: Orange cock with blue guinea fowl over
Wing: Brown squirrel over orange cock hackle fibres
Head: Black

The hair-wing dressing of the much lauded feather-winged standard has become very popular. It has largely been replaced, however, by the Munro Killer, which it strongly resembles.

Thunderflash (Robert Rattray)

PLATE 33

Hook: Heavyweight double, 6-10
Silk: Black
Body: Tight butting turns of oval gold, varnished
Hackle: Three full turns of orange cock, set at 45 degrees
Underwing: Gold Lureflash, four or five strands, to bend of hook
Wing: Black squirrel, sparse
Overwing: Six fibres of pearl Krystal Flash, extending beyond the squirrel
Head: Black

Robert Rattray is a salmon and sea-trout angler with wide experience throughout Scotland. He says that this is his best autumn fly when fishing a floating line. He stresses that the finished fly should look spare and sparse, but with plenty of sparkle and flash.

Thvera Blue (variant)

PLATE 34

Hook: Doubles & trebles, 8-12
Silk: Black
Tag: Fine oval silver or wire
Butt: Yellow floss
Tail: Yellow cock hackle fibres
Body: Pale blue floss
Rib: Oval silver
Throat: Light blue cock
Wing: Grey squirrel dyed a pale washed-out blue
Head: Black

Quentin Gardiner brought this fly back from Iceland and uses it to very good effect on the Dee, in very small sizes. He gave the above nameless recipe to Alan Donaldson and asked him to tie up a batch. I have searched for a name and can only assume that it is a variation on a well-known Icelandic pattern. Buckland and Oglesby list the Thvera Blue in A Guide to Salmon Flies, but advise its usage in large sizes. A pattern for those who like blue flies.

Tosh (tube & Waddington)

PLATE 35

Silk: Black
Body: Unribbed black floss
Wing: Quartered, black and yellow bunches
Head: Black

The Tosh is an universally appreciated tube and Waddington pattern and its sheer simplicity hints at a fundamental truth.

Many modern tyers add a silver rib, feeling that the naked body is an affront. But the original, tied by E. Ritchie, of the Delfur Beat on the Spey way back in 1957, lacked any such adornment. Ritchie's original also lacked any yellow hair and, if I may be so bold, could well have been a fore-runner of the much lauded Collie Dog. In the late John Ashley-Cooper's *Great Salmon Rivers of Scotland*, there is an illustration of a Tosh with a very long wing which lends some support to this theory.

Often referred to as a Black & Yellow, and wrongly as a Gordon's Fancy it is one of the best Spring patterns. It is popular on the Dee in all sizes throughout the season.

Tosh

PLATE 35

Hook: Doubles & trebles, 6-12
Silk: Black
Tag: Fine oval silver or wire
Tail: Yellow hackle fibres
Body: Black floss
Rib: Oval silver
Throat: Yellow cock

Wing: Black squirrel
Head: Black

In double and treble format, this is the most commonly encountered dressing of the Tosh and is very popular in the North and East. Personally, I would prefer to use an *unribbed* version, as a Stoat's Tail could quite effectively fulfil the function of the above, I'm sure.

Tosh (gold-bodied variant)

PLATE 35

Silk: Black
Body: Flat gold
Rib: Fine oval gold
Underwing: Hot orange Crystal Hair
Wing: Black squirrel
Head: Black

A gold-bodied Waddington version of the Tosh is a very popular dressing for the Dee, and other rivers of the region. It was given to me by Stuart Topp. Patterns for this area tend to be tied in smaller sizes than elsewhere, regardless of season, so choose your 'irons' accordingly.

Synthetic winging materials enhance the flash of tinsel bodies and are frequently used, in the modern idiom, to produce sparkly, 'ignore-this-if-you-can' patterns.

Watson's Fancy

PLATE 15

See page 92 in the section on Loch Flies.

Watson's Fancy is a useful sea-trout pattern for night work and a popular general purpose tool for spate rivers in the West.

Weasel (Robert Rattray)

PLATE 35

Hook: Low-water Doubles, 10 & 12
Silk: Black
Tag: Four turns of fine oval silver, varnished
Tail: Yellow cock hackle fibres
Body: Black floss

Rib: Medium flat silver (the black and silver bands should be of equal width)
Hackle: Black henny/cock, wound three turns and set at 45 degrees
Wing: Four or five fibres of pearl Krystal Flash, extending to the tip of the tail, with sparse black squirrel over
Head: Black, with a central band of fluorescent orange thread

Robert is a great proponent of the use of modern synthetic materials in salmon and sea-trout flies. This is a good summer salmon and grilse pattern for reduced flows and for sea-trout at almost any time.

The body should have three coats of clear nail varnish to protect the material and to produce a translucent effect. The original winging material came from a black labrador called 'Weasel', in the grand tradition of Scottish salmon flytying.

Whitewing (featherwing)

PLATE 35

Hook: Singles & Doubles, 4-10
Silk: Black
Tag: Fine oval silver
Tail: G.P. crest/topping and tippet strands
Body: In two halves: rear – red seal's fur, veiled with red ibis substitute; front – black seal's fur
Rib: Oval silver
Hackle: Black cock wound over front half of body
Throat: Blue cock
Wing: Strips of white swan, set horizontally
Head: Black

The Whitewing is one of the most successful of the featherwing patterns still in use today. The correct name for this fly is 'The Hunter' and it was originally devised for use on the Tay. It is now strongly associated with the Tweed and is often used on this river when the light starts to fade in the evening.

161

Whitewing (hairwing)

PLATE 35

Style: Tube & Waddington
Hook Dressing: Flat silver, varnished
Silk: Black
Body: Black floss
Rib: Oval silver
Wing: Bucktail in three bunches – red, blue and white
Head: Black

The hairwing version is a very popular and widely used pattern, strongly associated with the Tweed and other Border rivers. It is less used the further North one travels, although Mathieson likes it on the Beauly.

The assertion that white is an effective colour to use in fading light is open to debate, but many Southern anglers will fish no other pattern in such conditions. In Waddington format, the white bucktail should be tied so that it fishes uppermost in the water. This is rather harder to achieve with tubes.

Willie Gunn (longwing)

PLATE 36

Hook: Doubles & trebles, 4-10
Silk: Black
Tag: Fine oval gold
Body: Black floss
Rib: Oval gold
Wing: Mixed yellow and orange bucktail, over a few strands of pearl Flashabou, with black bucktail over – all twice the length of the body
Head: Black

Although many pundits might claim that this pattern is superfluous, due to its similarity to a Munro Killer, it refuses to go away. This version sees much use, particularly by those who dislike tubes and Waddingtons. Bill McLenan, of Elgin, supplied this pattern and rates it for Morayshire rivers for use in summer and autumn.

The major problem with this style of dressing is that the wing has a tendency to become caught up in the bends of the hooks. Rather

surprisingly, this doesn't seem to put off taking fish, but it will cause the fly to twist in a fast current, which can cause kinks and precipitate breakages in light monofilaments. I always make a point of Spey casting such long-winged patterns, as overhead casting seems to exacerbate the problem. The trailing tail does, however, seem very attractive to fish and so it is often a risk worth taking.

Willie Gunn (Davie McPhail)

PLATE 36

Hook: Doubles & trebles, 6-12
Silk: Red
Tag: Fine oval gold
Body: Black floss
Rib: Oval gold
Wing: Yellow, orange and purple bucktail mixed, with black squirrel over
Head: Red tying silk, varnished

I just had to add this variant to a somewhat embarrassingly long list of Willie Gunns. Davie tells me that it is very effective on his Ayrshire rivers, particularly in clear water, with fish coming in off the tide. He adds the purple hair to darken the wing. Willie Gunns tend to be tied in rather darker shades in Davie's part of Scotland. This version is a very pretty fly and I am sure it would stand its corner in any fly box.

Willie Gunn (tube)

PLATE 36

Silk: Black
Body: Black floss
Rib: Embossed gold
Wing: Mixed orange and yellow bucktail, with sparse black over

This is a popular northern version of the dressing. It is a brighter fly, with more sparkle for the heavily peat-stained waters of Spring and autumn.

Willie Gunn (Rob Wilson)

PLATE 36

Style: Waddington
Silk: Black
Tag: Flat gold
Body: Black floss
Rib: Oval gold, three turns above tag, then in open turns along the body
Wing: Bucktail – orange, under yellow, under black
Head: Black, with a central band of red (optional)

What can you say about this fly without drying up on superlatives? In recent years it has become the standard workhorse for Spring and autumn work throughout Scotland. There is considerable variation in the way the wing is rendered. In the far North, there is more yellow and orange and less black, while southerners prefer a predominance of black hair. Some tyers insist that the three colours should be 'pirled' (mixed) together, but this is the one I prefer for the northern rivers on which I do most of my salmon fishing.

It was named in honour of a Brora gillie, who died in 1996, but it has strong associations with the Helmsdale.

Willie Gunn, Gold (tube)

PLATE 36

Silk: Black
Body: Flat gold
Rib: Embossed gold
Wing: Mixed yellow, orange and black bucktail
Head: Black

This is a very popular alternative to the standard black bodied Willie Gunn and the version I prefer for bright Spring days.

Yabbie (J. Bett)

PLATE 37

Hook: Doubles & trebles, 6-12
Silk: Red

Tail: Red squirrel or goat, with strands of red Twinkle, tied very long
Body: Red floss
Rib: Oval silver
Hackle: Orange cock, with badger cock over
Head: Red

Yabbie is, I believe, an Australian name for a shrimp or prawn. Unlike most other shrimp fly dressings, the Red Yabbie is a 'doddle' to tie for even the least accomplished fly dresser. It has a somewhat strange appearance, but is well respected by those who know it. It fishes well on the Beauly, Carron, Conon and Spey.

Yellow Dolly

PLATE 37

Silk: Red
Body: Short length of red plastic tubing, from a quarter inch to three quarters of an inch long
Skirt: Yellow bucktail under black bucktail, trimmed exceedingly short, with the yellow protruding from beneath the black and *not* beyond the rear end of the tube
Head: Red varnish

Derek Knowles's fly is one that requires the right conditions and a deal of determination and faith in order to produce the goods. In conditions of low flow and high water temperature, when fish are comatose and unwilling to respond to standard patterns, a greased-up Dolly cast square and drawn across the stream just in front of a known lie will often precipitate some form of action. One often has to be persistent, covering the fish several times before a response is induced. On other occasions, a fish might come up for it at the first offering.

Hugo Ross, of Wick, has told me of his successful experiments with greased Muddler-headed patterns in the run-in to Loch Beg: a large pool on Beat 12 of the Thurso. The technique was identical and the results exciting and rewarding. Given that the correct conditions for this type of technique occur when salmon anglers are often tearing their hair out in frustration with standard techniques, further investigation is surely long overdue.

APPENDIX

Materials

Throughout this book the thread used in tying the patterns is referred to as 'silk', in deference to traditional terminology. In reality, these days, flytying threads are more likely to be modern synthetic textiles, such as nylon or polyester. For some patterns, however, authorities still insist on the use of the traditional material. The North-country 'spider' patterns, for example, are still specified as needing genuine Pearsall's 'Gossamer' silk.

Many of the patterns in this book have bodies made from dubbed seal's fur. The genuine material has a wonderful sparkle and lustre, that is hard to match. For a while, it looked as though seal's fur was going to disappear from the flytyer's palette, but this never actually came to pass and it is again readily available. Nevertheless, there are those who might prefer to use something else and there are some very acceptable substitutes. Veniard's seals fur substitute is a natural fibre (mohair, I believe) and is available in a wide range of dyed colours. Davy Wotton's 'SLF' (Synthetic Living Fibre) is an entirely man-made fibre that is also available in a wide range of colours and blends and in different textures, as well.

Modern Scottish loch fly patterns frequently make use of fluorescent materials. The Datam 'Glo-Brite' range has been specified in many of the patterns listed. Many flytyers will be completely familiar with these materials, but for newcomers to flydressing, or for traditionalists who have not yet become acquainted with them, the following information might be useful. Datam 'Glo-Brite' colours are available in three materials: a fine floss (that can be used for tails, wound bodies and even as the main tying thread); a thicker 'yarn' (useful for tails and wing additions, etc.) and as a suede (floc) chenille (used for wound bodies). The manufacturers produce a very handy shade card with a sample of each colour of the floss form.

DATAM Glo-Brite colours
1. Neon Magenta
2. Glo-Brite Pink
3. Glo-Brite Crimson
4. Glo-Brite Scarlet
5. Fire Orange
6. Glo-Brite Hot Orange
7. Glo-Brite Orange
8. Glo-Brite Amber
9. Glo-Brite Chrome Yellow
10. Glo-Brite Yellow
11. Phosphor Yellow
12. Glo-Brite Lime Green
13. Glo-Brite Green
14. Glo-Brite Blue
15. Glo-Brite Purple
16. Glo-Brite White

Index

165

Stoat, Thunder 158, Pl.32
Suspender Nymph 81, Pl.14

Tadpole (tube &
    Waddington) 159, Pl.33
Tana (tube & Waddington)
    159, Pl.33
Teal & Black 82, Pl.14
Teal & Black 128, Pl.22
Teal & Green (1) 82, Pl.14
Teal & Green (2) 83, Pl.14
Teal & Green (3) 83, Pl.14
Teal, Blue & Silver (variant)
    82, Pl.14
Technocat 83, Pl.15
Ted's Olive 83, Pl.15
Thunder & Lightning
    (featherwing) 159, Pl.34
Thunder & Lightning
    (hairwing) 159, Pl.34
Thunder Stoat see Stoat,
    Thunder
Thunderflash 160, Pl.33
Thvera Blue (variant) 160,
    Pl.34
Tosh (gold-bodied variant)
    161, Pl.35
Tosh (tube &
Waddington)160,
    Pl.35
Tosh 160, Pl.35
Treacle Parkin (variant) 84,
    Pl.15
Tup's Indispensable
    (variant) 84, Pl.15
Tup's Indispensable
    (variant) 128, Pl.22

Viva (variant) 84, Pl.15
Viva Spider (B. Peterson) 92
Viva, Cactus Head 84
Viva, Gold 92, Pl.15
Viva, Jungle Cock (Claret)
    92
Viva, Jungle Cock 92

Watson's Fancy 93, 161,
    Pl.15
Weasel 161, Pl.35
Wee Grey 128, Pl.22
Wee Man (dapping fly) 93,
    Pl.38
Wee Silver Nymph 128,
    Pl.22
Wet Daddy 93, Pl.15
White Cat see Booby Nymph
White Weazel 96, Pl.15
White Muddler see Muddler,
    White
White-Hackled Orangeman
    93, Pl.15
White-Hackled Invicta see
    Invicta, White-Hackled
Whitewing (featherwing)
    161, Pl.35
Whitewing (hairwing) 162,
    Pl.35
Wickham's Fancy(variant)
    96, Pl.15
Willie Gunn (Davie McPhail)
    162, Pl.36
Willie Gunn (longwing)
    162, Pl.36
Willie Gunn (Rob Wilson)
    163, Pl.36
Willie Gunn (tube) 162,
    Pl.36
Willie Gunn, Gold (tube)
    163, Pl.36
Wingless Wickham's (1) 96,
    Pl.15
Wingless Wickham's (2) 96,
    Pl.15
Woodcock & Green
    (variant) 97, Pl.16
Wormfly 97, Pl.16
Wormfly (longshank
    variant) 97, Pl.16
Wormfly, Black 97, Pl.16
Wormfly, Black (longshank
    variation) 100, Pl.16
Wormfly, Orange 100, Pl.16

Woven Nymph 128, Pl.22

Xmas Tree 100, Pl.16

Yabbie 163, Pl.3
Yellow Dolly 163, Pl.37
Yellow May Dun (Ron Glass)
    129, Pl.22
Yellow May Dun (Willie
    Miller)
    129, Pl.22
Yellow May Dun Emerger
    (Jimmy Fairgrieve) 129,
    Pl.22
Yellow Owl 101, Pl.16
Yellow Owl Muddler 101,
    Pl.16
Yellow-Eyed Damsel 101,
    Pl.16
Yellow-Tailed Daddy [dap]
    (J. Millar) 101, Pl.38

Zulu 102, Pl.16
Zulu, Blue 102, Pl.16
Zulu, Brown 102, Pl.16
Zulu, Gold 102, Pl.16
Zulu, Orange 104, Pl.11
Zulu, Pearly 104, Pl.16
Zulu, Red 104, Pl.16
Zulu, Slimline 104, Pl.16